YOU ARE A

HIGH VALUE TARGET

YOU ARE A

HIGH
VALUE
TARGET

DAVID L. JOHNSTON

PUBLISHING & MARKETING
Oviedo, FL

Published by HigherLife Development Services, Inc.
 PO Box 623307
 Oviedo, Florida 32762
 (407) 563-4806
 www.ahigherlife.com

ISBN: 978-1-951492-92-2 (Paperback)
ISBN: 978-1-951492-93-9 (Ebook)

Printed in the United States of America.

10 9 8 7 6 5 4 3 2 1

Contents

Chapter 1

What Is a High-Value Target?

Virtually every American who was alive on September 11, 2001, remembers where they were when the United States experienced the worst terrorist attack on homeland soil in the nation's history. Simultaneous attacks on the World Trade Center buildings, the Pentagon, and a downed plane in Shanksville, Pennsylvania, left nearly three thousand Americans dead and a terrified nation in mourning.

That September day also made famous the man who was ultimately behind the attacks—the founder of Al-Qaeda—and the one who directed the group that carried out the atrocities that shocked the world: Osama bin Laden became a household name. He was immediately the most wanted man in the world.

To our country and its military leaders, Osama bin Laden became a *high-value target*.

Nearly a decade later, on May 2, 2011, Americans celebrated the news that bin Laden was dead. Years of high-stakes intelligence work and meticulous military planning ultimately brought about his demise. Late that night, US President Barack Obama went on television to declare that United States Navy SEALs had located and killed America's number-one enemy.

History.com describes that historic event like this:

"On May 2, 2011, US Special Forces raided an [Al-Qaeda] compound in Abbottabad, Pakistan, and killed the world's most wanted terrorist: Osama bin Laden. The entire operation, which lasted only forty minutes from start to finish, was the culmination of years of calculated planning and training. Ultimately, bin Laden was found and killed within nine minutes, and SEAL Team Six was credited with carrying out a nearly flawless mission, the president announced."[1]

The mission had been dubbed Operation Neptune Spear, and it had been launched earlier that afternoon, around 3:30 p.m., Pakistan time (nine hours ahead of Washington, DC.). Twenty-five Navy SEALs, in a high-stakes and highly secretive maneuver, landed at bin Laden's compound in Abbottabad, Pakistan. Within ten minutes, the high-value target was located inside of the compound and summarily shot in the head. During the operation, three other men and a woman also were killed.[2]

The remains of bin Laden were placed in a body bag, and the team of Navy SEALs had cleanly exited the compound by 4:05 p.m. DNA samples were taken from the body before it was disposed of in the Arabian Sea. Those samples later confirmed, beyond any doubt, that the high-value target had been eliminated. Throughout the entire raid, President Obama was able to monitor the activity in the raid through footage being shot live by a drone flying over the terrorist's compound.

"Justice has been done," President Obama continued in his televised address to the nation that night. Not long after his announcement, large crowds assembled outside the White House, in Times Square in New York City, and at Ground Zero, celebrating the demise of America's most notorious enemy.[3]

---

1   "How SEAL Team Six Took Out Osama bin Laden," Julie Marks, History.com, updated August 2, 2019, https://www.history.com/news/osama-bin-laden-death-seal-team-six.

2   Ibid.

3   "Bin Laden Is Dead, Obama Says," Peter Baker, Helene Cooper, and Mark Mazzetti, *The New York Times*, May 1. 2011, https://www.nytimes.com/2011/05/02/world/asia/osama-bin-laden-is-killed.html.

The death of Osama bin Laden, the highest name on the US military's high-value target list, dealt a serious blow to enemy fighters in Afghanistan, Pakistan, and elsewhere. But his name wasn't the only one on this list.

High-value targets, when identified and sought out, are typically identified for either capture or assassination by the most elite of our nation's military forces. The systematic elimination of the targets on this "capture or kill" list is an important part of keeping the country safe.

Even following the death of bin Laden, officials at the International Security Assistant Force headquarters has maintained a collection of these strategically important "famous faces." This high-value target list is officially called the Joint Prioritization Effects List, and besides America's notorious, more famous enemies, it also includes largely unknown low- and mid-level enemy combatants who directly threaten US coalition troops in the field. Those local targets can include shadow government officials in enemy territories, financiers, gun runners, drug smugglers, bomb makers, and terrorist recruiters, some of whom are considered more important to the counterinsurgency mission than top insurgent leaders.[4]

"There are different types of high-value targets," Defense Department spokesman Colossians David Lapan has explained. "There are high-value targets that fall under the strategic level, but down at the battalion level, high-value targets are the guys that are affecting their operations on a regular basis."[5]

Major General Richard Mills was the commander of Marine Expeditionary Force I and other coalition troops in southern Afghanistan's Helmand and Kandahar provinces from June 2010 until late 2011. When he first arrived there, the insurgency was commanded by what he described as an "experienced leadership of pretty savvy guys that had been fighting for a number of years. Good leaders, good tacticians that could operate on the

---

4   "Changing the Face of the War One High-Value Target at a Time," Kevin Baron, *Stars and Stripes*, May 23, 2011, https://www.stripes.com/news/changing-the-face-of-the-war-one-high-value-target-at-a-time-1.144357.
5   Ibid.

battlefield." The average high-value target for General Mills was "a fairly experienced veteran on the battlefield. A man who knew how to allocate resources, knew how to command and control—and could inspire others."[6]

Mills's troops went to work on the high-value target list. "They went after the enemy's command and control to a really devastating effect," he said. "If you were a battalion commander in Helmand Province for the insurgency, your life expectancy was extremely short. Extremely short."[7]

The truth is, as long as enemies of the United States remain in power in this world, our nation's military will continue to maintain a high-value target list. They add targets to that list based on the direct level of threat they pose to our welfare, our security, and our way of life.

What If the High-Value Targets Are the Good Guys?

Did you know that you—yes, you—could also be a high-value target?

We can all appreciate the need to "take out" the bad guys – bad guys the likes of Osama bin Laden. But what if good people become the targets? What if the bad guys make *high-value targets* of the good guys? This is why we are warned in advance so many times. The wolves are after the sheep. And there are even wolves in sheep's clothing. Watch out! As Plato said, "No one is more hated than he who speaks the truth." Check these ancient but prophetic quotes:

> *"They gather themselves together against the soul*
> *of the righteous, and condemn the innocent blood."*
> (Psalm 94:21)

> *"Can Misrule have anything in common with you?*
> *Can Troublemaker pretend to be on your side?*

---

6   Ibid.
7   Ibid.

They gang up on good people, *plot behind the backs of the innocent."* (MSG)

"This know also, that in the last days perilous times shall come.
For men shall be...
*fierce, **despisers of those that are good**, traitors..."*
(2 Timothy 3:1, 3-4)

"Why the mean plots, peoples? Earth-leaders push for position, demagogues and delegates meet for summit talks, the God-deniers, the Messiah-defiers: 'Let's get free of God! Cast loose from Messiah!'" (Psalm 2:1-3 MSG)

"...the act of violence is in their hands.
Their feet run to evil, and they make haste to shed innocent blood: their thoughts are thoughts of iniquity; wasting and destruction are in their paths." (Isaiah 59:6-7)

"They weave wickedness, they hatch violence. They compete in the race to do evil and run to be the first to murder. They plan and plot evil, think and breathe evil, and leave a trail of wrecked lives behind them." (Isaiah 59:6-7 MSG)

Voltaire put it this way, "It is dangerous to be right in matters where established men are wrong." If you're a good person watch out! You are not just a target but a high-value target. The fact is that it is your high value that makes you a target.

It's highly unlikely that that US military has placed you on a terrorist watchlist. But there is another realm besides the natural one we usually consider in this world. All around us, battles are being waged in the spiritual world as God seeks to advance His kingdom on the Earth, and His archenemy, Satan, opposes Him at every turn. Good people are often targeted by the enemy, the devil, for attack. We may even be *high-value targets*, meaning that Satan has put a target on our backs because of the high purpose God has for our lives. He who would like nothing more than to steal our destiny, kill our dreams, and destroy our lives.

Jesus said this:

> *"The thief does not come except to steal, and to kill, and to destroy. I have come that they may have life, and that they may have it more abundantly."*
>
> (John 10:10 NKJV)

Most of us have experienced this threat at some point in our lives: a devastating medical report. A job loss. Divorce papers served to us unexpectedly. The late-night phone call telling of a loved one's sudden passing in a car accident.

Any number of problems may come our way that cause us to feel under attack. What can we do to fend off these attacks and ultimately gain victory in our lives? The first step is to gain knowledge. That's what this book is all about—to equip you with the knowledge to stand against the attacks of the enemy, especially the ones that indicate you are a high-value target, just like Osama bin Laden was to our United States military special operations teams.

When Are You under Attack?

Not long ago, I was standing with a group of men in the back of our church talking about this very subject. The men were each mentioning the problems they were experiencing in their lives and families, and they kept using the phrase that they were "under attack." Over and over, they kept saying, "I am under attack" or "The enemy is really attacking me in this area."

What they were saying may very well have been true. But the conversation was on my mind later that evening. In my own quiet prayer time, I said to God, "I think I am under attack, just like those men at church." I was also dealing with some issues in my life, and it seemed like a natural thing to mention to the Lord. But I heard His voice say to me: *"David, you are not under attack right now."* As I prayed further about the matter, I began to realize that sometimes the problems in our lives are not actually caused by the enemy and a direct attack from him. The truth is that we open the door to our problems through our own actions and attitudes.

That evening, I began to understand that certain situations in my life were creating the problems I was going through—and they had nothing to do with the devil's attacks! It may come as a surprise to you—as it did to me—that when we are going through difficult times in our lives, challenges that seem almost impossible to overcome, *our very first response* should be to check and see if we actually are being attacked. Addressing the actual root of the problem is what will make the biggest difference and propel us forward into God's destiny for our lives—not standing against an attack that isn't actually happening.

So, before we look at what to do to counter the attacks of the devil that wreak havoc in our lives, let's consider first what might be truly causing our problems—if we are not under attack. Here are five possible causes:

1. **We are overexposed to impurity.**

    Have you noticed that the culture around us seems to be growing more and more impure by the day? Things that would never have crossed the minds of our parents' and grandparents' generations have become commonplace in today's society. We are witnessing the undressing of America.

    Impurity surrounds us. And if we allow it into our lives in any way, we open ourselves up to all kinds of difficulties and challenges that we would not otherwise experience.

2. **We haven't renewed our minds.**

    When I prayed about these things that night, the Lord spoke very clearly to me. He said that my own personal challenges were the result of my living in an impure culture and not taking the steps I needed to take to renew my mind.

It can seem like an attack of the enemy when we allow our thought lives to run amok and we don't pull them under control. But it is really our own inattention to the renewal of our minds that is the problem.

The psalmist understood this when he wrote about what to do when we are surrounded by a society that does not take the ways of God seriously:

> *"Blessed is the man who walks not in the counsel of the ungodly, nor stands in the path of sinners, nor sits in the seat of the scornful;*
>
> *but his delight is in the law of the LORD; and in His law he meditates day and night.*
>
> *He shall be like a tree planted by the rivers of water, that brings forth its fruit in its season, whose leaf also shall not wither; and whatever he does shall prosper."* (Psalm 1:1–3 NKJV)

We must delight in the law of the Lord and meditate on it, no matter what is going on in the culture around us. When we do that, we will renew our minds.

3.   We are undisciplined.

If we are undisciplined in our lives, in any area—our finances, our health, our work ethic, our parenting skills—we will experience the consequences of that lack of discipline in negative ways. And that is not an attack of the enemy; that's just the natural consequences of our actions and attitudes.

Obedience to God and His Word will always reap positive rewards; laziness, slothfulness or a lack of discipline will not.

4.   We are not skilled in using the Word of God.

Many times, we could handle the problems we face in our day-to-day lives better if we were more aware of what God's Word says about our situations. Ignorance of the Bible's instructions and a lack of skill in applying the

Word in our lives will lead to challenges. We may even make our problems worse instead of better by floundering through them on our own. And again, that isn't necessarily an outright attack of the enemy; that is just a result of our own ignorance.

Get to know God's Word and what He has to say about how you should live your life! You won't regret it.

5. We are unyielded to the Holy Spirit.

God not only gave us His Word to help us through the situations and challenges we face in life; He also gave us His very Spirit to guide us through our own specific circumstances. But if we don't follow that still, small voice on the inside of us—which is actually the Holy Spirit whispering to us which way to go—then we will create further problems for ourselves. In these cases, the enemy doesn't need to attack us; we are filling our lives with trouble all on our own.

The Holy Spirit is available for you on a moment-by-moment basis to lead you and to guide you out of trouble successfully—to move you right on through it with the fewest repercussions. But you have to be tuned in to His voice and be obedient.

So, we are not always under attack from the enemy, even if it might seem that way at first. Keeping these points in mind, ask yourself the following questions to determine if you might, in fact, be experiencing a spiritual attack or if you are contributing to your own natural problems through your own actions or attitudes:

- Have I allowed the impure culture around me to creep into my life?

- Have I been actively renewing my mind on a daily basis, meditating on God's Word, and delighting in His truth?

- Have I been maintaining a life of discipline in every area, especially in those areas of life where I have been experiencing problems and challenges?

- How much of God's Word do I really know and apply to my life on a day-to-day basis? How much improvement do I need in this area?

- Is the Holy Spirit actively directing me each day in my specific situations—am I paying attention and listening for His voice, and then practicing an active and intentional obedience to His directives?

Consider your answers to each of these questions to see if you might be the cause of your own problems. But also know that even if you are not under a direct attack by the enemy at this moment, *you are certainly a high-value target*, and *you will certainly be under attack at some point* because of your incredible value in the kingdom of God.

How Do You Know You're Valuable?

Many of us have an understanding that God loves us and that we are valuable to Him—but do you know *why*? Just a vague concept of what your worth is to God's kingdom won't equip you to stand against the attacks of the enemy when they come. Ignorance won't cut it. You need a deep comprehension of who you are and what God has done for you so you can stand strong as a high-value target of the enemy and his kingdom. Here are eight assurances that you are valuable:

1. **You are made in the image of God.**

   Long ago, before God ever created people, Satan lived in heaven as one of God's most beautiful creations. He was an archangel, but when he rebelled, his fall was spectacular—and he became the ultimate archenemy of God and His purposes. His fall was so great that he took a third of God's angels with him, and he's been at war against God ever since. So how do you think he felt when God then created human beings, making them in His own image? Satan hates God—and anything that reminds him of God and the humiliation he suffered in his original fall. And now you, one of the very people who has been created in the image of the One he hates, remind him of everything he has lost.

The Bible says you were created in God's image:

> *"Then God said, 'Let Us make man in Our image, according to Our likeness; let them have dominion over the fish of the sea, over the birds of the air, and over the cattle, over all the earth and over every creeping thing that creeps on the earth.'*
>
> *So God created man in His own image; in the image of God He created him; male and female He created them."* (Genesis 1:26–27 NKJV)

You have been given the authority that Satan craves in this world.

You are a high-value target because you have been made in the image of God!

2. You were made to live forever.

You are an eternal being. You were made to live forever. Solomon, the wisest man who ever lived on the Earth, wrote that God *"has put eternity in [our] hearts"* (Ecclesiastes 3:11 NKJV). We are currently on this Earth with billions of other people, at this point in time—but this life here is not all there is. Every human being who lives now, who has ever lived, and who will ever live, is on a pathway that will never end. We are all eternal beings, destined for either heaven or hell.

Jesus mentioned this fact in John 10:27. He said, *"My sheep hear My voice, and I know them, and they follow Me."* Then He went on to say, *"I give them eternal life, and they shall never perish"* (27–28 NKJV).

Your life on Earth will continue until your physical death—but that is just a slight interruption before you move into your eternal destiny. Hebrews 9:27 tells us, *"It is appointed for men to die once, but after this the judgment"* (NKJV). That judgment doesn't have to be a frightening one if you have Jesus by your side: He took the punishment for all your sins, and He has opened the gateway to heaven for you. It is God's intention and His greatest desire to give you eternal life, for you to live in His presence forever.

I have many things in my life that were once valuable, but they aren't anymore. Maybe you do, too: old computers, televisions, and cell phones that are now obsolete. They have either worn out or lost their usefulness to us in whatever way, and they ultimately end up in the city dump or landfill. Those things have lost their value; you, as a human being made in God's image, will never lose your value. You will never end up in the trash heap of history because God has redeemed you and will bring you to His heavenly home on that glorious day when your life on this Earth is through. You have value because you were made to live forever!

3. **Jesus died for you.**

The most value that could be assigned to someone has already been assigned to you. Jesus Himself, the very Son of God, came to Earth and gave His life for yours. You may have heard it said that if you were the only person on this Earth who needed salvation, Jesus would have come and died—just for you. And that is the truth! The blood of Jesus is the price tag that has purchased the souls of each and every human being who will accept His offer of salvation—and that includes you:

> *"But God demonstrates His own love toward us, in that while we were still sinners, Christ died for us."* (Romans 5:8 NKJV)

You have immense, eternal value because Jesus gave His life—for you!

4. **Jesus lives in you (in the form of the Holy Spirit).**

The Good News doesn't end with your salvation from sin, bought by Jesus's death on the cross. No, it goes far beyond that. You can know that you are valuable because Jesus Christ Himself now is alive on the inside of you.

Can you grasp that concept? The Lord of the Universe, the One who spoke the galaxies into existence, now lives inside you in the form of the Holy Spirit. Can you understand just how much value that assigns to your life? How will your life change if you truly see yourself as the dwelling place of God?

The Scriptures put it this way: *"But we have this treasure in earthen vessels, that the excellence of the power may be of God and not of us"* (2 Corinthians 4:7 NKJV). And Paul tells us in the book of Romans, *"Much more then, having now been justified by His blood, we shall be saved from wrath through Him. For if when we were enemies we were reconciled to God through the death of his Son, much more, having been reconciled, we shall be saved by His life"* (Romans 5:9–10 NKJV). Much more than simply being reconciled to God by Jesus's death, we are saved by His life inside us! What is so valuable about that? You have the life of God inside you— God Himself. And with that life, you have His light: *"In Him was life; and the life was the light of men"* (John 1:4 NKJV).

Jesus is the Light that lights up the world—and He lights your life, too, so that you can be a witness for Him: *"You are the light of the world. A city that is set on a hill cannot be hidden"* (Matthew 5:14 NKJV). God needs you in this world to share His light with those around you. Your city needs you—and your community needs you. America needs you— now more than ever—because the greatest asset our country has in this day and age are citizens in whom Christ lives and through whom He can share His light. You have been given influence in your city, your nation, and your world—and that makes you extremely valuable in God's kingdom.

5. **You have the ability to affect the future.**

What you do matters! Here is what the Bible has to say about your potential:

> *"Those from among you shall build the*
> *old waste places: you shall raise up the*

> *foundations of many generations; and you*
> *shall be called the Repairer of the Breach, the*
> *Restorer of Streets to Dwell In.*
>
> *If you turn away your foot from the Sabbath,*
> *from doing your pleasure on My holy day, and*
> *call the Sabbath a delight, the holy day of the*
> *Lord honorable, and shall honor Him, not*
> *doing your own ways, nor finding your own*
> *pleasure, nor speaking your own words,*
>
> *then you shall delight yourself in the Lord."*
>
> (Isaiah 58:12–14 NKJV)

You have a divine destiny to raise up the waste places of this Earth, to repair the breaches of broken relationships, and to restore the paths, or "streets," that the people of this world will follow. You are an important influencer for God's work on this Earth—and under your influence, the future will be changed. You will build up the generations that are coming behind you, and you will help to set the foundation for the future that is yet to come. Imagine glancing into a film about the future. Notice faces. Hear the stories. Because of your influence, the world changed. God has given you the ability to do that.

6.   You help shape your spouse.

Not only do you have an effect on the future of the world in general, you have an extremely strong influence on the people who are closest to you. For most of us, that person is our spouse. You are an extremely valuable influence on your husband or your wife. Spouses affect each other in an infinite and intimate number of ways—and together, a husband and wife can do more for God's kingdom than they ever could do on their own. The ways in which you shape your spouse and the influence you can have on the world together make you extremely valuable to the kingdom of God. They also make the two of you a high-value target to the enemy.

7. **Your children will be what you are.**

In addition to your influence on your spouse, arguably the person closest to you on this Earth, you have an incredible influence on the children whom God blesses you with. In fact, your children will not just do as you do—they will actually be what you are. They follow our example, sometimes to a T—and they are the ones we send directly into the future to continue our influence on this world when our own time here is over.

The Bible tells us, *"You are our epistle written in our hearts, known and read by all men"* (2 Corinthians 3:2). That means that, as the examples God has made us to be for our children, we ourselves—who we are, the lives we live out before them—are the actual "epistle," or Word of God, that they see and "read" every single day. Both fathers and mothers have extraordinarily important roles to play in their children's lives: they are the epistles of the Lord to their children. As a parent, you are extremely valuable to God's kingdom!

8. **Your children's children will be what you are.**

When you have children, you are stretching your godly influence into the future. And your spiritual heritage doesn't stop with the sons and daughters you bring into this world. Not only will your children become who you are—but their children will also become who you are, because you have taught your children the ways of the Lord. They will, in turn, teach those ways to your grandchildren, who will teach them to your great-grandchildren, and so on.

Let's consider the math here for just a moment. If you were to have four children of your own, and you lived a godly life before them, inspiring them to have godly children of their own—imagine if each of them had four children of their own. If the same thing happens to the next generation, and the generation after that, can you see how the multiplication process leads to an incredibly strong godly influence in this world?

———

Given all these reasons you are so valuable to God's kingdom, is it any wonder that Satan would put a target on your back? You have incredible value in God's eyes—not just as His amazing creation, made in His very image—but because of the design and purpose He has for you, for your spouse, for your children, and for your children's children on this Earth.

Sometimes the troubles you face have nothing to do with an attack by the enemy. But rest assured: you are valuable to the kingdom of God. You have a destiny to fulfill on this Earth. And that makes you a high-value target to God's enemy, the devil. He will attack you—if not now, then someday soon. Keep reading to learn what to do when you find yourself targeted by the enemy.

> *"Be sober, be vigilant; because your adversary the devil walks about like a roaring lion, seeking whom he may devour.*
>
> *Resist him, steadfast in the faith, knowing that the same sufferings are experienced by your brotherhood in the world."*   (1 Peter 5:8–9 NKJV)

Chapter 2

Who Is the Enemy?

T he first rule of warfare is pretty basic, but it is extremely important if we are going to win the battle: know your enemy. Remember the advanced tactics that the United States used to capture Osama bin Laden: months of sophisticated intelligence gathering and planning for the strike and then, after the successful strike, the collection of DNA evidence to confirm the target. The United States works proactively with its intelligence operatives to gather information about our nation's biggest threats— so that we can remain always prepared for a potential attack. The same is true in our spiritual battles: Satan uses advanced tactics against Christians to defeat God's purposes in the world. We must know our enemy and learn his tactics, his "devices," the tricks he will use to try to deceive us:

> *"Lest Satan should get an advantage of us:*
> *for we are not ignorant of his devices."*
>
> (2 Corinthians 2:11)

If we are aware of Satan's devices, he has less of a chance of getting an advantage over us. We want to minimize his ability to infect our lives by learning about him and how he operates:

> *"Be sober, be vigilant; because your adversary*
> *the devil, as a roaring lion, walketh about, seeking*
> *whom he may devour:*

Whom resist steadfast in the faith, knowing that the same afflictions are accomplished in your brethren that are in the world." (1 Peter 5:8–9)

To be sober means to be serious. To be vigilant means to be on guard. Our adversary, the devil, walks around as a roaring lion seeking whom he may devour. This is a very important phrase: "whom he may devour." His ability to devour any of us is determined by whether or not we know what's going on and whether or not we allow it to happen. We are to resist the devil, which will prevent him from devouring us, our families, and our ministries. We are to resist him steadfast in the faith.

Also, we are not wrestling against flesh and blood. Your enemy is not other people. Your enemy is Satan, the devil. Even those people who seem to be enemies of godly Christians, those people who plot evil against the United States, including terrorists and those we would call "evil" in nature may have been captured by the true enemy, Satan. And because they have been captured by him, he is able to coerce them and manipulate them into doing his will. But they themselves are *not* the enemy. People are not your enemy. And our ultimate task is to win them back from Satan unto the Lord:

"For we wrestle not against flesh and blood, but against principalities, against powers, against the rulers of the darkness of this world, against spiritual wickedness in high places."

(Ephesians 6:12)

Although we do not wrestle against flesh and blood, we still have to deal with principalities, powers, and spirits that are positioned in the hierarchy of Satan's kingdom. I am referring to Satan and his evil spirits.

Notice that the Bible says we wrestle "against the rulers *of the darkness* of this world." The enemy is not *the ruler of this world*. He is the ruler of the *darkness* of this world. These rulers are those evil spirits intent on bringing the world into darkness and out of the light. And then there is spiritual wickedness in high places. Each of these demonic spirits has a position in the rank and file of the hierarchy, and they are in high locations. But we must always remember that our enemy is not flesh and blood, but principalities and powers, rulers of the darkness of the world, and spiritual wickedness in high places.

What should we learn about the enemy? We don't want to be ignorant of his devices. Let's look at ten of his characteristics:

1. Satan is an accuser.

First, Satan is an accuser. There are people, his instruments, who are territories already occupied by him, human beings under his sway, under his leadership, under his servanthood. And they will become his instruments used by him to accuse you:

> *"And I heard a loud voice saying in heaven,*
> *Now is come salvation, and strength, and the*
> *kingdom of our God, and the power of his*
> *Christ for the accuser of our brethren is cast*
> *down, which accused them before our God day*
> *and night."*   (Revelation 12:10)

At the point in time when Jesus died on the cross at Calvary, salvation had come. At that point, salvation, strength, the kingdom of God, and the power of Christ all came to the human race. And this crucifixion, this bearing of our sin, this resurrection of Christ changed Satan's status. After Calvary's victory, the accuser (Satan) of the brethren (that's you) was cast down. He used to accuse us before God day and night, but he has now lost his status. God is no longer on talking terms with him. He was defeated at Calvary. Before that defeat at Calvary, he was the legal leader on the Earth. Adam turned his authority over to him, and because God is a God of law, He didn't violate His law. Satan used to accuse the human race before God, but now he has lost that status and has been cast down.

However, Satan is still the accuser—it's in his nature, and he hasn't stopped accusing. It's so important to remember that when he accuses you now, you do not have to believe his accusations. He will often include part of the truth in his accusations, and because people know that part of what he is saying is true, they think *everything* he says is true. But he is a liar, and if we believe his lies, they will bring destruction into our lives. He says things like, "You're not forgiven," "You're not cleansed," "You're the same as you always were," "You're never going to amount to anything," "You're stupid," "You can't do anything right," "There's no meaning to your life," and "You think God loves you? You're kidding yourself." On and on the accusations go. Those voices will keep coming at you because that's his nature. He's an accuser.

Don't believe his lies! Stand against him and remember: he was defeated at Calvary!

2. Satan is a tempter.

Our enemy is also a tempter:

> *"And when the tempter came to him, he said, If thou be the Son of God, command that these stones be made bread.*
> *But he answered and said, It is written, Man shall not live by bread alone, but by every word that proceedeth out of the mouth of God."* (Matthew 4:3–4)

Don't ever think you are immune from temptation—Jesus Himself wasn't, so why should you be? When the tempter came to Jesus, he tempted Him three different times. In this instance, he said, "If you're the Son of God, command these stones to be turned into bread." Remember, Jesus hadn't eaten for forty days and forty nights. So, Satan came to Jesus to tempt Him in an area in which He might have had some weakness. Do you ever wonder sometimes why temptation is so escalated in your life, whatever nature of temptation he uses against you? Sometimes it is due to the weaknesses we have in our own flesh:

> *"Let no man say when he is tempted, I am*
> *tempted of God: for God cannot be tempted*
> *with evil, neither tempteth he any man:*
>
> *But every man is tempted, when he is drawn*
> *away of his own lust, and enticed."*
>
> (James 1:13–14)

God is never the one who is tempting you. The Bible tells us that every man is tempted when he's drawn away by his own lusts and enticed. We have enough problems at that level, the level of the flesh, but then, on top of that, to exacerbate the problem, Satan comes along and escalates that temptation.

> *"For this cause, when I could no longer*
> *forbear, I sent to know your faith, lest by some*
> *means the tempter have tempted you, and our*
> *labour be in vain."* (1 Thessalonians 3:5)

Satan comes to accuse you, and he comes to tempt you. He will tempt you to lie and to deceive. He will tempt you into lust. He will tempt you to be bitter. He will tempt you to speak evil. He will tempt you in a million different ways. He is a tempter.

3. Satan is a murderer.

Our enemy is a killer. He has no scruples at all. He kills children. He kills babies. He has no conscience whatsoever:

> *"Ye are of your father the devil, and the lusts*
> *of your father ye will do. **He was a murderer***
> ***from the beginning."*** (John 8:44)

Satan, the devil, was a murderer from the beginning. And he is not about to change.

4. Satan is a liar.

> *"Ye are of your father the devil, and the lusts*
> *of your father ye will do. . . When he speaketh*
> *a lie, he speaketh of his own: for he is a liar,*
> *and the father of it."* (John 8:44)

The enemy is a liar. Do you ever wonder why you may suddenly have thoughts that are so opposite from the truth? Where do these thoughts come from? They are assaults. You are under attack. The enemy is going to tell you things about people that are not true. He's going to create suspicion in you about others. He will tell you outright lies. And he has a way of embellishing them to make them seem true. He will grab some fragment of evidence and drag it into your thinking, if you allow him to. He will turn you into a distrusting, negative-thinking person because of the lies he whispers into your ears. When he speaks a lie, the Bible says that "he speaketh of his own." He is not repeating someone else's lie—he is the originator of all lies. He is a liar and the father of lies. In life, you might not always keep a lie from being stated. But you can choose to not believe that lie. That is how to respond to Satan. Don't believe a word he says. That is the choice you must make.

5. Satan is a thief and a destroyer.

> *"The thief cometh not, but for to steal, and to*
> *kill, and to destroy: I am come that they might*
> *have life, and that they might have it more*
> *abundantly."* (John 10:10)

The enemy is a thief. He wants to steal. He has no constructive reason to be in your life. There is nothing good that will happen to you because of him, ever. He may try to use some things that may seem better for you in order to trick you. But he comes to steal, he comes to kill, and he comes to destroy. Now, this destruction may be physical.

Satan hates your body because it is the temple of the Holy Spirit. Your body belongs to God, and the enemy is the arch-hater of everything that is God's—and so he has a very strong hatred for your physical condition. If he can put disease and sickness on you, he will. Now, granted, there are many different causes of disease. Not all of them can be directly attributed to Satan, but some of them can. There are some sicknesses and some diseases that can be dealt with only by first dealing with the devil.

But the enemy doesn't just want to kill your body; he also wants to destroy you psychologically. Psychological warfare is a big deal going on in the world right now. And Satan is the originator of it. He wants you to lose your sanity. He's not interested in your mental health. If you allow his accusations; his deceit; and his mental, emotional, and psychological manipulation in your life, he will ultimately destroy you.

I am absolutely persuaded that the wisest psychological and psychiatric help that you can ever get comes from Jesus:

> *"The thief cometh not, but for to steal, and to kill, and to destroy: I am come that they might have life, and that they might have it more abundantly."* (John 10:10)

Jesus came so that we might have life and that we might have it more abundantly. We have not been given a spirit of fear, but a spirit of power, love, and *a sound mind*. Satan's destruction is not merely physical; he wants to destroy your mind, your emotions, your very soul. But Jesus wants to bless you and give you abundant life.

6. **Satan is a provoker.**

> *"And Satan stood up against Israel, and provoked David to number Israel."* (1 Chronicles 21:1)

The enemy is a provoker. In this particular case, Satan himself stood up against the whole nation of Israel and provoked David. Now, to "provoke" means "to incite, to aggravate to a wrong reaction." You might think you have a few people in your life who do this pretty well, so you don't need the devil to provoke you. But remember, if somebody's provoking you, that person is not the problem. People are just conquered territory, and they're doing what they do best because they don't know any better. It is really the enemy provoking you through them.

7.   Satan is a blinder.

"In whom the god of this world hath blinded
the minds of them which believe not, lest the
light of the glorious gospel of Christ, who is
the image of God, should shine unto them."

(2 Corinthians 4:4)

It is no accident that Satan is referred to as that "old serpent the devil." Did you know that certain kinds of serpents make a hissing sound? They have hollow front teeth, and before they attack their prey, poison is dropped down into those hollow teeth, and when they hiss, they are actually blowing the poison into the face of their prey, and it blinds them. Satan, that old serpent, uses this same tactic to blind us, his prey. He blinds unbelievers to the truth of the Gospel. He blinds us to the knowledge of how much God loves us.

But the Spirit of the Lord came upon Jesus, and He is coming upon us, to open the eyes of those who have been blinded, to bring deliverance to the captives. The Spirit gives us a new way of seeing life. Through Him we are no longer blinded by the foe.

8.   Satan is a deceiver.

The enemy is a deceiver:

> *"And the great dragon was cast out, that old
> serpent, called the Devil, and Satan, which
> deceiveth the whole world: he was cast out
> into the earth, and his angels were cast out
> with him."*   (Revelation 12:9)

Satan is called the "great dragon that was cast out."
Where is he now? He has been cast out of heaven—and
now he deceives the whole world. The world is in its present
condition right now because of the deception of the enemy.
Now, his packages look innocent enough. If you want to
deceive somebody, if you want to poison somebody, you
don't give them a bottle to drink that says "arsenic" on
it. No, you slip it into the cherry pie. You deceive people
into thinking of doing what they otherwise wouldn't even
contemplate.

That's what the enemy does. He's a deceiver. When he
was cast out into the Earth, his angels were cast out with
him. He's not alone. One-third of the host of heaven fell with
Satan, and they are now the demons who seek to deceive us
every day.

> *"And no marvel; for Satan himself is
> transformed into an angel of light. Therefore
> it is no great thing if his ministers also be
> transformed as the ministers of righteousness;
> whose end shall be according to their works."*
>   (2 Corinthians 11:14–15)

Satan's ability to deceive is quite remarkable. Satan
himself appears to be transformed into an angel of light.
He appears to be a good guy if we aren't paying attention.
He's wearing a white hat, not a black hat. Therefore, it's
not a stretch to understand that his ministers, those other
angels that fell with him, would also be transformed into
appearing as ministers of righteousness. Not everything that
talks "Christianese" is Christian. The way to lead people to
hell isn't to show up as a devil with a red suit, horns, and a

pitchfork. The way you really lead people to hell is to look like you're leading them to heaven. Thus, our enemy is a deceiver. Do not listen to his lies.

9. **Satan entraps.**

The enemy also sets traps:

> *"And that they may recover themselves out of the snare of the devil, who are taken captive by him at his will."* (2 Timothy 2:26)

The devil ensnares people. He tricks them:

> *"Woe unto them that call evil good, and good evil; that put darkness for light, and light for darkness; that put bitter for sweet, and sweet for bitter!"* (Isaiah 5:20)

What is the magnitude of his treachery? It's described for us here in Scripture: "Woe unto them that call evil good, who call good evil." That's what he does: He switches the price tags on the merchandise. He sets people up in snares. That's why you need to know the enemy.

Have you ever felt trapped in a situation or a place—literally or figuratively? Stuck. Unable to move. That is our enemy's plan—to entrap us.

10. **Satan complicates.**

The enemy complicates everything:

> *"But I fear, lest by any means, as the serpent beguiled Eve through his subtilty, so your minds should be corrupted from the simplicity that is in Christ."* (2 Corinthians 11:3)

The devil beguiled Eve through his subtlety, his ability to deceive. Paul was concerned that the Corinthian believers would have their minds corrupted away from the simplicity of the Gospel. Satan loves to confound, to make things complicated, but God's ways, God's plans—the Gospel itself—is simple:

> *"And an highway shall be there, and a way,*
> *and it shall be called The way of holiness; the*
> *unclean shall not pass over it; but it shall be*
> *for those: the wayfaring men, though fools,*
> *shall not err therein. "*   (Isaiah 35:8)

In fact, the Scripture says that God's way is so simple that a foolish, wayfaring man would be able to follow it. It's not complicated. But the enemy complicates things. He is treacherous, and he loves to deceive people's minds, just like he did to Eve. He tries to do the same thing to people today.

How to Watch for
Early Warning Signs of Enemy Activity

It is possible to stop the enemy in his tracks by knowing the early warning signs of one of his attacks. Watch out for the following seven signs:

1. The intrusion of unscriptural thoughts

One of the first signs that you are under an attack from the enemy is the intrusion of unscriptural thoughts in your mind. When you get a thought that is unscriptural, it should send you into immediate alert, and you should make an immediate response. The way you are constructed—spirit, soul, and body—was designed on purpose that way by God. God speaks to the spirit to change the mind, but everybody else, including the enemy, must speak to the mind to change the spirit. Satan does not have direct access to your spirit unless you've already been demonized. He must get to your spirit through your mind. God, on the other hand, speaks to your spirit to affect your mind. So, one of the first signs of an enemy attack is that Satan will try to intrude into your mind with unscriptural thoughts.

How should you respond? Purposefully think on these things:

> *"Finally, brethren, whatsoever things are true,*
> *whatsoever things are honest, whatsoever*
> *things are just, whatsoever things are pure,*
> *whatsoever things are lovely, whatsoever*
> *things are of good report; if there be any*
> *virtue, and if there be any praise, think on*
> *these things.*
>
> *Those things, which ye have both learned, and*
> *received, and heard, and seen in me, do: and*
> *the God of peace shall be with you."*
>
> (Philippians 4:8–9)

If the thoughts you have been having do not meet the criteria of Philippians 4, then you can know that they are not from God. Begin to think thoughts that are of God to defeat this first line of attack from the enemy.

If a deceiving, deceptive thought occurs, you know it's not a biblical thought. Begin to think on things that are true. Your mind was not designed to entertain the gross, the wicked, the evil. It was designed to think lovely thoughts. And so, when your thoughts are being intruded by thoughts that are contrary to Philippians 4, beware: this is an early warning sign that you are under attack.

2.   A spirit of heaviness

The second early warning sign is when you develop what we call a "heavy spirit." The response to this sign of attack is to put on the garment of praise for the spirit of heaviness:

> *"Why art thou cast down, O my soul? and*
> *why art thou disquieted within me? hope thou*
> *in God: for I shall yet praise him, who is the*
> *health of my countenance, and my God."*
>
> (Psalm 42:11)

When your spirit starts to feel cast down, ask it: "Why are you cast down, O my soul? Why are you disquieted? Why are you perturbed and disturbed within me?"

We would not be allowed on an airplane carrying luggage which was too heavy. We should not expect to travel where God is taking us in life if we hold the heavy weight from the enemy. It holds us back. It knocks us down.

You need to immediately, and consciously, determine to place your hope in God. When you praise Him, He will then be the health of your countenance. Watch out for a heavy spirit. It's an indication of a Satanic attack on your mind and your spirit.

3. The interruption of peace

And third, the interruption of your peace is a strong sign that you are under an attack of the enemy:

> *"Peace I leave with you, my peace I give unto you: not as the world giveth, give I unto you. Let not your heart be troubled, neither let it be afraid."* (John 14:27)

Jesus has told us that He has given us His peace—and His peace is not like the peace of the world. When the world gives you something, it almost always tries to take it back. The peace from the world lacks sincerity and depth. Did you know that a lack of peace will affect your whole well-being? But Jesus's peace will fill your entire being. He wants you to live in His peace in your heart and your soul. He told us to not let our hearts be troubled. We are not to live in fear when He is with us. So you can know that when your peace is interrupted, it is an early warning sign that you are under attack.

4. The loss of joy

Fourth, the loss of your joy signals an enemy attack:

> *"And ye now therefore have sorrow: but I will*
> *see you again, and your heart shall rejoice,*
> *and your joy no man taketh from you."*
>
> (John 16:22)

When you are filled with the Spirit of the Lord, your heart will rejoice, and no one will be able to take your joy away from you. So, if you are starting to experience a loss of joy, you can know you are under attack.

5. The presence of fear

The presence of fear is a strong indication that you are under attack from the enemy.

> *"For God hath not given us the spirit of fear;*
> *but of power, and of love, and of a sound*
> *mind."*
>
> (2 Timothy 1:7)

God has not given us a spirit of fear! For every fear that Satan thrusts at you, God has a biblical antidote to that fear. There is a promise, a commitment, from God to counteract every fear that could come your way. God has also given you power to conquer your fears. You can have a sound mind every minute of the day—God has made that provision for you. So watch out when fear tries to come against you; that indicates an enemy attack.

6. A sense of bondage

> *"Now the Lord is that Spirit: and where the*
> *Spirit of the Lord is, there is liberty."*
>
> (2 Corinthians 3:17)

7. A division between you and fellow Christians

Finally, you can know you are under attack from the enemy when division comes between you and your fellow brothers and sisters in Christ. Satan is a divider. One of his favorite strategies is to divide and conquer:

"But he, knowing their thoughts, said unto them, Every kingdom divided against itself is brought to desolation; and a house divided against a house falleth."   (Luke 11:17)

Every kingdom divided against itself is brought to desolation. That includes churches and families—if they are divided against themselves, they are going to fall.

It's good for brothers and sisters in the Lord to dwell together in unity. When something is fracturing your relationship with a fellow believer, you can assume that you're under attack from the enemy.

Our adversary, the devil, walks around like a roaring lion, seeking whom he may devour. He is our enemy. If we stop him, we win, we conquer! And then we will have the chance to set other people free as well. Be aware of his strategies so you can stand against him in whatever attack he may send your way. See the victory in sight. Stand up and believe the enemy has been defeated.

Chapter 3

Beware!

I t has been said that the most dangerous enemy is the one you don't know is there.

Some years ago, a man backed his bright, shiny new Cadillac out of his driveway and headed for the interstate on his daily commute to the office. As he listened to the music on the radio, he busied himself shaving at the stoplights—a common practice for him. He turned to the news and traffic reports as he made his way to work that morning. All was completely normal, until, witnesses say, he suddenly reached up behind his neck—and then slumped over the wheel.

The car swerved wildly, and then, out of control, flew into a culvert. The car was completely demolished, and the man was killed.

An autopsy told the real story of what had happened to this man. A small pinprick behind the man's ear indicated a wasp sting. The insect had likely flown from behind the seat, or another part of the car, and stung the man. He was temporarily blinded with pain as the wasp's sting temporarily hit a nerve in his neck. He slumped across the wheel, lost control of his brand-new Cadillac, and consequently lost his life.

Normally, a full-grown man would be able to swat aside a tiny insect with no problem. But when that insect hit its mark that day, the result was fatal.

Our enemy is not a wasp or any kind of insect. It's not even any kind of animal or other human being on the earth. Our enemy is the devil himself, and if we are not careful—if we do not remain vigilant of his subtle attacks—we could fall victim to something we didn't see coming, just like the driver of the Cadillac on his way to work.

Being on guard against the enemy—especially when you realize that you are a high-value target and on Satan's "hit list"—is the first step you should take to protect yourself. Increasing your awareness of his tactics and his strategies to take you out—to steal your God-given dreams and destiny—is what this book is all about. And the first step to accomplishing this is to *beware*.

That might seem obvious to you at first glance. Of course, we should beware of our enemy! But what does that actually mean? *Merriam-Webster* has given us a clue in its definition: To *beware* means "to be cautious, to be on one's guard, to be wary, to take care, and to take heed, especially in reference to a danger." Again—obvious, right? We must be on our guard against what's coming at us from the enemy. The real question is this: what, exactly, should we beware of? What specifically are the enemy's tactics that we should be on guard against? When we identify these strategies of the devil, we will not only be aware of them, and gain an advantage in that way—but we will also be able to turn and go on the offense against him—not giving up an inch of our own destiny. We also will move forward and take back the things he has stolen from us, restoring what God has intended for us to have all along.

The good news is that I have identified ten different strategies of the enemy, described in the Scriptures, that God wants us to be on guard against. The even greater news is that these strategies do not have to bring fear into our lives. In other words, when we *beware* of them, we don't need to find ourselves cowering behind a tree or hiding in the bushes, looking for Satan's work at every turn. No, we use the wisdom that comes from God and His Word, we take a good hard look at the situations and the possible "attacks" we are facing, and we, soberly and with good judgment, consider whether one or more of the devil's tactics are wreaking havoc in our lives.

Beware of These Ten Things

Let's look at these ten strategies of the enemy—things we are to beware of, to guard against occurring in our lives:

1. Beware that you do not forget God.

This is perhaps the most important warning we ever receive in the Scriptures. God has made it clear that He must be first in our lives; if that is not the case, then everything else in our lives will eventually fall apart. The devil's number-one strategy will always be to tempt us away from God, from staying close to Him, from trusting Him with every area of our lives.

Sometimes the enemy does this by tempting us away with good things. God Himself warned against this happening to His people all the way back in the book of Deuteronomy in the Old Testament:

> *"**Beware that you do not forget the Lord your God** by not keeping His commandments, His judgments, and His statutes which I command you today,*
>
> *lest—when you have eaten and are full, and have built beautiful houses and dwell in them;*
>
> *and when your herds and your flocks multiply, and your silver and your gold are multiplied, and all that you have is multiplied;*
>
> *when your heart is lifted up, and you forget the Lord your God who brought you out of the land of Egypt, from the house of bondage."*
>
> (Deuteronomy 8:11–14 NKJV)

Did you catch that? The very first word in this passage of Scripture is *Beware!* We are to beware that we never forget the Lord our God.

Is it possible to discern when a person has forgotten God in his or her life? Sure, it is. Look at these verses again. Many times, God's people don't forget about Him in their minds—they still remember Him, and they usually remember what He has called them to do. That is not really what we are asked to "beware" against. What we are to watch out for is forgetting God *in not keeping His commandments, His judgments, and His statutes.* We know we have forgotten God when we quit keeping His commandments.

There is an antidote to help us keep this from ever happening in our walk with the Lord, and it is given in this famous passage in Proverbs. We may have memorized it—but have we really applied it to our lives? Could that be a summary of how we choose to live?

> *"Trust in the Lord with all your heart, and lean not on your own understanding; in all your ways acknowledge Him, and He shall direct thy paths."* (Proverbs 3:5–6 NKJV)

If we want to stay safe from the attacks of the enemy, if we want to stand guard against every evil plan he has for our lives, *we must not forget about God!* We must keep Him first in our lives—in anything that applies to us. In my own life, before I ever speak, act, or make a decision in any given situation, I first check to see if God has a commandment that applies to what I am considering. If He does, I obey that commandment immediately, without compromise, and joyfully—all the time, every time.

Beware that you don't forget God!

2. Beware of false prophets.

The second thing we are to guard against, according to God's Word to us, are false prophets. The word *prophet* isn't used that much in our society today. Occasionally, we may hear of someone on the news who is trying to predict the end of the world who has labeled himself a "prophet" and who believes he can forecast the future. Most of us know to stay away from those types. But that is not the only "false prophet" we should be wary of. These people may not call themselves "prophets." But they do tend to move in religious circles and try to influence people in ways that are outside God, His Word, and His ways. And when you spot one—watch out.

When traveling, you should only trust the right people or devices for directions. Why would you receive guidance from someone who doesn't want you to reach you desired destination? False prophets provide dangerous information—which we must reject.

Most of the false prophets, if you want to know the truth, are found in churches all across our land. They're also quite prevalent on Christian television. That means every time you watch Christian television or even set foot in a church you've never been to before, you need to beware. Not all churches are the safe zones we think they should be. There could be a false prophet in charge, or false prophecies being given—and that is why you need to know how to judge a prophecy by God's Word.

Four Kinds of Wolves

The Bible describes false prophets as "wolves in sheep's clothing." You may remember this analogy from the fairy tale involving Little Red Riding Hood. The consequences of not watching out for false prophets can be costly—even deadly—in our lives:

> *"Beware of false prophets, who come to you in sheep's clothing, but inwardly they are ravenous wolves...*
> *Therefore by their fruits you will know them."*
>
> (Matthew 7:15, 20 NKJV)

There are four types of these wolves that God has described to us in His Word—wolves we need to beware of:

1. Judges

The first type of wolf is a *judge*. The Old Testament book of Zephaniah talks about corrupt judges being wolves who prey upon the people: *"Her princes in her midst are roaring lions; her judges are evening wolves that leave not a bone till the morning. Her prophets are insolent, treacherous people; her priests have polluted the sanctuary, they have done violence to the law. The* LORD *is righteous in her midst, He will do no unrighteousness. Every morning He brings His justice to light; He never fails, but the unjust knows no shame"* (Zephaniah 3:3–5 NKJV). God even describes them as having "done violence to the law"—isn't that an interesting phrase?

Judges—and this included the leaders, the magistrates, the princes of the nations of that time—who do not represent God are referred to as *wolves*. They are placed in their seats of power to be the voice of God for the people, but when they abuse those positions of power, they become as ravenous wolves. They kill one time, but they will eat the results of the killing the next day. They gnaw on the bones the next day. These false prophets, these wolves, were not present only in Old Testament times; they are still alive and active in our own nation today. Our just God will bring justice to the corrupt false prophets in our country as we cry out to Him—I am so glad that, as Zephaniah has said, He is still in our midst!

2. Selfish Spiritual Leaders

Secondly, selfish spiritual leaders wreak havoc on the people, and the Bible calls them *wolves* as well. The prophet Ezekiel had this to say about these evil priests who were meant to do the work of God but were only in it for themselves: *"Her priests have violated My law and profaned My holy things: they have not distinguished between the holy and unholy, nor have they made known the difference between the unclean and the clean; and they have hidden their eyes from My Sabbaths, so that I am profaned among them. Her princes in her midst are like wolves tearing the prey, to shed blood, to destroy people, and to get dishonest gain"* (Ezekiel 22:26–27 NKJV).

When God's leaders violate His law and profane His holy things, they show no difference between the unclean and the clean. Can you see how this has become a huge problem in America today? It is a problem in America because it is a problem in the Church. As the Church goes, so goes a nation:

> *"For the time has come for judgment to begin at the house of God; and if it begins with us first, what will be the end of those who do not obey the gospel of God?*
>
> *Now 'if the righteous one is scarcely saved, where will the ungodly and the sinner appear?'"*   (1 Peter 4:17–18 NKJV)

Judgment must begin at the house of God. The problem in America today is a spiritual problem, and the foundation of all the spiritual issues we face in America right now is the Christian Church. The greatest need we have in America today is not a political solution—it is a spiritual revival in the Church. Until we have that, until our spiritual leaders stop behaving like wolves—shedding innocent blood and destroying souls for their own selfish, dishonest gain—we will never see revival in our nation.

Leaders in the Church had better never be in the ministry to make money, and our decisions should never be made based on our budgets, on how much is in the offering plates, or how much certain programs will bring in. We must listen to God's voice first—the great Shepherd of the sheep—whose motivation is love and care for His people, and whose anger is stoked when selfish leaders in His Church take advantage of His sheep.

3. False Prophets

Third, false prophets seek to destroy the people by masquerading in sheep's clothing—but the Bible says that they are easy to spot: *"Therefore by their fruits you will know them"* (Matthew 7:20 NKJV). You will know them by their fruit—that is, the results that are visible in their lives will betray their true motivations. And when you judge them by the standard of New Testament prophecy—whether or not their words edify (build you up), exhort (challenge you to do better), or comfort you—you can also know whether or not they are of God.

The purpose of prophecy is not to tear you down but to build you up. Not to take from you but to point you in the right direction. Also, if a prophet can't quote a Scripture to back up the direction he or she is giving to you, do not listen—instead, *beware*.

4. False Teachers and Church Leaders

Finally, false teachers and church leaders are the fourth kind of wolves the Bible speaks of: *"Therefore I testify to you this day that I am innocent of the blood of all men. For I have not shunned to declare to you the whole counsel of God. Therefore, take heed to yourselves and to all the flock, among which the Holy Spirit has made you overseers, to shepherd the church of God which He purchased with His own blood"* (Acts 20:26–28 NKJV).

Paul used interesting words in this passage: *"I am innocent of the blood of all men...I have not shunned to declare to you the whole counsel of God."* Now, that's what you want to look for in a pastor, a prophet, or a teacher—whomever you allow to speak for God into your life. That kind of person will give you the whole counsel of God. People like these share God's truth because they don't want the blood of the people on their hands. They know that the people they are giving counsel to are those who have been purchased with Jesus's own blood.

The most frightening thing I do in my life is to stand before people each week to deliver the Word of God. The highest priority on my schedule in a given week is not the hundreds of duties of things that most people would see as needing to be done. No—it's the fact that I am going to minister to those whom *Jesus purchased with His own blood.* That goes for you, too. You're not one person out of a mass of billions. You are someone who needs this Gospel of grace, and you are a person whom Jesus has purchased with His blood.

In America, we need to start judging what's going on in the Church because the wolves are loose. The people exist for the leadership—not the other way around. It can be tempting for churches to just give people what makes them feel good: It doesn't take a genius to figure out that the fastest way to build a crowd—or a congregation—is to give people what they want. Change the diet, promote the product, sell the gimmick. But if we are not careful, the wolves will enter, and they will not spare the flock. They will draw God's disciples away from Him and pull them to follow their own agendas.

Paul feared this after his time in leadership was over: *"For I know this, that after my departure savage wolves will come in among you, not sparing the flock"* (Acts 20:29 NKJV).

Let's watch for all four of these types of wolves in our midst.

3. Beware of men.

After taking care that we do not forget God, and that we are watching out for false prophets, our next priority is protecting ourselves from other people (the ones we typically "beware of" first):

> *"But beware of men, for they will deliver*
> *you up to councils and scourge you in their*
> *synagogues.*

*You will be brought before governors and
kings for My sake, as a testimony to them and
to the Gentiles.*

*But when they deliver you up, do not worry
about how or what you should speak. For
it will be given to you in that hour what you
should speak;*

*for it is not you who speak, but the Spirit of
your Father who speaks in you.*

*Now brother will deliver up brother to death,
and a father his child; and children will rise
up against parents and cause them to be put to
death.*

*And you will be hated by all for My name's
sake. But he who endures to the end will be
saved."*   (Matthew 10:17–22 NKJV)

Beware of men—and I am sure you know this also means to beware of women. We are to beware of other people. Watch out who you allow into your inner circle, those whom you allow to be your confidants. This verse is likely talking about other people giving a literal scourging because, back in Bible times, that was more likely than it is today. But you can still get a tongue lashing behind your back in our modern times. Thankfully, the Word also tells us that the Spirit of our Father will remain within us when those times come. Even though we must beware of men and women, if we get into trouble, we can count on the Holy Spirit. A day is coming, the Bible tells us, when brother will deliver brother to death—children will rise up against their parents, and we will be hated by all men for the sake of Jesus's name. But the person who endures to the end shall be saved.

In our own modern Church, we have suffered at least thirty years of indoctrination by the "how to win friends and influence people" crowd. I'm not against Dale Carnegie personally, and I'm certainly all for honorable, respectful manners in dealing with other people. But we have become so conditioned to "be nice" that we don't speak up—we don't think other people will respond the "right way." We don't want to offend people, and because of this, our mouths have been silenced—and the Gospel has become watered down. In America today, the mouth of the Church—the true Church, the righteous Church—has been stopped. We have decided to just send our money to the televangelists and let them broadcast the Gospel for us. Now, there is nothing wrong with television per se, but there *is* something wrong when we are willing to substitute a microphone and a camera for our own personal witness.

Here is the Bible's proven method for spreading the message of Jesus: *"Therefore those who were scattered went everywhere preaching the word"* (Acts 8:4 NKJV). The Christians were scattered abroad throughout the regions of Judea and Samaria, all except the apostles—they were in jail. That is what must begin to happen in America and throughout the world—not necessarily that we get thrown in jail for our faith, but we must *go everywhere* preaching the Gospel. We need to leave the sanctuaries of our churches and preach about our God everywhere we go. If we get people to Christ, if we get people back to God's Word, we will save America—and this world.

> *"For I am not ashamed of the gospel of*
> *Christ: for it is the power of God to salvation*
> *for everyone who believes, for the Jew first*
> *and also for the Greek."* (Romans 1:16 NKJV)

There are three types of ways we need to beware of other people, according to the Scriptures.

First, we must beware of the wrath of men. This one is the one we usually focus on—we are trying so hard to make people like us that we fear their wrath. In reality, we are to beware of their wrath, especially if it creates a hindrance to spreading the Gospel in this world.

Second, we are to beware the fear of men. As Proverbs 29:25 says, *"The fear of man bringeth a snare: but whoso putteth his trust in the* LORD *shall be safe"* (KJV). Fearing men leads us into traps. The fear of God, on the other hand, brings liberty. It gives us the freedom to do what He asks us to do.

And finally, we are to beware of the *praise* of men, which is probably the most subtle trap of all. First Corinthians reminds us: *"You were bought at a price; do not become slaves of men"* (1 Corinthians 7:23 NKJV). We are not to be slaves of other people or what they think—we are God's servants only. When we have our priorities straight in this way, nothing that mere people can do will ever get to us, and we will be able to move forward into the destiny that God has for our lives. As the Scriptures say, *"Who art thou that judgest another man's servant? to his own master he standeth or falleth. Yea, he shall be holden up: for God is able to make him stand."* (Romans 14:4) Don't become a slave to the opinions of others. To your own Master you rise or fall.

> *"How can ye believe, which receive honour one of another, and seek not the honour that cometh from God only?"*   (John 5:44)

4. Beware the leaven of the Pharisees.

Fourth, we are to beware of the leaven of the Pharisees:

> *"Jesus said to them, 'Take heed and beware of the leaven of the Pharisees and the Sadducees.'*
>
> *And they reasoned among themselves, saying, 'It is because we have taken no bread.'*
>
> *But Jesus, being aware of it, said to them, 'O you of little faith, why do you reason among yourselves because you have brought no bread?*

> *Do you not yet understand, or remember the*
> *five loaves of the five thousand and how many*
> *baskets you took up?*
>
> *Nor the seven loaves of the four thousand and*
> *how many large baskets you took up?*
>
> *How is it you do not understand that I did*
> *not speak to you concerning bread?—but to*
> *beware of the leaven of the Pharisees and*
> *Sadducees.'*
>
> *Then they understood that He did not tell them*
> *to beware of the leaven of bread, but of the*
> *doctrine of the Pharisees and Sadducees."*
>
> (Matthew 16:6–12 NKJV)

Jesus told us to beware of the leaven of the Pharisees, the religious leaders of His day. When the Lord said this to His disciples, they thought He was talking about literal bread, because leaven is the yeast that makes the bread rise. Are we to be careful of religious leaders who use yeast in their bread? If we aren't careful, we will miss the spiritual application of this. Jesus realized that danger in His disciples, and so He said, "O ye of little faith. Why do you reason because you have brought no bread? Do you not understand? Don't you remember the five loaves? Don't worry about the bread—I can make bread!" (my paraphrase). Instead, we are to beware of *the doctrine* of the religious leaders. Doctrines are the belief systems that are being preached in our churches, and doctrine is vital to our salvation. Consider this verse:

> *"Take heed to yourself and to the doctrine.*
> *Continue in them, for in doing this you will*
> *save both yourself and those who hear you."*
>
> (1 Timothy 4:16 NKJV)

We are to take heed of ourselves—and of our doctrine! Why? Because in doing this, we will save ourselves—and those who hear us. It takes *accurate* doctrine to get saved.

Here is a passage of Scripture that tells us how to get saved. It's a great example of accurate doctrine:

> *"For 'whoever calls on the name of the Lord shall be saved.'*
>
> *How then shall they call on Him in whom they have not believed? And how shall they believe in Him of whom they have not heard? And how shall they hear without a preacher?*
>
> *And how shall they preach unless they are sent? As it is written: 'How beautiful are the feet of whose who preach the gospel of peace, who bring glad tidings of good things!'"*
>
> (Romans 10:13–15 NKJV)

Whoever calls upon Jesus's name will be saved. But how can people call on Him if they don't know who He is? How can they believe in Someone they have never heard of? And how will they ever hear without a preacher to tell them? Certain information must be given to people for them to have a genuine conversion. It is not a matter of *inspiration* as much as it is a matter of *information*. The Gospel must be preached! And you don't have to be a preacher to preach it.

5. Beware of the scribes.

Fifth, we are to beware of the scribes:

> *"Then He said to them in His doctrine, 'Beware of the scribes, who desire to go around in long robes, love greetings in the marketplaces,*
>
> *the best seats in the synagogues, and the best places at feasts,*
>
> *who devour widows' houses, and for a pretense make long prayers. These will receive greater condemnation.'"* (Mark 12:38–40 NKJV)

What made the scribes different from the other religious leaders was precisely this: their form of "religious marketing" was based on appearances, on showmanship. The scribes liked to wear long robes as their clothing because it showed that they were the intellectual religious leaders of their day; they thought it made them look cool. They also liked to speak in the marketplaces, take the chief seats in the synagogues, and eat in the higher and best rooms at the feasts. The scribes were far more concerned with style than substance. Beware of "Christian showmanship" that is attractive in its style. Unfortunately, the generations in the Church today have been educated in a lot of style, and so we have begun to cater to them.

We are trying to sell Christianity to our young people, but selling anything has to do with style. *How can we enhance the appearance of the faith?* we wonder. *How can we put better music behind it, put more color on the page? How can we "Hollywood it up" a bit? It's too drab-looking just the way it is; we need to stylize it.* When people are more attracted to style than substance, we need to beware!

6. **Beware of hypocrisy.**

Sixth, we are to beware of hypocrisy. Now, earlier we saw that the leaven of the Pharisees could relate to false doctrine being preached in the Church (see Mark 16:6–12). But here, we can see that the leaven of the Pharisees is also hypocrisy:

> *"Beware ye of the leaven of the Pharisees,*
> *which is hypocrisy."* (Mark 12:1)

We must beware of hypocrite leaders.

The Pharisees not only taught false doctrine but were hypocrites as well. The single greatest need is for authenticity. Hypocrisy is assuming a false appearance of virtue and goodness. It is fake and sham, all show, no go. They weren't *"fair-you-see."* They pretended to be pure and holy. The only time Jesus spoke scathing remarks was about the hypocrites. Check this:

> *"Woe unto you, scribes and Pharisees,*
> *hypocrites! for ye make clean the outside of*
> *the cup and of the platter, but within they are*
> *full of extortion and excess.*
>
> *Thou blind Pharisee, cleanse first that which*
> *is within the cup and platter, that the outside of*
> *them may be clean also.*
>
> *Woe unto you, scribes and Pharisees,*
> *hypocrites! for ye are like unto whited*
> *sepulchres, which indeed appear beautiful*
> *outward, but are within full of dead men's*
> *bones, and of all uncleanness.*
>
> *Even so ye also outwardly appear righteous*
> *unto men, but within ye are full of hypocrisy*
> *and iniquity."*   (Matthew 23:25-28)

To help grasp the sting of Jesus's criticism of the fake religious leaders, read the Message:

> *"You're hopeless, you religion scholars and*
> *Pharisees! Frauds! You're like manicured*
> *grave plots, grass clipped and the flowers*
> *bright, but six feet down it's all rotting bones*
> *and worm-eaten flesh. People look at you and*
> *think you're saints, but beneath the skin you're*
> *total frauds."*
>
> *"For there is nothing covered that will not be*
> *revealed, nor hidden that will not be known."*
>   (Luke 12:2 NKJV)

The Bible tells us here that all hypocrisy will someday be revealed for what it is. Your secret thoughts—and mine—will one day be projected for all the world to see. The words that I speak out of earshot will be heard by all. Realizing this truth will bring the fear of God into your life! And that is the cure for hypocrisy: the fear of God. The fear of God is based on this truth, that nothing will stay covered up that will not be revealed eventually:

> *"Therefore whatever you have spoken in the dark will be heard in the light, and what you have spoken in the ear in inner rooms will be proclaimed on the housetops."* (Luke 12:3 NKJV)

Hypocrisy is contagious. If children see it in their parents, the children will grow up to be hypocrites themselves. If a wife sees it in her husband, or if the husband sees it in his wife, they will soon be practicing hypocrisy as well. It's contagious. When it is allowed to remain in the Church, it will spread. And because we have allowed a floodgate of hypocrisy in our midst, we are faced with pretension in the Church. The Bible tells us the result:

> *"Now the Spirit expressly says that in latter times some will depart from the faith, giving heed to deceiving spirits and doctrines of demons,*
>
> *speaking lies in hypocrisy, having their own conscience seared with a hot iron."*
>
> (1 Timothy 4:1–2 NKJV)

Within our churches, we have been speaking lies in hypocrisy. And when hypocrisy is allowed to run unattended, we soon have a conscience that is seared. It's one thing to be a hypocrite; it's another thing to have been a hypocrite so long that your conscience doesn't even bother you about it anymore!

In George Barna's recent report *What Americans Believe*, he shared some astonishing—and disturbing—statistics of what is going on in the Church today. He reveals that 52 percent of Christians say there is no such thing as absolute truth; 41 percent of Christians believe that all people are basically good; 31 percent of those who claim to be "born again" say that we all pray to the same God, but we just use different names for Him; 43 percent of those who claim to be "born again" believe that Satan is not a person, but merely a symbol of evil; 52 percent of those who claim to be "born again" attend church on a given Sunday; and only 42 percent actually function as members. Also, only 22 percent of those who claim to be "born again" read the Bible every day, and 31 percent of those who claim to be "born again" say the Bible is not the Word of God.[8]

Do any of these statistics shout a warning at you like they do to me? Each of us is being targeted by Satan—and God's first response for each of us is to beware! Beware of hypocrisy. Do not tolerate it in your life or in your church:

> *"For what is the hope of the hypocrite, though*
> *he hath gained, when God taketh away his*
> *soul?"*   (Job 27:8)

There is no hope for the hypocrite when God takes away his or her soul.

7.   Beware of covetousness.

Seventh, we are to beware of covetousness:

> *"And He said to them, 'Take heed and beware*
> *of covetousness, for one's life does not consist*
> *in the abundance of the things he possesses.'"*
>   (Luke 12:15 NKJV)

We must beware of covetousness because our lives do not consist of the abundance of *things* we have. Most of us have too much stuff! Our treasure lies in our salvation:

---

8   "New Barna Survey: More Americans Believe in Satan Than Believe in God," Steve Warren, CBN News, April 24, 2020, https://www1.cbn.com/cbnnews/us/2020/april/new-barna-survey-more-americans-believe-in-satan-than-believe-in-god.

> *"Then He spoke a parable to them, saying:*
> *'The ground of a certain rich man yielded*
> *plentifully.*
>
> *And he thought within himself, saying, "What*
> *shall I do, since I have no room to store my*
> *crops?"*
>
> *So he said, "I will do this: I will pull down my*
> *barns and build greater, and there I will store*
> *all my crops and my goods.*
>
> *And I will say to my soul, 'Soul, you have*
> *many goods laid up for many years; take your*
> *ease; eat, drink, and be merry.'"*
>
> *But God said to him, 'Fool! This night your*
> *soul will be required of you; then whose will*
> *those things be which you have provided?'*
>
> *So is he who lays up treasure for himself, and*
> *is not rich toward God.'"*   (Luke 12:16–21 NKJV)

In Jesus's parable, the rich man ultimately lost everything. Have you ever heard the phrase "You can't take it with you"? Well, it is true! Covetousness—wishing you had more material possessions, especially if your friend or neighbor has more than you—is a trap, of which we need to beware. Exodus 20 tells us:

> *"You shall not covet your neighbor's house;*
> *you shall not covet your neighbor's wife, nor*
> *his male servant, nor his female servant, nor*
> *his ox, nor his donkey, nor anything that is*
> *your neighbor's."*   (Exodus 20:17 NKJV)

Coveting things you don't have can ruin your life—and quickly. It is an attitude of ungratefulness for the things that God has already given you, an attitude that God Himself hates:

> *"For the wicked boasts of his heart's desire;*
> *he blesses the greedy and renounces the*
> *Lord."*   (Psalm 10:3 NKJV)

Covetousness is also rooted in iniquity.

Iniquity and sin are NOT the same thing. However, we will speak of iniquity a little late. It is sufficient to know that it's a big issue, with 365 verses about it in the Scripture. While it's difficult to cover much of it in this book, you may purchase our book, *How You See Yourself* originally published as, *How to Conquer Iniquity.* (It's also available as an audio book on Audible.)

Iniquity is one of the four reasons for the cross: *"He was wounded for our iniquities…"* (Isaiah 53:5). It's what turned a very good angel, Lucifer, into the devil. For of him, the anointed cherub, it is noted, *"Thou wast perfect in thy ways from the day that thou wast created, till iniquity was found in thee"* (Ezekiel 28:15).

You can tell that this is a pertinent subject. For now, though, let us notice that iniquity being the cause of many damaging behaviors is here referred to being the cause of covetousness.

> *"For the iniquity of his covetousness I was*
> *angry and struck him; I hid and was angry,*
> *and he went on backsliding in the way of his*
> *heart."*   (Isaiah 57:17 NKJV)

The driving force behind covetousness is usually a desire for something we don't already have, something we don't need.

Did you know that covetousness can destroy your marriage? It will replace the love that you have for your husband or wife or in any other relationship in your life:

> *"So they come to you as people do, they sit*
> *before you as My people, and they hear your*

words, but they do not do them; for with their
mouth they show much love, but their hearts
pursue their own gain."   (Ezekiel 33:31 NKJV)

When your heart is fixated on getting more and more and more—in other words, covetousness—it will destroy whatever love you once experienced. It will destroy your love for God, along with your love for your spouse, for your children, and for your parents. Covetousness, or jealousy, is one of the primary reasons for the destruction that's taking place in America right now—because people are voting based on what? Economics. And what is that about? Covetousness. Decisions made at the polls are typically determined by what will bring the biggest benefits to our own selves—and the root of that is the condition of covetousness. Most Americans no longer vote on the basis of principle; they vote selfishly for which candidate will give them the most benefits.

Every born-again, true, authentic Christian who casts a ballot must cast that ballot for God. We must ask ourselves, "Who is God in favor of in this election? And who is God against?" The true answer to that question will never be found if covetousness is in our hearts.

Covetousness also brings a false sense of security because we are putting our hope and our faith in the material things we have. Advertisers know this is true about human beings, and they try to create a sense of insecurity to get us to buy their products. They play on our inferiorities and insecurities and propose their products as the solution to resolve that insecurity. That's not a new strategy at all. Look at what the Bible tells us:

"Woe to him who covets evil gain for his
house, that he may set his nest on high, that he
may be delivered from the power of disaster!"
(Habakkuk 2:9 NKJV)

Covetousness operates from a false sense of security, but we can be delivered from this evil power in our lives. And it is *evil*:

> *"For from within, out of the heart of men,*
> *proceed evil thoughts, adulteries, fornications,*
> *murders, thefts, covetousness, wickedness,*
> *deceit, lewdness, an evil eye, blasphemy, pride,*
> *foolishness.*
> *All these evil things come from within and*
> *defile a man."*   (Mark 7:21–23 NKJV)

All kinds of evil can be found in the hearts of men. But right there in the middle, we find covetousness. It is a serious issue! It's serious from God's perspective because it is so destructive. It is a misdirecting of our energy, resources, and attention, and it takes us off the track we should be following. It consumes us—and is actually the root of all evil:

> *"But they that will be rich fall into temptation*
> *and a snare, and into many foolish and hurtful*
> *lusts, which drown men in destruction and*
> *perdition.*
> *For the love of money is a root of all kinds*
> *of evil, for which some have strayed from*
> *the faith in their greediness, and pierced*
> *themselves through with many sorrows. But*
> *you, O man of God, flee these things and*
> *pursue righteousness, godliness, faith, love,*
> *patience, gentleness."*   (1 Timothy 6:9-10 NKJV)

The love of money—in other words, covetousness—is the root of all evil because it prevents us from pursuing what is good. If you want to know how covetous you are, you only have to look at your money in terms of percentages. Take a look at your giving and your tithes. Are you giving ten percent of your money to God's work? Are you giving anything above that as an offering to Him? If not, covetousness might be at work in your life.

Covetousness can take over your life if you aren't careful. It will hijack your communication, especially if you only talk about the things you are hoping to obtain. And it will surely destroy any contentment you had in your life:

> *"Let your conversation be without*
> *covetousness; and be content with such things*
> *as ye have: for he hath said, I will never leave*
> *thee, nor forsake thee."* (Hebrews 13:5)

Covetous people talk about whatever they're coveting, whether it's houses, land, or vehicles—anything, really. If you do this, it will take over your conversations and destroy your contentment. It is a state of idolatry that must be terminated and ripped out of your life.

> *"Mortify therefore your members which are*
> *upon the earth; fornication, uncleanness,*
> *inordinate affection, evil concupiscence, and*
> *covetousness, which is idolatry."* (Colossians 3:5)

The word *mortify* means "to kill." We are to kill any "inordinate affection," any affection that is out of balance, out of the ordinary, all-consuming. If we can't eat or sleep, if everything we do concerns the thing that consumes us, then we have an affection that's ruling us. An affection has taken over—and we must kill it.

That's why we are taught to guard our affections. Covetousness relates to our affections—the things we so strongly desire to have in our lives. Covetousness is a form of idolatry because it replaces the leadership in your life that only God should have. Covetousness dictates how we spend our time. It becomes what we think about. And when it controls us, all the good and positive things that would be happening in our lives if God were in the management position are replaced by an idol.

You're a target for this! You are so filled with potential for the kingdom of God—but the enemy would love to trip you up with the insidious trap of covetousness, *"covetousness which is idolatry..."* Beware of it!

8. Beware of devourers, evil workers, and abusers.

The great potential that God has for you is being targeted by the enemy. who doesn't care how he stops you. He comes to steal, to kill, and to destroy. Now, this destruction is meant to keep you from doing what you should be doing, what you have the power to do, what you have the potential to do. So, beware. The eighth thing we are to beware is devourers, evil workers, and abusers:

> *"Beware of dogs, beware of evil workers,*
> *beware of the mutilation!*
> *For we are the circumcision, who worship*
> *God in the spirit, rejoice in Christ Jesus, and*
> *have no confidence in the flesh."*
> (Philippians 3:2–3 NKJV)

In the Bible, dogs are not the cute and faithful companions we keep as pets in our homes today; no, they always represent "devourers" in the Scriptures:

> *"Do not give what is holy to the dogs; nor cast*
> *your pearls before swine, lest they trample*
> *them under their feet, and turn and tear you to*
> *pieces."* (Matthew 7:6 NKJV)

Should I give the holy things that God has shared with me, to "dogs," to evil people who would only seek to devour me? We need to beware of the devourers who show up in our lives. Who or what is "devouring" your time? Who is siphoning off the spiritual energy that God has birthed in you?

Beware of those who would try to manipulate you to accomplish less than your purpose in the kingdom of God.

The devourer wants you working at a job for more time than you should, probably for reasons that you shouldn't, spending all your mental and emotional energy on things that don't really matter in the long run.

We are also to beware of abusers. Now, abuse has many forms. Today, we are seeing unprecedented levels of child abuse; whether it's physical or sexual abuse, it is on the rise in our society. But abusive behavior doesn't involve just children. God's Word tells us that abuse of anyone is wrong, and it should not be promoted in a society:

> *"Righteousness exalts a nation, but sin is a reproach to any people."* (Proverbs 14:34 NKJV)

Abuse can be emotional, social, or even spiritual. You can be in a church where abuse takes place, with manipulation due to ungodly motives that its leadership acts on.

9. Beware of being spoiled through the philosophy of humanism.

Ninth, we are to beware of being spoiled through the philosophy of humanism:

> *"Beware lest anyone cheat you through philosophy and empty deceit, according to the tradition of men, according to the basic principles of the world, and not according to Christ.*
>
> *For in Him dwelleth all the fullness of the Godhead bodily;*
>
> *and you are complete in Him, who is the head of all principality and power."*
>
> (Colossians 2:8–10 NKJV)

We need to watch out for the nice-sounding but unbiblical ideas that come our way, ideas that are after the tradition of men, including the false doctrine of humanism. Humanism is one of the traditions of men, but it is not a doctrine of Christ.

Humanism teaches that people are the masters of their own destiny and that we should simply do whatever feels good in the moment. Humanism is the exclusion of morals and/or God. God's ways are higher. Beware this false doctrine and philosophy that will lead you astray from the things of God. Now we are facing trans-humanism which is the embedding of technology to supposedly enhance and move us beyond present human limitations. We used to carry technology. Then we were able to wear it. Now the attempt is to embed it. We are facing perhaps the greatest demonic attempt to control the minds of the masses. (As a side note: beware of bionic checkout technology. It's the Book of Revelation coming to pass.)

10. Beware of not being a diligent learner of Scriptures.

Finally, we are to beware of not being diligent learners of the Scriptures. When we are not immersed in God's Word, we will begin conformity to the world's thinking and lose our steadfastness in following Him:

> *"Paul...has written to you,*
>
> *as also in all his epistles, speaking in them of these things, in which are some things hard to be understood, which untaught and unstable people twist to their own destruction, as they do also the rest of the Scriptures.*
>
> *You therefore, beloved, since you know this beforehand, beware lest you also fall from your own steadfastness, being led away with the error of the wicked;*
>
> *but grow in the grace and knowledge of our Lord and Savior Jesus Christ. To Him be the glory both now and forever. Amen."*
>
> (2 Peter 3:15-18 NKJV)

Paul mentions the *"things that are hard to understand."* But what do you do when you come across something in the Bible that is hard to understand? The danger would be to ignore it, but these verses ask us to work to learn things that are hard to understand. In fact, some of the greatest blessings you will ever experience in your life come about when you begin to understand something that was hard for you to comprehend before. It brings a freedom to you that you otherwise would not experience—but at first it was hard for you to understand.

Jesus put it this way:

> *"Ask, and it will be given to you; seek, and you will find; knock, and it will be opened to you."* (Matthew 7:7 NKJV)

Some things in life are worth pursuing! The gold doesn't sit on the surface; you have to mine it. And so it is with God's Word.

I believe that God has a totally sensible, logical, reasonable response to every issue and every question that mankind will ever face. God has the answer to every human ill. There is no philosophical issue that God and His Word do not have a profound and accurate response to. Studying the Scriptures can make you wise—and there ought to be no sense of intellectual inferiority among us when we have such a great wealth of information given to us in the Bible:

> *"Wisdom has built her house, she has hewn out her seven pillars."* (Proverbs 9:1 NKJV)

> *"The fear of the LORD is clean, enduring forever; the judgments of the LORD are true and righteous altogether.*
> *More to be desired are they than gold, yea, than much fine gold; sweeter also than honey and the honeycomb."* (Psalm 19:9–10 NKJV)

"Forever, O Lord, Your word is settled in heaven." (Psalm 119:89 NKJV)

———

Whether we like it or not—whether we know it or not—the enemy has set his sight on us. You are a high-value target! But God has clear directions for you, telling you what to do. Even though you're targeted, the enemy will have no power to hurt you if you beware the things He has pointed out to you in His Word. We don't have to fear; we have Jesus's promise, even when we are the targets of the enemy:

> *"Behold, I give you the authority to trample on serpents and scorpions, and over all the power of the enemy, and nothing shall by any means hurt you."* (Luke 10:19 NKJV)

Nothing shall, by any means, hurt you! Isn't that great news? That's God's intention for you, for your life, and for your purpose in His Kingdom.

Now that we know the things we should actively *beware* of as high-value targets, let's look at another list—this one composed of the things of which we should *take heed*.

Chapter 4

Take Heed!

Y ou are valuable! You have a purpose to serve—but again, there is a target on your back. As you have seen so far in this book, the enemy wants nothing more than to deter you from your calling and "take you out," limiting your impact as a follower of Jesus.

In the last chapter, we looked at the many tactics our enemy will use to try to knock us off course. These are things that we must beware of—things that come at us from the outside, things we need to defend ourselves against when we see them heading our way. We are taking a defensive posture when we *beware*.

But there are other things we need to actively pay attention to—things we need to *heed*—and this requires an active, offensive posture. We need to take notice of certain things, proactively making sure we are doing these things so we can survive, thrive, and fulfill God's purpose for us. To take heed means to give careful attention to, to mind, regard and take notice.

> *"For they shall eat, and not have enough: they*
> *shall commit whoredom, and shall not increase:*
> *because they have left off to take heed to the Lord."*
>
> (Hosea 4:10)

There is tremendous value in taking heed. This verse tells us that when people stop taking heed to the Lord, certain things will happen. One of the first is that people will eat, but they will not have enough. In other words, they will be caught up in an insatiable lifestyle. The word "eat" here certainly refers to physical food—

but it also refers to more than that. In all of life, if you do not take heed to the Lord, you will never have enough. You can buy everything the world has to offer, and it still will not be enough. You will never be satisfied—because we were made to find our satisfaction in our relationships with God and others.

Second, without taking heed to the Lord, this verse helps us see that people will commit "whoredoms." Now, this could mean a number of things. In the Bible, God calls many things "whoredoms"—but most of them begin in just one unexpected place. They don't begin in our physical bodies, in our appetites, or even when we see things and lust after them with our physical eyes. Most whoredoms begin in our *minds*. Whoredom is a condition of the mind.

We are targeted by the enemy, and we need to beware of his attacks when they come. We need to be proactively taking heed of what we think about—not focusing on the sinful thoughts that crop up in our minds, but rather, focusing on the things of God. Knowing that we are high-value targets, we must eliminate the power of the enemy! And one of the ways the enemy destroys us is with whoredoms. These whoredoms exist because we have stopped taking heed to certain things.

Look at the third consequence found in this verse: *"They shall not increase."* Have you ever thought, *The faster I go, the behinder I get*? That is what it means to *not increase* in your life. People can spend a lifetime trying to get ahead, but they never get there. They never increase, and the reason is because they have stopped taking heed to the Lord. The apostle Paul gave us the answer to this particular problem:

> *"Not that I speak in regard to need, for I have learned in whatever state I am, to be content."*
>
> (Philippians 4:11)

In whatever state I find myself, I am to be content. I know how to abound because my sense of "having arrived," and my ability to achieve fulfillment and increase in my life, is not based on outward circumstances. Instead, I have been taking heed of the things of God, and that brings blessing, power, and purpose to my life.

So, what things should we be proactively watching out for, "taking heed of," in our lives? Let's take a look.

Things We Must Heed

The following are the things we must heed, or pay attention to, as we stand against Satan's attacks:

1. Take heed to your heart.

First of all, we must take heed to our hearts, guarding them from unbelief:

> *"Take heed, brethren, lest there be in any of you an evil heart of unbelief, in departing from the living God."* (Hebrews 3:12)

We need to believe sufficiently so that we are never detached from God:

> *"So they said, 'Believe on the Lord Jesus Christ, and you will be saved, you and your household.'"* (Acts 16:31 NKJV)

Mental assent is not enough. Our faith is what counts! And faith is a function of the heart:

> *"For with the heart one believes unto righteousness, and with the mouth confession is made unto salvation."* (Romans 10:10 NKJV)

Faith is a function of the heart. And we must take heed to avoid an evil heart of unbelief. It is *unbelief in the heart* that brings evil into our lives.

Dietrich Bonhoeffer was a modern-day martyr of the faith—and one of my personal heroes. He was executed by hanging in 1945, in Germany, for resisting the Nazi regime and for contending for the Gospel in that place and at that time in history. He was one of the voices that denounced what Nazism was doing. He declared that while the Nazi regime was touting themselves as a "Christian" movement, what they were doing was not Christian at all. Bonhoeffer was right, and they were wrong—and it cost him his life.

If you are looking for a good book to read, give *The Cost of Discipleship* by Dietrich Bonhoeffer a try. In it, Bonhoeffer wrote that "only those who *really* believe—obey. And only those who obey really believe." Think about that: only those who really believe obey, and only those who obey really believe.

In other words, we need to take heed to our hearts. One great way to do this is to look out for each other and encourage each other in our faith:

> *"But exhort one another daily, while it is*
> *called 'Today,' lest any of you be hardened*
> *through the deceitfulness of sin."*
>
> (Hebrews 3:13 NKJV)

Let's exhort one another daily. Pick up the phone and actively call somebody else because collectively, the enemy has targeted us. But the book of Hebrews tells us how to be consistent and firm until the end: *"For we are made partakers of Christ, if we hold the beginning of our confidence steadfast unto the end"* (Hebrews 3:14). When we encourage each other, let's ask the hard questions: "Did you partake of Jesus this week? Did you extract from His willing offerings, from the magnitude of His blessings, from the fullness of His fountain, from the reservoir of His resources, from the vigor of His virtue, from the luster of His love, from the burnish of His beauty? Did you get something of Christ's life this week? Did you get it today? Did you get it yesterday? Do you get it every day?"

My friend, this Jesus who rose from the dead, the One who lives to make intercession for us, has sent the Holy Spirit as His chief administrator to be everything we need. He holds nothing back! But to receive these blessings, we must be partakers. We must cultivate hearts of belief, not hearts of unbelief.

2. Take heed to yourself and your doctrine.

Paul wrote Timothy, the eighteen-year-old pastor, and said, "Take heed."

> *"Take heed to yourself and to the doctrine.*
> *Continue in them, for in doing this you will*
> *save both yourself and those who hear you."*
>
> (1 Timothy 4:16 NKJV)

Timothy got it and was able to pass it on to others, "take heed to yourself." Now, this has nothing to do with selfishness—but recall that we are to love our neighbor *as ourselves*. If you don't look out for yourself, you'll be in big trouble. You are the only steward of your thoughts, your body, and your motives. And so, we must take heed to ourselves.

The second thing is to take heed to the doctrine—and continue in it by walking it out. If you do this, you will see two wonderful results. First, you'll save yourself from a whole lot of pain, a whole lot of anguish, and perhaps hell itself. Also, you will save those around you:

> *"And with many other words he testified and*
> *exhorted them, saying, 'Be saved from this*
> *perverse generation.'"*　　　(Acts 2:40 NKJV)

Peter actually said, *"save yourselves from untoward generation"* (KJV) in one of his sermons. He boldly told those around him to save themselves from the perverse generation that was all around them. He said, "Don't go where they go, do what they do, think the way they think, behave the way they behave, or believe the way they believe. Save yourselves from them!" Now, of course we understand that nobody can truly save themselves in the eternal sense. Jesus is the Savior of the world. But He cannot save us if we refuse to assume personal responsibility for ourselves. So, save yourself—take heed to what you do and with whom you are doing it. When you do, you will help to save others by your example and those who give you a listening ear.

Believe it or not, we are all contagious. Whatever you have is contagious and will rub off on others. If you are depressed, those around you will soon find themselves fighting depression. If you have a negative way of thinking, those around you will soon have the same mind-set. Each of us is contagious. That is why the Scriptures tell us to be very particular about the friends we keep and the associations we have. Now, I can *relate to* the worst sinner that I meet, but I cannot bring him into a position of friendship in my life because friends of the world are enemies of Christ. Jesus said that whoever is not for Him is against Him. If a person's not for Christ, he is against Christ. That means he's against what I am for, so we are at odds. He's fortunate, though, because being my enemy, I will love him because we love our enemies, right? As I like to say, with enemies like us, they don't need friends!

So, watch out because you are contagious. Every decision you make, everything you do, affects your children, your family, and others around you. Take heed to yourself and to your doctrine because *you're* going to affect *you*—and *you're* going to affect *others*:

> *"But take heed to yourselves, lest your*
> *hearts be weighed down with carousing,*
> *drunkenness, and cares of this life, and that*
> *Day come on you unexpectedly."*
>
> (Luke 21:34 NKJV)

Take heed to yourself—and watch over your heart, especially when it gets overtaken by the cares of life:

> *"Only take heed to yourself, and diligently*
> *keep yourself, lest you forget the things your*

eyes have seen, and lest they depart from your
heart all the days of your life. And teach them
to your children and your grandchildren."

(Deuteronomy 4:9 NKJV)

And finally, take heed to yourself so you do not forget the things the Lord has shown to you. Remember what the Lord has shown you. Refuse to forget those things. Rejoice in them.

3.   **Take heed to your attitude.**

Third, take heed to your *attitude*—your mental position, feeling, or emotion:

"Therefore let him who thinks he stands take
heed lest he fall."   (1 Corinthians 10:12 NKJV)

Don't be cocky about how strong you are, how great you are, how wonderful you are, or how sufficient you are—watch out for your attitude:

"Pride goes before destruction, and a haughty
spirit before a fall."   (Proverbs 16:18)

I am sure you have heard this before! Watch out for pride entering your heart. Too much of your attention is just on you. Beware. What is the attitude we should have? Humility. We should be more like Jesus, who said this:

"Take My yoke upon you and learn from Me,
for I am gentle and lowly in heart, and you
will find rest for your souls."

(Matthew 11:29 NKJV)

Jesus's attitude must become our own. That's what makes a person a servant—meek and lowly, not trying to flaunt and dominate. We should not be out trying to get the upper hand because that process is based on style, not substance. We win with *substance*. And when you have substance, you can be meek and lowly. Why? Because that is how we will be blessed:

> *"Blessed are the meek, for they shall inherit*
> *the earth."*   (Matthew 5:5 NKJV)

Did Jesus say, "Blessed is the super-salesman because he shall inherit the earth"? "Blessed are the loud and incompetent"? "Blessed are the self-assured"? "Blessed are those who know how to push buttons and pull strings"?

No. The Lord tells us, "Let the one who thinks he is standing *take heed* lest he fall." Watch your attitude. Stay meek and lowly, like the Master.

Jesus also said this:

> *"Take heed that you do not do your charitable*
> *deeds before men, to be seen by them.*
> *Otherwise you have no reward from your*
> *Father in heaven."*   (Matthew 6:1 NKJV)

Don't do what you do so you can be seen by other people—if you do, that will be your only reward. Do what you do so Jesus can be seen by other people through you.

Jesus also tells us, *"Take heed and beware of the leaven of the Pharisees and of the Sadducees"* (Matthew 16:6). That leaven was hypocrisy, another problem with the attitudes of the religious leaders of that day—and it's a problem in our own lives as well. Let the words you say reflect what you do, and let what you do be actions that spring from a heart of love and humility, a heart filled with gratitude for what God has done for you.

4.   **Take heed what you hear.**

> *"Then He said to them, 'Take heed what you*
> *hear. With the same measure you use, it will be*
> *measured to you: and to you who hear, more*
> *will be given.'"*   (Mark 4:24 NKJV)

Be very careful what you allow yourself to hear, what you actively listen to. You are your faith, and your faith comes from what you hear:

> *"So then faith comes by hearing, and hearing*
> *by the word of God."* (Romans 10:17 NKJV)

You are your faith, and your faith comes from what you hear—you will obey your faith. You believe something only when you act on it as if it were true. And if you hear something enough times, you will start to believe it. If somebody says, "I hate you" enough times, you'll believe them—whether it's true or not. And if somebody says, "I love you" enough times, you'll believe them—whether it's true or not because faith comes from hearing. When you have faith in what you have heard, you will then *always* act on your faith. Jesus wants to save you a whole lot of trouble. So, He has told us to take heed what we hear—what we allow ourselves to speak and listen to.

In the present social networking culture this requires acute diligence. "Fools delight in scorning," and that's about the essence of news broadcasting these days... each side scorning and mocking the other without authentic unvetted facts. Watch out! Don't study evil, for *"I would have you wise unto that which is good, and simple concerning evil"* (Romans 16:19).

5. Heed what you see.

In addition to heeding what we hear, we must also heed what we see.

The two main paths of access to our spirit are our ears and our eyes. Of course, we have five senses, and we certainly receive input from our senses of smell, touch, and taste. But the main access to our spirit is through our ears and eyes:

> *"The lamp of the body is the eye. If therefore*
> *your eye is good, your whole body will be full*
> *of light.*

*But if your eye is bad, your whole body will be
full of darkness. If therefore the light that is in
you is darkness, how great is that darkness!"*
(Matthew 6:22–23 NKJV)

When our eyes become evil, our bodies will be full of
darkness. How does the darkness get into our bodies? It gets
into our bodies through our eyes. If we see dark things, our
bodies will be full of darkness. But if our eyes see only what
is just, right, true, pure, and holy, our entire bodies will be
full of light.

If darkness gets in our eyes, our feet will take us where
we should not go. If we get darkness in our eyes, our hands
will do what they should not do. If we get darkness in our
eyes, our mouths will speak what they should not speak. If
we get darkness in our eyes, the sexual parts of our bodies
will do what they should not do. Is that plain enough? Take
heed to what you allow your eyes to see!

6. **Take heed how you build your life.**

You are the builder of your life. Yes, other people can
give input into your life, and you may look to others for help
and support. But ultimately, whether or not you are effective
in life is up to you:

*"According to the grace of God which was
given to me, as a wise master builder I have
laid the foundation, and another builds on it.
But let each one take heed how he builds on
it."* (1 Corinthians 3:10 NKJV)

What makes a wise master builder? A wise master builder
is one who has laid a foundation that others can build on. A
wise master builder builds a foundation first.

Every life has a foundation. Some people have founded
their lives on their feelings; whatever they feel like doing, they
do. Some people have founded their lives on intellectualism.
Whatever they think and see, through their humanistic-tinted

glasses, becomes the foundation or the basis of their choices, their decisions, and their behaviors. But Paul said we must lay a foundation that anybody else can build on. What must that foundation be?

> *"For no other foundation can anyone lay than*
> *that which is laid, which is Jesus Christ."*
>
> (1 Corinthians 3:11 NKJV)

The foundation cannot be somebody else's life, example, education, or anything else. The foundation of our lives must *always* be Jesus Christ. And if that foundation is not laid, the rest of it will crumble. The walls are going to crack, and the ceiling is going to fall in. Make no mistake about it: the wisest decision that any walking, living, breathing human being on this planet can make is to place Jesus Christ as the very foundation of his or her life and then establish every decision, every thought, and every process of life on that sure foundation. He will never fail you. He's the one Person in the whole universe who is really watching out for you. And when you build your life on Him, anything you build on top of that foundation will be sure because *He* is sure.

7. Take heed to your relationships.

Our relationships make up another area of life to which we should actively "take heed."

> *"But if ye bite and devour one another, take*
> *heed that ye be not consumed one of another."*
>
> (Galatians 5:15)

So many people bite and devour each other in relationships. The first step comes after the "honeymoon phase" is over: we become snippy—taking little bites at one another. Stop it...just stop it, because before long, you will have devoured one another. So many good relationships can become bad ones. They can become consumed with hatred and disgust because the power of death and life is in the tongue. You may think that the little things we do in our day-to-day relationships don't matter that much—but they do. A little bite here, a little bite there—and before you know it, it will be too late. Before you realize it, your relationship will have been consumed.

What are we to do instead? Love one another! And walk in the Spirit of love. That's the Holy Spirit.

> *"I say then: Walk in the Spirit, and you shall not fulfill the lust of the flesh."*
>
> (Galatians 5:16 NKJV)

Walk in the Spirit because it is the lust of the flesh that makes you bite at somebody. It is the lust of the flesh that makes you accuse, demean, call down, dishonor, and disrespect another person. The cure—the best way to take heed to your relationship—is to walk in the Spirit.

8. Take heed that you keep the Lord's Day.

> *"Thus says the Lord: 'Take heed to yourselves, and bear no burden on the Sabbath day, nor bring it in by the gates of Jerusalem;*
>
> *nor carry a burden out of your houses on the Sabbath day, nor do any work, but hallow the Sabbath day, as I commanded your fathers.'"*
>
> (Jeremiah 17:21–22 NKJV)

Many people say that directive was for the those who lived in Old Testament days. But if you knew your Bible, you would know two things. You would know that the Sabbath was an everlasting covenant. And you would know that in the New Testament, Jesus did not do away with the Sabbath principle; He merely switched the Lord's Day from the seventh to the first—which for us is Sunday.

What does it mean to "bear no burden on the Sabbath day"? It means, don't even think about your work on Sundays! Now, you may not understand this rule of God, but if you live it and obey it, you'll understand the benefits of it. You'll get more done in six days if you have a seventh day of rest to spend with the Lord, dedicated to the Lord, to spend quality time with your family, and to rest and relax. Remember, *"Six days shalt thou labor and do all thy work."* Not six days and nights and not seven days.

9. Take heed to your liberty.

> *"But take heed lest by any means this liberty of yours become a stumbling block to them that are weak."*   (1 Corinthians 8:9)

Liberty is not the right to do wrong but the power to do right! We need to take heed to our views about liberty and not only how they affect us, but how they affect others as well. This is becoming a real problem today in America. We are a liberty-conscious people, but we've seen liberty from only one side. We have not understood what true liberty really is. We have concluded erroneously that liberty is the right to do wrong, the freedom to do evil. Nothing could be further from the truth. Nobody has the right to do wrong. When we do wrong we exchange freedom for slavery. We have been given the freedom to *do the right thing*! Watch for these opportunities in your life.

10. Take heed to whom you follow.

> *"Take heed to yourself that you are not ensnared to follow them, after they are destroyed from before you, and that you do not inquire after their gods, saying, 'How did these nations serve their gods? I also will do likewise.'"*   (Deuteronomy 12:30 NKJV)

Take heed to yourself that you do not follow the wrong example, even when the people you are following are destroyed before you. Watch out who your heroes are—because you will become like them. Be careful whom you admire—because you will become like them, probably before you even realize it. The news reports about leaders who have made terrible decisions should remind us. Do not follow such leaders.

11. Take heed to disregard iniquity.

> *"Take heed, do not turn to iniquity, for you*
> *have chosen this rather than affliction."*
> (Job 36:21 NKJV)

We are to take heed to disregard the energy that comes from iniquity. Iniquity is the biblical word for narcissism. It involves the exaltation of ourselves, when what we should really be seeking is to be exalted by God Himself:

> *"Behold, God is exalted by His power; who*
> *teaches like Him?"* (Job 36:22 NKJV)

The reality is this: you don't get anywhere in the world on your own. You may think you do, but truthfully, you get where you are only because God has placed you there. Even though in the world we are constantly seeking for other people to promote us, God says that He is the One who will promote us by His power. That happens only if we are not following after iniquity. Take heed of this!

> *"For promotion cometh neither from the east*
> *nor from the west, nor from the south.*
> *But God is the judge: he putteth down one,*
> *and setteth up another."* (Psalm 75:6-7)

12. Take heed to the ministry you have.

> *"Take heed to the ministry which you have*
> *received in the Lord, that you may fulfill it."'*
> (Colossians 4:17 NKJV)

Seven ministry gifts are listed in Romans 12. I refer to them as **E**mbedded **N**atural **A**bilities (ENA). We need to take heed to the ministry that the Lord has given us. Now, you can operate in each of these gifts in part, but you will be *especially* gifted in just one of them. The Scripture in 1 Corinthians 12 tells us this:

> *"Now ye are the body of Christ, and members*
> *in particular."*   (1 Corinthians 12:27 NKJV)

You are a particular member of the body. That means you have a particular ministry. What makes one member of the body different from the other members of the body?

> *"Having then gifts differing according to the*
> *grace that is given to us, let us use them: if*
> *prophecy, let us prophesy in proportion to our*
> *faith."*   (Romans 12:6 NKJV)

God has endowed each of us with a gifting that enables us to minister—whether we are proclaimers to proclaim, servers to serve, teachers to teach, exhorters to exhort, givers to give, rulers to rule, or showers of mercy to show mercy. Take heed to which ministry gift you have received—and then go out into the world and fulfill it. In other detailed writings I have referred to them as the Messenger, the Helper, the Explainer, the Encourager, the Provider, the Administrator, and the Care Giver. Same giftings, or ENAs, but different insights.

Don't think that what you have in you is not important! You need to take heed to your particular ministry because Satan is targeting you to take you out of that very ministry! The gift that's in you, the ENA, is so valuable, and so important, it's part of the reason the enemy is targeting you. Take heed to the ministry that you have received from the Lord—and then begin to operate in it!

13. Take heed to those you influence.

Once you have taken heed to your particular ministry, you must also take heed to those you influence. Don't just minister to someone through your gift—influencing him or her, and then letting that person go. Follow up. Follow through. Be consistent. Take heed to those you influence:

> *"For I have not shunned to declare to you the*
> *whole counsel of God."*   (Acts 20:27 NKJV)

The people you influence need the whole counsel of God from you. Don't specialize in just being able to fix somebody with a marriage problem. That may be good, but they need more than just help in their marriage. They need to know how to live life *in its entirety*. Make sure you give the whole counsel of God:

> *"Therefore take heed to yourselves and to all*
> *the flock, among which the Holy Spirit has*
> *made you overseers, to shepherd the church*
> *of God which He purchased with His own*
> *blood."*   (Acts 20:28 NKJV)

We also need to take heed to the flocks we find ourselves placed over. Now, this was certainly written with the context of a pastor in a church in mind, but there are a lot of different kinds of flocks—including your family. You also have a circle of three friends. And then you have a circle of twelve, just like Jesus had the twelve disciples. After that, He had a group of seventy, and then a group of five hundred, and finally there is the whole world. Each of these different levels of relationships gives you the opportunity to minister at different levels, to different people, in different areas of your life.

14. Take heed that you do not despise children.

These are the very words of Jesus:

> *"Take heed that you do not despise one of*
> *these little ones, for I say to you that in heaven*
> *their angels always see the face of my Father*
> *who is in heaven."*   (Matthew 18:10 NKJV)

The word "angel" in this verse refers to a messenger who is always reporting to the Father what is going on in the life of a child. Did you know that every time you find Jesus in the Bible, you will find children nearby? He, in fact, rebuked His disciples because they were sending the children away as if they didn't matter. What is it about children that Jesus loved so much? The answer can be found in Jesus's words. He brought a child to Himself and then turned to the crowd: *"Whoever humbles himself as this little child is the greatest"* (Matthew 18:4 NKJV). And He said, *"of such is the kingdom of heaven"* (Matthew 19:14, Mark 10:14, Luke 18:6).

Greatness in the kingdom is measured by humility. In our culture of evangelical stardom, we do not particularly exonerate or exalt the humble. But Jesus says that the greatest in the kingdom are those who are like children in their humility.

Jesus's teaching gets even more stunning.

> *"Except ye be converted, and become as little children, ye shall not enter into the kingdom of heaven.*
>
> *Whosoever therefore shall humble himself as this little child, the same is greatest in the kingdom of heaven.*
>
> *And whoso shall receive one such little child in my name receiveth me.*
>
> *But whoso shall offend one of these little ones which believe in me, it were better for him that a millstone were hanged about his neck, and that he were drowned in the depth of the sea."*
>
> (Matthew 18:3-6)

You can always tell how civilized a culture is by two things: how it treats women, and how it treats children. Civilized means a stage of social and cultural development marked and characterized by the highest standards of behavior, refinement, and moral intelligence. Love, compassion, care for the poor, the less fortunate and the impaired. Sensitivity, courtesy, politeness, being obliging, respectful and decenct in contrast with coarseness, crudeness, selfishness, narcissism, ego-centricity, and being demeaning… the list could go on and on.

So what has America become?

Imagine targeting babies and children! On January 22, 1973 the Supreme Court of the United States of America (SCOTUS) in a 7-2 decision decided that a baby in the womb of a mother was not a human. It therefore followed that it could be killed without it being murder. So now we have killed 62 million plus babies. 62 million plus targets!

Jews in Germany were described as rats and laws were passed based on the supposed "pure blood doctrine" that determined them to be less than human so they could be killed without it being murder. In November of 1945 Robert Jackson, a former Attorney General and a member of the Supreme Court was appointed by Harry Truman to be the main prosecutor at the Nuremburg Trials. In his opening remarks he said, "The wrongs which we seek to condemn and punish have been so calculated, so malignant, and so devastating, that civilization cannot tolerate their being ignored because it cannot survive their being repeated."

But America has repeated it. Like the Nazis legally determined that the Jews were less than human and could be killed without it being called murder, SCOTUS and American politicians have determined that babies are less than human and can killed without it being called murder (although you can be fined and/or imprisoned for disturbing unborn turtles near the beach 400 feet from my home).

It was no surprise that of the 22 men tried, a predominant defense was, "we broke no laws." In America we kill babies but "break no laws." Really?

Dear Reader: I beg your indulgence to carry this dialogue forward. Duty to you and to God demands it!

In the historical account from Jeremiah chapter 19, God says:

> *"Because they have forsaken me, and have estranged this place, and have burned incense in it unto other gods... and have filled this place with the blood of innocents;*
>
> *They have built also the high places... **to burn their sons with fire** for burnt offerings unto Baal, which I commanded not, nor spake it, **neither came it into my mind**:"*
>
> (Jeremiah 19:4-5)

When you leave God the value of human life goes down! These people had places to burn their sons. Likewise in America we have places where we burn our children, vacuum them out like picking up dirt... your tax dollars at work.

This was so abominable, so unequivocally detestable, so revolting, disgusting and despicable that God said, "it had never entered His mind."

In the meantime where is the church on this matter? Forever teaching that babies are born sinners! And the pro-abortionists love this doctrine... that babies are born sinners because now all they are doing is killing dirty little sinners. Shame on the church, the historic church, the modern church that teaches such heresy. So let's examine the Scriptures.

False Doctrine Number 1: We are guilty because of Adam's transgression

If parts are missing out of the truth then what remains is heresy. "Adam made us all guilty sinners," so the heresy starts. The rest of the truth is rarely mentioned. Here's the whole truth:

> *"Therefore as by the offence of one judgment came upon all men to condemnation even so **by the righteousness of one the free gift came upon all men unto justification of life.**"*
>
> (Romans 5:18)

Notice that what Adam did was counteracted and thwarted by Jesus. Note that what Jesus did affected *"all men."* And what was the effect? *"Justification of life!"* Everyone is born justified.

Breathes there a man with mind so skewed as to believe that a loving, just and intelligent God will punish a person for what someone else has done? This is the essence of what is called the Federal Headship Theory. It dishonestly and dishonorably claims that since mankind was in the loins of Adam, therefore we sinned in him.

False Doctrine Number 2: Sin is inherited

Sin is a wrong moral choice. Yet some speculate that sin is biologically transmitted. That's the reason why some cults forbid blood transfusions because it is assumed that sin is in the blood. If morality could be transmitted through the blood, then a blood transfusion from a saint would make a man more holy. When asked to defend the notion of infant baptism, the answer generally given is that Adamic sin is the sin of which infant baptism absolves a person. *"But every one shall die for his own iniquity..."* (Jeremiah 31:30) *"The soul that sinneth, it shall die. The son shall not bear the iniquity of the father, neither shall the father bear the iniquity of the son"* (Ezekiel 18:20).

False Doctrine Number 3: David was born a sinner

Often quoted to support the view that babies are born sinners is this verse from Psalm 51:5:

> *"Behold, I was shapen in iniquity; and in sin did my mother conceive me."*

The iniquity of the mother and father was that they were not married to each other. The sin in the Scripture is the mother's sin. Here's the Amplified translation, *"my mother was sinful who conceived me."* David admitted in the present tense that he was indeed a sinner. In fact, Psalm 51 is his remorseful penitent Psalm, ashamed over his adulterous sin with Bathsheba.

How tragic that some translations miss the mark and mistranslate this verse as, "I was born a sinner...." Please just read the Scripture with me again asking yourself who is the sinner in the sentence? "In sin did my mother...." The obvious answer is David's mother. Further David's mother was in a relationship deemed as an iniquity. What was that?

Perhaps David was referring to his illegitimacy. It appears that David's mother may not have been married to his father Jesse but was in fact a prostitute or some other man's wife. Much historic speculation implies that David's mother was not yet married to Jesse when she became pregnant—that perhaps she was still married to Nahash when she conceived David. David's mother is never named in the Bible. David was never accepted in the family with the same status as his seven brothers and two sisters. Here's the evidence from several translations:

> *"Even my own brothers pretend they don't know me; they treat me like a stranger."* (NLT)
>
> *"My brothers shun me like a bum off the street. My family treats me like an unwanted guest."* (MSG)
>
> *"I am become a stranger unto my brethren, and an alien unto my mother's children."*
> (Psalm 69:8)

When the Prophet Samuel came to anoint one of the sons of Jesse as the upcoming king, David was not included. The theologians don't want to refer to his illegitimacy, so they spin the story by saying that David was not among them because he was too young. However, it was common in those days to anoint an upcoming king at a young age. For example, Uzziah became king at the age of 16. (See 2 Chronicles 26:1.) You find the history recorded in 1 Samuel 16:11.

It is true that, *"all we like sheep have gone astray"* (Isaiah 53:6). Astray means going away from the correct path or direction, off course, off track. How can one get off course if he's never been on track. That sort of like trying to come back from some place you've never been. This is false reasoning.

The Truth:

Let's simply put the false notion of babies being born sinners next to Scriptures and see if the concept is not contradicted repeatedly. Beside each Scripture is a box for you to vote. If you think the Scripture supports the **false** idea of babies being born sinners and guilty mark "√" in the box. If the Scripture does NOT support the doctrine place an "X" in the box. Here we go!

Matthew 18:3 *"Verily I say unto you, Except ye be converted, and become as little children, ye shall not enter into the kingdom of heaven."* ❑

Matthew 19:14 *"Jesus said, Suffer little children, and forbid them not, to come unto me: for of such is the kingdom of heaven."* ❑

Isaiah 11:6 *"A little child shall lead them."* ❑

Matthew 18:4 *"Whosoever therefore shall humble himself as this little child, the same is greatest in the kingdom of heaven."* ❑

Matthew 21:16 *"And Jesus saith unto them, Yea; have ye never read, Out of the mouth of babes and sucklings thou hast perfected praise?"* ❏

The religious leaders were, "sore displeased," "indignant," "up in arms" because the children were crying in the temple, and saying, *"Hosanna to the Son of David."* And it was the adults that were shouting, *"Crucify Him! Crucify Him!"*

It's amazing that if a baby cries or screams we say it's the devil instead of hunger, or a pain, or a need for love and attention.

Babies are targets! And so are children!

Is there anything so despicable as a mother marching for the right to kill her baby. As one little girl said, "If women would control their own bodies, they wouldn't need an abortion."

27% of all human trafficking are children and two out of three child victims are girls. In the United States children represent 51.6% of trafficking. Trafficking includes sex trafficking, forced prostitution, forced labor, domestic servitude, organ trafficking, debt bondage, and recruitment of children as child soldiers. All of this is according to the United Nations Office on Drug and Crime.

California consistently has the highest human trafficking rates in the United States. It is estimated that there are 20 to 40 million in modern day slavery. The real numbers are not known. The United Nations refers to this as "the hidden figure of crime."

Then Jesus went on to say that if someone offends one of the little ones it would be better for that person for a millstone, a rock, to be hung about his or her neck and that they would be drowned in the depths of the sea. That is how much Jesus cares about children. He was forever taking them up in His arms and blessing them. Take heed to children, that you are not offending them or hindering their faith. Don't call them sinners. They'll become sinners soon enough.

15. Take heed that you be not deceived.

> *"And He said, 'Take heed that you not be deceived. For many will come in My name, saying, "I am He," and, "The time has drawn near." Therefore do not go after them.'"*
>
> (Luke 21:8 NKJV)

Who are the ones we need to watch out for? Jesus said that many will come *in His name*. The deceit we will need to take heed of is going to come from people *who are bearing the name of Jesus*. If they came in the name of Buddha, Allah, or Confucius, they couldn't deceive you—because it would be too obvious. The greatest possibility for deceit comes from those who speak and act in the name of Jesus! These false prophets and deceivers will show signs and wonders to try to seduce you into believing their words. But take heed so that you are not deceived.

16. Take heed to what you say.

We are to take heed to our ways so that we do not sin with our tongues:

> *"I said, I will take heed to my ways, **that I sin not with my tongue: I will keep my mouth with a bridle**, while the wicked is before me."*
>
> (Psalm 39:1)

Remember, the power of death and life is in the tongue. Be careful what you say, or you'll make the biggest speech you'll ever live to regret! That's why certain words should never appear in our vocabulary. If we say the wrong thing to our children, we can damage them for a lifetime. The same is true for our spouses and other family members and loved ones. Heed what you say!

———

Because you are a high-value target, it is so important that you proactively begin to take heed of these things in your life! Close up each of these potential areas of attack from the enemy, and do not allow him to gain any kind of foothold.

As you *beware of* the potential areas of trouble listed in chapter 2, and now *take heed of* the potential vulnerable areas listed in this chapter, your next step is to prepare yourself with the weapons and armor that God has provided to His kingdom warriors. Even though you are a high-value target, you have been given everything you need to withstand any attack!

Chapter 5

Stay Armed

In December 2004, a single question from a young soldier touched off a storm of controversy. US Secretary of Defense Donald Rumsfeld had traveled to Kuwait to deliver a spontaneous pep talk to the American troops stationed at Camp Buehring there. But the usually calm politician found himself a bit flustered when, in front of the rolling news cameras, Army Specialist Thomas Wilson of the 278th Regimental Combat Team, boldly spoke up: "Why do we soldiers have to dig through local landfills for pieces of scrap metal and compromised ballistic glass to up-armor our vehicles?"

Good question! The American soldiers in that camp clearly felt they were being sent into battle with inadequate protection against the enemy.

That is not the case with God's army.

As Christians, we should not have that fear. Our Commander in Chief, the Lord of the armies, knows that we are high-value targets and that the enemy has his sight set on us. Because of that, He has generously equipped us with all we need to not only defend ourselves, but also to go on the offense against the enemy. The belt of truth, the breastplate of righteousness, the gospel of peace, the shield of faith, the helmet of salvation, and the sword of the Spirit: these are all ours to use. It's up to us to put them on—and then put them to use. Let's look at how to do that.

We Are at War

We are in a war. Our enemy is strong. He is cunning. His desire is to take out those of us who are meant to accomplish great things in God's kingdom and in this world—and that includes you!

What good is it to go into a battle unprepared? How quickly would you be defeated if you went into a war against a well-equipped opponent if you had no weapons to go on the offense, and perhaps even worse, no defensive equipment to protect you from the enemy's onslaught?

This may seem obvious, but God's Word reminds us of the importance of this step—and what it does for us: It allows us to stand against the wiles of the devil!

> *"Finally, my brethren, be strong in the Lord and in the power of His might.*
>
> *Put on the whole armor of God, that you may be able to stand against the wiles of the devil."*
>
> (Ephesians 6:10–11 NKJV)

. You're the target. When you are targeted, make sure that you stay armed because this will render the enemy incapable of damaging you.

We must also know our enemy—and we must know who we are fighting for:

> *"For we wrestle not against flesh and blood, but against principalities, against powers, against the rulers of the darkness of this world, against spiritual wickedness in high places."*
>
> (Ephesians 6:12)

The battles we are facing have nothing to do with flesh and blood. They have everything to do with the spiritual battle that is taking place in our world, in our country, in our culture, in our families—and in our own hearts.

Seven Things to Know about God's Armor

There are certain things we need to know about the armor of God for it to have a maximum impact in our lives. Here are seven of them:

1. The armor is designed by God.

> *"Put on the whole armor of God, that you may*
> *be able to stand against the wiles of the devil."*
>
> (Ephesians 6:11 NKJV)

God is the designer of the armor; He is also the Maker.

2. The armor is made by God.

God is the manufacturer of the armor. That means the armor will fit you perfectly. It's going to be comfortable. God designed it with ultimate perfection in mind.

3. All the armor is necessary.

Each piece of the armor is necessary to ensure your success. You can't pick and choose, putting on one piece but rejecting another. If you do that, you will be a vulnerable target. Every part is necessary.

4. You must put on the armor.

You must actively put on the armor of God. It is not sufficient to know what the six pieces of armor represent. We must actually put the armor on every day to be able to withstand the attacks of the enemy.

5. You must keep the armor on.

Next, you must keep the armor on. The armor of God is designed for use 24/7. Even when you're sleeping, you must sleep with your armor on.

6. The armor is real, not imagined or mystical.

We aren't pretending to put on God's armor when we follow this practice. This armor is real. It is not imaginary. And it is not based on magic. I have known people who stand in front of the mirror every morning and literally go through the motions of putting their arms through the breastplate of righteousness, or they put on the helmet of salvation by lifting their hands up to their head. Such a mystical application of these spiritual truths will cause you to believe you are armed, when in fact you are not. That's a dangerous place to be.

7.   **Each piece of armor serves a specific function.**

If we're going to be able to take a hit from the enemy, we'd better have the armor on, and it'd better be functional so it can achieve the purposes that God intends. The following two verses state why we must wear God's armor:

> *"Put on the whole armor of God, that you may be able to stand against the wiles of the devil."*
> (Ephesians 6:11 NKJV)

> *"Therefore take up the whole armor of God, that you may be able to withstand in the evil day, and having done all, to stand."*
> (Ephesians 6:13 NKJV)

Whatever the devil comes at you with, you will be able to stand against it when you wear the armor of God. Because you're a target, you want to beware. You want to take heed. But you also want to have your armor on. The purpose of the armor is so that you can stand against the enemy's attacks.

Again, I need to emphasize the need for the *whole* armor. If you leave off one of the pieces, then you can expect the enemy to penetrate that area. Let's look at each of the target zones the enemy will try to attack—and the piece of armor for each zone that is intended to stop him in his tracks.

Target Zone 1: Loins (Your Genitals)

The first target zone where the enemy will try to attack you is in the area of your loins—the upper and lower abdominal regions and the region about the hips, which contain the reproductive organs. (See Genesis 35:11 and 46:26, 1 Kings

8:19, and Acts 2:30 for instances when "loins" is used in this way.) It's an area of the body that says it's about your genitals!

But the Bible tells us what to do:

"Stand therefore, having your loins girt about with truth, and having on the breastplate of righteousness." (Ephesians 6:14)

Your loins are the first part of your body that God wants you to protect. And how do you protect them? With truth.

We are to stand, having our loins girded with truth, which is our first armament in standing against the enemy.

Armament 1: Truth

Now, the first armament, truth, is given to help us protect the number-one target zone, our private parts. This piece of armor—truth—covers this most precarious part of our body that God wants protected, from our earliest childhood through our adult years and until we exit from this planet. It's something that God, with a whole lot of divine wisdom behind it, emphasizes. It is not difficult to understand why Satan wants to attack you in your sexuality first—because he knows how important it is to God. He also knows that if he can defeat you there, he can defeat you anywhere and everywhere.

Target zone number one is the loins, and armament number one is the truth.

Now, this does not refer to the whole truth of Scripture; we will cover that later, when we come to the sword of the Spirit, which is the Word of God. But the loins are protected by the truths in the Bible that are designed to protect your genitals, your sexuality, and your procreative ability.

What are these truths?

"Finally then, brethren, we urge and exhort in the Lord Jesus that you should about more and more, just as you received from us how you ought to walk and to please God;

for you know what commandments we gave you through the Lord Jesus.

For this is the will of God, your sanctification; that you should abstain from sexual immorality;

that each of you should know how to possess his own vessel in sanctification and honor,

not in passion of lust, like the Gentiles who do not know God;

that no one should take advantage of and defraud his brother in this matter, because the Lord is the avenger of all such, as we also forewarned you and testified.

For God did not call us to uncleanness, but in holiness.

Therefore he who rejects this does not reject man, but God, who has also given us His Holy Spirit."   (1 Thessalonians 4:1–8 NKJV)

The first truth that protects your loins is that you must obey the commandment so you can please God more and more. One of the primary commandments of God in this matter is to avoid fornication and uncleanness:

"Do you not know that your body is the temple of the Holy Spirit who is in you, whom you have from God, and you are not your own?

For you were bought at a price; therefore glorify God in your body and in your spirit, which are God's."   (1 Corinthians 6:19–20 NKJV)

Second, understand that your body is the temple of the Holy Spirit. You are not your own. You have been bought with a price. Your body belongs to the Lord:

> *"Flee also youthful lusts; but pursue*
> *righteousness, faith, love, peace with those*
> *who call on the Lord out of a pure heart."*
> (2 Timothy 2:22 NKJV)

Finally, the pastor Timothy tells us to flee youthful lusts. That's pretty self-explanatory!

So, how do we put on this particular armor, the truth about God's will regarding our sexuality? First, memorize these specific passages of the Bible, with the understanding that they are designed for the protection of that area of your body. And second, meditate on these verses because meditation is the process by which we move truth from our minds to our hearts.

Embedding this truth about your loins down into your heart from your mind, and keeping it there, *will* stop Satan from being able to reach you at target zone number one. How do we know this?

> *"Your word I have hidden in my heart, that I*
> *might not sin against You."* (Psalm 119:11 NKJV)

David wrote those words. He knew there would be a contest of ideas—humanistic ideas, demonic ideas, seducing spirits, and doctrines of demons. They will come at you when you drive down the street, bombarding you from the billboards, when you open up a newspaper, when you flip through the cable stations looking for the news—filthy, immoral ideas are going to come at you. These are the assaults of the enemy. When these assaults come, and they will come, the armor that God has designed for these attacks will be effective in stopping the intrusion of these missiles, the projectiles that the enemy sends your way in this area of life.

There have been times when I waged tremendous battles in my mind over ideas that were not godly, such as these. But I can tell you what my problem was: I didn't have the armor on. I didn't have my loins girded with the truth. It is that simple.

So, where's the armor? Where's the truths we need to memorize in order to protect our private parts? Here are the passages:

- Memorize Proverbs 5, 6, 7 and 9!

- Memorize 1 Thessalonians 4:1-8!

- Memorize 2 Timothy 2:22!

- Memorize Job 31:1!

- Memorize 1 Corinthians 7:2-5!

Target Zone 2: Your Heart

> *"Stand therefore, having your loins girt about with truth, and having on the breastplate of righteousness."* (Ephesians 6:14)

Second, we must put on the breastplate of righteousness, to protect Target Zone 2, your heart. If the enemy cannot get you in the loins, he will go for the heart. That's why the Scripture tells us to do this:

> *"Keep your heart with all diligence, for out of it spring the issues of life."* (Proverbs 4:23 NKJV)

The issues of life proceed from your heart. It's a vital organ to you and to your ability to survive! Here is what Romans 10:10 says about the heart:

> *"For with the heart one believes unto righteousness, and with the mouth confession is made unto salvation."* (Romans 10:10 NKJV)

There are six clear reasons why our hearts are central to our connection with God.

First, the heart is the home of faith. With the heart we believe unto righteousness. You don't believe with your head; you believe with your heart. There's nothing wrong with having doubts—as long as you don't believe them! Believe your beliefs and doubt your doubts.

Second, the heart is the home of your conscience:

> *"For if our heart condemns us, God is greater than our heart, and knows all things.*
>
> *Beloved, if our heart does not condemn us, we have confidence toward God."*
>
> (1 John 3:20–21 NKJV)

God has constructed the heart in such a way that when you start to do something that is not right, your heart corrects you; it pricks your conscience.

Third, the heart is the home of wisdom—as evidenced by the purpose of the entire book of Proverbs, which is to get wisdom into our hearts.

Fourth, the heart is the home of joy. Happiness can come and go within twenty minutes—but not joy. The joy that Jesus brings, nobody can take away (see John 16:22). It is resident—where? In your heart.

Fifth, the heart is the home of your enthusiasm. The very word *enthusiasm* means, by definition, "God in you"—*en theo*. *Theo* means "God." God in you is what will bring you genuine enthusiasm—and it all starts in your heart. There are a lot of fake displays of enthusiasm. Just look at a car salesman on a television commercial! Real enthusiasm is found with God in you, pouring all His life into you until it bursts forth out of you to others. This enthusiasm—this God in you—will come from your heart.

Sixth, the heart is the home of discernment in your life. This may be the reason that Satan targets your heart as the second zone—because it is the home of discernment:

> *"But as it is written, 'Eye has not seen, nor ear heard, nor have entered into the heart of man the things which God has prepared for those who love Him.'*
>
> *But God has revealed them to us through His Spirit. For the Spirit searches all things, yes, the deep things of God.*
>
> *For what man knows the things of a man except the spirit of the man which is in him? Even so no one knows the things of God except the Spirit of God."*   (1 Corinthians 2:9–11 NKJV)

God reveals important things to us by His Spirit—to our hearts. That is discernment.

Finally, your heart is the home of your creativity and your peace. No wonder it is so very important to protect it!

Armament 2: Righteousness

When the enemy fails to reach you in your loins, he will go after your heart because of its great importance in your spiritual life. So, God has designed a second armament to protect the heart: righteousness. This second piece of armor is the breastplate that covers the heart, made of righteousness. If you have righteousness in your heart, it will protect your heart from every option of going astray. It will protect your heart from every attack of the enemy:

> *"Stand therefore, having your loins girt about with truth, and **having on the breastplate of righteousness**."*   (Ephesians 6:14)

How can you put on this righteousness?

First, you must remember that you're made righteous by the Lord Jesus Christ. You can't do this on your own:

> *"Not by works of righteousness which we have*
> *done, but according to His mercy He saved*
> *us, through the washing of regeneration and*
> *renewing of the Holy Spirit."*   (Titus 3:5 NKJV)

Only by His mercy and His grace are we saved:

> *"For He has made Him who knew no sin*
> *to be sin for us, that we might become the*
> *righteousness of God in Him."*
>
>   (2 Corinthians 5:21 NKJV)

We receive our righteousness because of the work of Christ Jesus...we become righteous only in Him. Righteousness is not simply the absence of sin. Righteousness is a positive deposit put in you by the Lord Jesus Christ. It's really in there. It comes to you from Jesus, and it comes by faith:

> *"For with the heart one believes unto*
> *righteousness, and with the mouth confession*
> *is made unto salvation."*   (Romans 10:10 NKJV)

God wants you to live in a state of being aware that you are righteous. When that is in place, every time the enemy comes at you and points his finger, he can't get through because you know that the righteousness of Jesus is in your heart. How do you know you have the righteousness of Jesus?

> *"Little children, let no one deceive you. He*
> *who practices righteousness is righteous, just*
> *as He is righteous."*   (1 John 3:7 NKJV)

If you practice righteousness in your life—if you are doing "right" things—then you are righteous. It's pretty simple! The fruit, or the evidence that it's there, is that you are practicing doing right all the time and in every situation.

97

The opposite of that is a consciousness of sin. If you are conscious of sin in your heart, I encourage you to repent before the Lord and allow His righteousness to reenter your life. When you do, you will be protecting your heart with the breastplate of righteousness.

Target Zone 3: Feet

> *"And having shod your feet with the*
> *preparation of the gospel of peace."*
>
> (Ephesians 6:15 NKJV)

In the world of military warfare, it is astonishing how important the feet are to the soldiers on the battlefield. In fact, you can immobilize an entire army if you can sabotage their boots. Without the right socks, without the right footwear, it doesn't matter what other kind of weapons or armor you have. You won't be moving forward against the enemy; you will be lucky to stand your ground. Our enemy knows that— and that is why the feet are one of his top-three targets!

Our defense against an attack to our feet is being adequately prepared to preach the Gospel, the Gospel of Peace. If we are not adequately prepared to preach the Gospel, we don't have our spiritual boots on. We're immobilized. We may be living righteous lives, but we are not moving forward against the enemy. He has stopped us because we didn't put our boots on:

> *"For 'whoever calls on the name of the Lord*
> *shall be saved.'*
>
> *How then shall they call on Him in whom they*
> *have not believed? And how shall they believe*
> *in Him of whom they have not heard? And how*
> *shall they hear without a preacher?*
>
> *And how shall they preach unless they are*
> *sent? As it is written: 'How beautiful are the*
> *feet of those who preach the gospel of peace,*

who bring glad tidings of good things!'"
(Romans 10:13–15 NKJV)

I don't know about you, but I don't tend to think of the feet as a "beautiful" part of the body. And back at the time of the writing of these verses, the messengers who would have carried "good tidings" from town to town often ran up the mountains barefooted. When they finally arrived with the Good News, their feet were usually bloody, broken, and bruised. But those feet were beautiful to the recipients of the Good News!

The enemy's goal is to stop you from sharing the Good News of peace. So, how do you put your boots on? By being prepared to preach. I am not just talking about pastors or evangelists; this refers to the whole body of Christ. This verse applies to us all:

"And He said to them, 'Go into all the world and preach the gospel to every creature.'"
(Mark 16:15 NKJV)

Preparing Your Feet

Here are six ways to prepare yourself to share God's Good News with other people. Get your feet ready!

1. Be properly motivated.

You have to be properly motivated. Now, I'm going to just review some of the adequate motivations for preaching the Gospel. This can come out of necessity (see 1 Corinthians 9:16), which means that God comes into our lives so powerfully that we don't have a choice—we have to share His love with others. He commands it; it's an absolute necessity that we obey His will in this matter.

We also become motivated out of obligation (see Romans 1:14–15), out of obedience and the fear of the Lord (see 2 Corinthians 5:11). We understand that there will be a payday someday, and because we love other people, we want them to understand the consequences of the choices they are making (see Jude 1:23). We know a reward is coming for being obedient to share the Gospel (see Hebrews 11:6), and we want to see God glorified in the process (see 1 Corinthians 10:31).

2. Understand the Gospel.

It is important to understand the true Gospel of the lordship of Jesus Christ. The true Gospel is based on what Jesus did for us on Calvary and the fact that if we will respond appropriately, He will save us. The appropriate response is that we must surrender our whole lives to His leadership. We must repent—and *repentance* is a change of heart, a change of lordship. Repentance is not stopping or terminating one, or even a thousand, sins; that would be like cutting off the limbs of a tree when, in fact, the whole tree needs to come down. Faith is the key to pleasing Him:

> *"But without faith it is impossible to please*
> *Him, for he who comes to God must believe*
> *that He is, and that He is a rewarder of those*
> *who diligently seek Him."*　　(Hebrews 11:6 NKJV)

Without faith, it's impossible to please God:

> *"For with the heart one believes unto*
> *righteousness, and with the mouth confession*
> *is made unto salvation."*　　(Romans 10:10 NKJV)

And then we must continue in our belief and in promoting the Lordship of Jesus in our lives:

> *"Then Jesus said to those Jews who believed*
> *Him, 'If you abide in My word, you are My*
> *disciples indeed.'"*　　(John 8:31 NKJV)

3. Check your attitude.

Third, before we preach the Gospel, we need to adopt the right attitude. The first component of a God-seeking attitude is *meekness*—our strength under God's control. When we go to talk to somebody about the most important thing in his or her life—eternal destiny and the lordship of Christ in his or her life—we need to do so with a meek spirit and in the fear of the Lord, with an awareness that God is listening to what we say to people, as well as how we say it:

> *"In meekness instructing those that oppose themselves; if God peradventure will give them repentance to the acknowledging of the truth."*
>
> (2 Timothy 2:25)

However, we also need to cultivate an attitude of boldness when preaching to others. *Boldness* is confidence that what I have to say has lasting value. But we must temper that boldness with the spirit of a servant (see 2 Timothy 2:24).

4. Be filled with the Spirit.

To be prepared to preach the Gospel, we must be filled with the Spirit:

> *"But you shall receive power when the Holy Spirit has come upon you: and you shall be witnesses to Me in Jerusalem, and in all Judea and Samaria, and to the end of the earth."*
>
> (Acts 1:8 NKJV)

5. Be ready to seize every opportunity.

We will be prepared to share God with others only when we are truly ready to seize every opportunity to do so:

> *"Preach the word! Be read in season and out of season. Convince, rebuke, exhort, with all longsuffering and teaching."*
>
> (2 Timothy 4:2 NKJV)

101

6. **Know how to handle objections and opposition to the Gospel.**

And finally, we're prepared to preach the Gospel when we know how to handle people's resistance, their objections, and their opposition to it. Take a Christian apologetics class. Read books on witnessing and sharing your faith. Writers such as Josh McDowell and C. S. Lewis have compiled some amazing arguments to back up the Christian faith. Learn what you can do to handle any objections or opposition that people might have as you share your faith.

Target Zone 4: Your Whole Body

The next piece of armor is more all-inclusive. The following Scripture reveals what it does for us:

> *"Above all, taking the shield of faith with which you will be able to quench all the fiery darts of the wicked one."* (Ephesians 6:16 NKJV)

"Above all" means that this piece of armor is very important, and you need to be sure you are holding the shield of faith to protect your entire body. How many fiery arrows of the enemy will this shield defeat? Just one fiery dart can take you out. You want to quench them all.

Armament 4: Shield

What is this shield of faith? It has four important characteristics.

1. **The shield is the first line of defense.**

The shield of faith is your first line of defense against an attack from the enemy. If an arrow is incoming, yes, you can stand there with your shield on the ground, and you still have a breastplate that will protect your chest and a helmet to protect your head. But your *first* line of defense should be your shield. You must stop the incoming attack at the shield level, before it ever reaches you.

2. **The shield protects the whole body.**

   The helmet protects the head, and your boots protect your feet, but the shield protects the entire body. If you've seen a shield, you know that it is a large piece of equipment. Shields from biblical times were about two feet wide and about four feet high. An entire man's body can fit behind such a shield, and no matter what comes at him, he will survive.

3. **The shield protects the other armor.**

   The other pieces of armor can do their job if a strike gets through or around the shield of faith, but it is meant to be the second line of defense. The shield protects the other armor.

4. **The shield quenches all the fiery darts of the wicked.**

   The shield of faith stops the attacks from the enemy and prevents them from taking any kind of toll on your life. The fiery darts of the wicked are thoughts and false ideas intended to destroy.

Fiery Darts

What are the fiery darts that the enemy launches toward you in his attacks? Let's look at how the Bible describes them.

1. **They are swift.**

   You don't get time to prepare for incoming darts. The word *dart* implies quickness of speed. They are swift. Darts come at you quickly.

2. **They are secret.**

   Darts are often secret. You won't detect them until they are already upon you.

3. **They have a wounding, hurting, killing nature.**

The enemy's intent is to steal, kill, and destroy. He uses fiery darts to accomplish these goals. The darts wound. They hurt. They kill.

4. **They come from the enemy, the wicked one.**

It is important to remember the true source of these darts. They come from the enemy, not from other people. The devil can send you a fiery dart whenever he would like. He has many evil spirits working for him who can launch a fiery dart at you at any time.

5. **They come through wicked people.**

Although their true source is the enemy, darts often come *through* wicked people. Wickedness is usually disguised. It may not come through a sinful person, but it may come through a wicked person.

> *"For look! The wicked bend their bow, they*
> *make ready their arrow on the string, that they*
> *may shoot secretly at the upright in heart."*
> (Psalm 11:2 NKJV)

Wicked people keep their arrows ready upon the string. And they shoot privately at the upright in heart. It is possible that you could experience a fiery dart from a parent, from a spouse, from a child, or from a friend—especially if you are doing what you should be doing, and they are not. They will want to tear you down. Sometimes the fiery dart comes straight from the enemy, the adversary, the devil, but other times it comes from other people.

6. **They often appear in the form of bitter words.**

Fiery darts are very often bitter words. Here's what the Scripture says about fiery darts:

> *"Hide me from the secret plots of the wicked,*
> *from the rebellion of the workers of iniquity,*

> *who sharpen their tongue like a sword, and*
> *bend their bows to shoot their arrows—bitter*
> *words.* " (Psalm 64:2–3 NKJV)

What arrows are being shot? The darts are words, which come off the tongue, and the power of death and life is in the tongue. These poisonous darts that are aimed at you are words that come either from the enemy when he accuses you directly, or they are accusations that come through other people who, at that moment at least, are operating as instruments of the devil's will. Satan is using them to send bitter and condemning words at you. Make no mistake about what fiery darts are—they are messages. They are ideas that are carried in words to get inside of you and destroy you. These are fiery darts of the enemy—and the only thing that can stop them is the shield of faith.

So, how do you take up the shield of faith? This is rather simple because faith has only one origin:

> *"So then faith comes by hearing, and hearing*
> *by the word of God."* (Romans 10:17 NKJV)

Faith comes by hearing the Word of God. In ancient times, the shield was covered with leather, and during a military operation, soldiers would put the leather in water until it was soaking wet because what was coming at them were arrows that were on fire—literally fiery darts. But when a fiery dart hit the shield, it didn't just stop the dart; it also stopped the fire that was in the dart. God wants you to have so much faith that when the darts strike your shield of faith they are immediately quenched. Smile as you are reading this. Realize the victory is yours through Christ. Celebrate today as you hear the Word and receive it by faith.

Target Zone 5: Head

*"And take the helmet of salvation, and the
sword of the Spirit, which is the word of God."*
(Ephesians 6:17 NKJV)

Now we put on the helmet of salvation because the fifth
target zone is the head.

Armament 5: Helmet

The armament that is used to protect the head is the helmet
of salvation. And the helmet is exactly that—salvation.

*"O God the Lord, the strength of my salvation,
You have covered my head in the day of
battle."*
(Psalm 140:7 NKJV)

What does the Bible tell us about salvation? Here are
seven truths of salvation:

1. **Salvation is God's.**

   *"I long for Your salvation, O Lord, and Your
   law is my delight."*
   (Psalm 119:174 NKJV)

   Salvation is God's. It was His idea. And it is the result
of His work in us:

   *"Behold, God is my salvation, I will trust
   and not be afraid: 'For YAH, the LORD, is my
   strength and song; He also has become my
   salvation.'"*
   (Isaiah 12:2 NKJV)

   Salvation is found in a living Person. It is not a
salvation that comes because of a prayer or something
that occurred mystically in the past. It comes because
God is in your life right now. He is your salvation.

2. Salvation is found in Christ Jesus alone.

> *"Nor is there salvation in any other, for*
> *there is no other name under heaven given*
> *among men by which we must be saved."*
>
> (Acts 4:12 NKJV)

Salvation is in Christ alone. There is only one way to God, and it comes through a provision that He made personally when He visited this planet and died on a cross to redeem our soul from sin. And then He rose from the grave to prove it. He lives to this day to guarantee it. And He is coming back again to demonstrate it. Jesus is the only way. There is no inclusiveness about salvation. It is exclusive:

> *"Because narrow is the gate and difficult is*
> *the way which leads to life, and there are few*
> *who find it."*   (Matthew 7:14 NKJV)

Make no mistake about it—salvation is found in Christ alone.

3. Salvation is deliverance from sin.

True salvation is deliverance from sin:

> *"For sin shall not have dominion over you,*
> *for you are not under law but under grace."*
>
> (Romans 6:14 NKJV)

It brings us eternal life:

> *"But now having been set free from sin, and*
> *having become slaves of God, you have your*
> *fruit to holiness, and the end, everlasting*
> *life."*   (Romans 6:22 NKJV)

This is not a salvation that brings some theoretical relationship with God whereby He pretends you are righteous when you're really not. He *actually* makes you free from sin. You will live a life of righteousness. And in the end, you will receive everlasting life.

4. **Salvation is deliverance from iniquity.**

> *"To you first, God, having raised up His Servant Jesus, sent Him to bless you, in **turning away every one of you from your iniquities.**"* (Acts 3:26 NKJV)

Most people know what *sin* is, but they don't know what *iniquity* is. Iniquity is the biblical word for narcissism. The two, sin and iniquity, are very different. Isaiah 53 tells us that Jesus's ultimate sacrifice on the cross saves us from both:

> *"But He was wounded for our transgressions, **He was bruised for our iniquities**; the chastisement for our peace was upon Him, and by His stripes we are healed."* (Isaiah 53:5 NKJV)

5. **Salvation brings peace with God.**

When you receive salvation, you have peace with God:

> *"And by Him to reconcile all things to Himself, by Him, whether things on earth, or things in heaven, having made peace through the blood of His cross."*
> (Colossians 1:20 NKJV)

6. Salvation is deliverance from sickness and disease.

Salvation isn't just eternal life in heaven when we die; it is also deliverance from sickness and disease in the here and now:

> *"But He was wounded for our transgressions, He was bruised for our iniquities; the chastisement for our peace was upon Him, and **by His stripes we are healed**."* (Isaiah 53:5 NKJV)
>
> *"Who forgives all your iniquities, who heals all your diseases."* (Psalm 103:3 NKJV)

God not only forgives all our iniquities; He also heals all our diseases.

7. Salvation is deliverance from poverty.

Salvation also includes deliverance from poverty. Jesus especially wants His Gospel to be preached to the poor. He wants the poor to have the Gospel so they won't be poor anymore:

> *"The blessing of the Lord makes one rich, and He adds no sorrow with it."*
>
> (Proverbs 10:22 NKJV)

Putting on the Helmet of Salvation

So, how do you put on the helmet of salvation? You must firmly establish salvation thoughts in your mind so that no contrary thoughts can rival or prevail. Next, follow these four steps:

1. Work out your salvation with fear and trembling.

> *"Therefore, my beloved, as you have always obeyed, not as in my presence only, but now much more in my absence, work out your own*

salvation with fear and trembling."

(Philippians 2:12 NKJV)

You need to "work out"—ponder, understand, consider—your salvation, and you should do this with fear and trembling. Work it out. Sit down with the Bible and perhaps a pen in hand, and get thoroughly acquainted with what salvation has done for you.

2. Don't neglect your salvation.

In addition, don't neglect your salvation:

> *"How shall we escape if we neglect so great a salvation, which at the first began to be spoken by the Lord, and was confirmed to us by those who heard him."* (Hebrews 2:3 NKJV)

Don't neglect all those details that you considered when you worked out your salvation with fear and trembling. Don't make any presumptions and don't make any assumptions. Work it out with fear and trembling in the presence of Almighty God. And don't neglect your salvation. Nurture your relationship with God through regular prayer, reading His Word, and abiding by His principles. Those actions continue strengthening the relationship with God.

3. Think salvation thoughts.

Third, think salvation thoughts exclusively:

> *"Let the wicked forsake his way, and the unrighteous man his thoughts; let him return to the Lord, and He will have mercy upon him; and to our God, for He will abundantly pardon."* (Isaiah 55:7 NKJV)

Here's the reason why:

> *"'For My thoughts are not your thoughts, nor are your ways My ways,' says the Lord."*
>
> (Isaiah 55:8 NKJV)

God's thoughts are not our thoughts—and thank Him for that! The thoughts we have after salvation should not in any way be the thoughts that we had before Calvary. If you are still thinking pre-Calvary thoughts, you do not have your helmet on.

4. Rejoice in your salvation.

Finally, rejoice in your salvation. You ought to experience a continual fountain of joy based on what the Lord has done for you: What a great reason to rejoice. God has done so much for us—we should celebrate.

> *"Therefore with joy you will draw water from of the wells of salvation.*
>
> *And in that day you will say: 'Praise the Lord, call upon His name; declare His deeds among the peoples, make mention that His name is exalted.'"*   (Isaiah 12:3–4 NKJV)

Target Zone 6: The Enemy!

God hasn't just given us defensive armor to protect us from what the enemy might send our way. He has provided us with a powerful offensive weapon to use against the enemy.

Go on the offensive! Make the target zone the enemy!

> *"And take...the sword of the Spirit, which is the word of God."*   (Ephesians 6:17 NKJV)

When we go on the offensive, the target zone is not part of our bodies; it is the enemy. Now let me clarify. The target isn't really the enemy; it is the attacks the enemy launches at us. Why is it not the enemy himself? Because he's already been dealt with.

On the cross, our Lord defeated Satan. This means that the attacks the enemy is launching at us now are illegal. His attacks on you are unlawful! There are two mistakes you can make about the devil: the first is to ascribe to the devil *more* power than he really has, and the other is to ascribe to him *less* power than he actually has. You may overestimate him, or you may underestimate him. Both are a problem! Thankfully, we have the offensive weapon of the sword of the Spirit. All the other weapons are defensive armaments. But not this one. With the sword of the Spirit, we can defeat the attacks of the enemy.

Armament 6: The Sword

Here are eight facts to learn about the sword of the Spirit, which is the Word of God:

1. The sword of the Spirit is made out of the Word of God.

> *"For the word of God is living and powerful, and sharper than any two-edged sword, piercing even to the division of soul and spirit, and of joints and marrow, and is a discerner of the thoughts and intents of the heart."*　　(Hebrews 4:12 NKJV)

2. It is used by the Holy Spirit through us.

This is the sword of the Spirit—and *Spirit* here takes the capital "S." It's not just a sword that's used in the spirit realm; it is the sword that is personally endorsed and empowered by the Holy Spirit. When you use the sword, you are not using it alone. The Spirit is using the sword with you.

3. The sword is designed to defeat every enemy effort, including overcoming temptation.

Jesus Himself used this sword when the enemy came against Him with temptation:

> *"Then Jesus said to him, 'Away with you, Satan! For it is written, "You shall worship*

the Lord your God, and Him only you shall
serve."'
Then the devil left Him, and behold, angels
came and ministered to Him."

(Matthew 4:10–11 NKJV)

4. The sword overcomes heresies.

One of the great tragedies of our day is that when we think of heresy, we think of some of those strange cults, like Jonestown or Waco, full of weirdos. They had heresies in their doctrine, and it got them off track. But heresy isn't committed just by the outliers, living on the fringes of society:

"Now the Spirit expressly says that in latter times some will depart from the faith, giving heed to deceiving spirits and doctrines of demons." (1 Timothy 4:1 NKJV)

We are told that in the last days, there will be such a proliferation of heresy that it would deceive even the elect. What is the cure for this problem? Jesus tells us:

"Sanctify them by Your truth. Your word is truth." (John 17:17 NKJV)

God's Word is the truth. That's why I make no apology that this book and its content should be first and foremost in every one of our lives. You want to get fanatical about something? Get fanatical about following God's Word!

5. The sword overcomes corruption and lust.

If a person is bound up by lust or corruption, either that person has yet to be converted to Christ, or he or she hasn't gotten the armor on and hasn't used the sword of the Spirit.

6. The sword overcomes afflictions.

> *"Unless Your law had been my delight, I would then have perished in affliction."*
>
> (Psalm 119:92 NKJV)

7. The sword overcomes depression.

> *"So shall My word be that goes forth from my mouth; it shall not return to Me void, but it shall accomplish what I please, and it shall prosper in the thing for which I sent it."* (Isaiah 55:11 NKJV)

Watch what happens when God's Word, or the sword, goes forth:

> *"For you shall go out with joy, and be led out with peace; the mountains and the hills shall break forth into singing before you, and all the trees of the field shall clap their hands."* (Isaiah 55:12 NKJV)

You will go out with joy. You will be led forth with peace, and the mountains and the hills shall break forth before you into singing. In my own life, I have had my share of battles. But I have learned that this sword of the Spirit always works!

8. The sword overcomes ignorance.

> *"Your word is a lamp to my feet and a light to my path."* (Psalm 119:105 NKJV)

God's Word is a lamp, bringing light to our ignorance and confusion. The following verse is worth repeating here because it holds the key to how the sword overcomes ignorance:

*"Your word I have hidden in my heart, that I
might not sin against You."*

(Psalm 119:11 NKJV)

How to Take Up the Sword of the Spirit

We must do three things with the Word of God to understand the essence of how to take up the sword of the Spirit:

1. Learn how the Word of God addresses every subject.

Whatever subject you are ignorant about, that is where the enemy will attack you. You must learn the Word of God about every subject and allow the Holy Spirit to enliven those Scriptures to you. That's what He does best—and He loves to do that for us. In fact, it is His mission:

*"However, when He, the Spirit of truth, has
come, He will guide you into all truth; for
He will not speak on His own authority, but
whatever He hears He will speak; and He will
tell you things to come."* (John 16:13 NKJV)

The Spirit of Truth will bring to your mind the things you have already learned from the Word of God.

2. Allow the Holy Spirit to bring the Word alive for you.

Once you know what the Word of God has to say, you must allow the Holy Spirit to enliven it to you.

3. Quote the Word at every sign of opposition.

Finally, you must quote the Word whenever the fiery darts of the enemy come your way. And this is not only for your benefit; it will benefit other people as well. You cannot teach what you do not know; you cannot lead where you do not go. The Word will work mightily in us so that it can work mightily in others.

God has given us an ample arsenal of armor to help us withstand the attacks of the enemy, especially since we are high-value targets in the conflict that is raging between the armies of the Lord and the armies of Satan. Put on the armor and keep it on—every day and every night. It will guard your heart, your mind, your loins, and your feet. And with the offensive and powerful weapon of the sword of the Spirit, you will turn the tables on the enemy, making him the target instead!

Chapter 6

Know Your Enemy and His Devices

The battle of Antietam in 1862 was, without a doubt, the bloodiest day in the entire Civil War. In just twelve hours, the fierce fighting left ten thousand Confederate soldiers dead and even more than that killed on the Union side. One historian wrote: "At last the sun went down and the battle ended, smoke heavy in the air, the twilight quivering with the anguished cries of thousands of wounded men."

Although it seemed that the battle ended in a draw, Union General George McClellan had, that day, put a stop to the Southern advance into Maryland. The Confederate army, led by Robert E. Lee, was forced to retreat across the Potomac.

The reason for this tipping of the scales toward a later Union victory? The bravery of two young Union soldiers, who found a copy of Robert E. Lee's battle plans and delivered them to General McClellan before the battle.

In many respects, we are no match for our enemy. And as a high-value target, we may feel especially outnumbered by his tactics. But just as with General McClellan's good fortune that day, our Commander has given us a copy of the enemy's playbook. His plans have fallen into our hands. We can see his strategies to entice us with deceit, lust, greed, covetousness, and all manner of temptations—and we can prepare ourselves against his onslaught.

Learn about the Enemy

Even in modern warfare, one of the most important rules that our nation's military personnel follow is a simple one: Know the enemy. This is an important rule of combat, one that saves lives when it is put into practice. Our soldiers must learn the enemy: What are his strengths? What are his weaknesses? What artillery is he using? What capacity to damage us does he have? What weapons is he carrying? What are his battle plans in the war he is waging against us?

The reason this is valuable should be obvious: If you know the enemy's devices, you can protect yourself! This is precisely what the Scriptures tell us about the enemy we face each and every day in our own lives:

> *"...lest Satan should take advantage of us; for we are not ignorant of his devices."*
>
> (2 Corinthians 2:11 NKJV)

We cannot be ignorant of the enemy's devices! What tricks, what tactics, what devices does the enemy of your soul possess in order to damage, hurt, steal from, and destroy you and yours?

The best way to avoid this kind of ignorance is to study the devices of Satan so you will know how to not only protect yourself, but also wage war, and go on the offensive, against him. Know your enemy! Here are the devices Satan uses to separate us from our Lord and Savior.

Device #1 of the Enemy: Keep Christians in Unforgiveness

When Christians refuse to forgive each other, Satan starts winning battles. My friend, there is not a sin so great that forgiveness cannot leap over it. There's not a wall so high that forgiveness cannot tear it down:

> *"For to this end I also wrote, that I might put you to the test, whether you are obedient in all things."*
>
> (2 Corinthians 2:9 NKJV)

Paul wrote to the Corinthian believers to "put them to the test." He wrote about two types of tests. On one occasion, Paul had asked people about their faith, which was one of the "tests" of their belief. But in this instance, the test was whether or not they were obedient in all things. They could not be selective, just obeying the Lord in some things; the test was whether they were obedient in *all* things. This was made more obvious in the next verse that Paul wrote, which indicated one of the most difficult areas in which to practice this obedience:

> *"Now whom you forgive anything, I also forgive. For if indeed I have forgiven anything, I have forgiven that one for your sakes in the presence of Christ."*　　　　　　　　　(2 Corinthians 2:10 NKJV)

Paul said that if the Corinthians forgave anybody of anything, he would forgive that person also. Forgiveness is not simply a one-on-one issue. If you forgive your child, the rest of the family should also forgive that child. If the mother forgives the daughter, the father also needs to forgive the daughter. Satan's intention is to keep us in unforgiveness, even toward those who haven't offended us. Why is forgiveness so important? To keep Satan from gaining an advantage!

Unforgiveness gives an advantage to Satan in at least two ways. First, if we are not forgiving, we are not forgiven. Jesus made this clear at the end of His Lord's Prayer, that if we forgive others, our heavenly Father will forgive us, but if we do not forgive others, our heavenly Father will not forgive us. Forgiveness is the first step in the redemptive process. Second, Satan will gain an advantage because if you have unforgiveness in your heart, your prayers will not be heard. Jesus told us that when we stand praying, we are to *forgive*. Unforgiveness hinders the effectiveness of our prayers. If Satan can get a Christian to be unforgiving toward any other person, he can stop that Christian's prayers. If he can get a Christian to be unforgiving toward any other person, he has pulled that Christian out of a proper, right relationship with God. Let's not be ignorant of this first device of Satan—let's always walk in forgiveness toward other people!

Device #2 of the Enemy: Have Christians Question the Word of God

The inclination to question what God has said goes all the way back to the beginning—to Eve's temptation by Satan in the Garden of Eden:

> *"Now the serpent was more cunning than any beast of the field which the Lord God had made. And he said to the woman, 'Has God indeed said, "You shall not eat of every tree of the garden"'?"*
>
> (Genesis 3:1 NKJV)

From the very beginning, Satan's tactic has been to plant seeds of doubt in God's people and prompt them to question what the Lord has said. This is exactly what he did with Eve. And as this Scripture shows us, our enemy can be very *subtle*. He will plant thoughts such as this in our minds: *Did God really say that? Do you think He really meant what He said? Do you think He really wants good things for my life?* He wants you to question the Word of God.

Device #3 of the Enemy: Exaggerate the Standards of the Word of God

Look at this next tactic of the enemy: he exaggerates the standards of the Word, and we see it in the very same verse:

> *"Now the serpent was more cunning than any beast of the field which the Lord God had made. And he said to the woman, 'Has God indeed said, "You shall not eat of every tree of the garden"'?"*
>
> (Genesis 3:1 NKJV)

Now, we just looked at this Scripture. But in this tactic, it seems as if Satan repeats back to the woman what God said—but look closely. He actually asks the question, "Did God say, 'You shall not eat of every tree in the garden'?" Guess what? That's not what God said! Satan put a twist on it and exaggerated the claim. Now, let's look at the next verse:

> *"And the woman said to the serpent, 'We may eat of the fruit of the trees of the garden;*
>
> *but of the fruit of the tree which is in the midst of the garden, God has said, "You shall not eat it, nor shall you touch it, lest ye die."'"* (Genesis 3:2–3 NKJV)

Eve was actually able to correct the serpent's words, telling him that they could eat of all the other trees, but they could not eat or touch the fruit of *the one tree*, or they would die. Satan rephrased what God had said. He twisted God's words—and this is an important tactic he uses on all of us. Watch out for it!

Device #4 of the Enemy: Contradict the Word of God

Fourth, the enemy contradicts the Word of God:

> *"Then the serpent said to the woman, 'You will not surely die.'"* (Genesis 3:4 NKJV)

The serpent told Eve that she would not die, that what God had said to her was not true. He flat-out contradicted the Word of God. You need to understand that at a most primary level, Satan is against the Bible—probably because the Bible is against him. He may do it in obvious ways, or he may do it in subtle ways, but he will contradict the Word of God.

Device #5 of the Enemy: Put a Wrong Interpretation on the Word of God

In addition to exaggerating or contradicting the Word of God, the enemy will also place a wrong interpretation on the Scriptures. Now, we know that the Bible has only one correct interpretation and many applications. But Satan will bring a wrong interpretation to what God has said:

> *"For God knows that in the day you eat of it your*
> *eyes will be opened, and you will be like God,*
> *knowing good and evil."*   (Genesis 3:5 NKJV)

The enemy made the false claim to Adam and Eve that their eyes would be opened if they only disobeyed God. He proposed that God didn't want them to have the knowledge of good and evil like He did. Of course, the story went downhill from that point because Adam and Eve fell for the lies the enemy told them:

> *"So when the woman saw that the tree was good*
> *for food, that it was pleasant to the eyes, and a tree*
> *desirable to make one wise, she took of its fruit and*
> *ate. She also gave to her husband with her, and he*
> *ate."*   (Genesis 3:6 NKJV)

Eve looked…and she saw that the tree was good for food, and it was pleasant to the eyes. So was ushered in the greatest tragedy of all time. Satan's attempt was to discredit what God had said. His tactic was successful then, and it still works today.

Device #6 of the Enemy: Tempt God's People

Another device of Satan is to tempt believers to disobey what they know to be right:

> *"Then Jesus was led up by the Spirit into the*
> *wilderness to be tempted by the devil….*
> *Now when the tempter came to Him, he said, 'If*
> *You are the Son of God, command that these stones*
> *become bread.'"*   (Matthew 4:1, 3 NKJV)

In these verses, the tempter, the devil, came to Jesus; he was proactive about it. It's in his nature: Satan is a tempter. But I want to share with you some good news about his tempting:

> *"No temptation has overtaken you except such as*
> *is common to man; but God is faithful, who will not*
> *allow you to be tempted beyond what you are able;*

> *but with the temptation will also make the way to escape, that you may be able to bear it."*
>
> (1 Corinthians 10:13 NKJV)

In other words, we are all in the same boat! Satan is going to use the same temptations with everybody. But God is faithful to each of us as well! He will make a way of escape for us so that we can bear the temptation and not fall. God watches closely to make sure that any tempting never becomes so great that we can't overcome it. And He provides the way of escape so that we can bear the temptation.

That's good news! You can hang in there during times of temptation. Temptation is a form of *influence*, but it is not *brute force*. Satan has the ability to *influence* you, but he doesn't have the power to *force* you. You see the difference? The tempter is only a tempter, and the temptation is not a force greater than you can deal with. He will sure make it seem enticing, but you are the only one who can agree to follow the temptation—again temptation is an influence, not a force. It's a tactic of the enemy—but it is one that you can overcome!

Device #7 of the Enemy: Accuse God's People—Whether They Are Guilty or Not

Seventh, the enemy is an accuser. He will point his finger at you over almost anything you do. If you do something wrong, he will drag it back up in front of you; if you do something right, he'll accuse you of having false motives. There is no winning with him because he is an adversary who knows no rules. The Geneva Conventions that govern our modern-day warfare do not cover him. He accuses—and he doesn't play fair. He'll accuse you to yourself.

One of the worst things that could ever happen to you is to believe his accusations. But his tactic is to accuse you so consistently, and so perpetually, that the risk becomes great that you will join your faith to him and to his accusations. He'll tell you that God doesn't love you. He'll tell you that there's no hope. That you can't change your life. That you're a failure—and you always will be a failure. That you can't keep your marriage together. That you can't keep your family together. That you're a lousy mother. *That's what he does.*

Accusation is one of his favorite devices. And his tactic is to wear you down until you finally give in and agree with him. But when you agree with him, despair is the end result. Then you will live under the accusation of the enemy all the time. You will gradually begin to weaken until you fall into despair. And when you despair, the next step is to give up…

Don't give up! Consider the end result of the "accuser":

> *"Then I heard a loud voice saying in heaven, 'Now salvation, and strength, and the kingdom of our God, and the power of His Christ have come, for the accuser of our brethren, who accused them before our God day and night, has been cast down.'"* (Revelation 12:10 NKJV)

In the end, the "accuser of our brethren"—Satan, our enemy—is cast down. Notice his tactic, though: He would accuse God's people before God day and night. He used to have that ability—but he doesn't any longer. He used to go before God and the angels and accuse people to them; in fact, that's what he did with Job. But he can't do that anymore. He got cast down at Calvary. He's still an accuser, though, and it's one of his favorite tactics to use against God's people.

Device #8 of the Enemy: Operate through Demons Who "Possess"

There are several things you need to know about Satan. First, he is not omniscient. He does not know everything. God and God alone can do that. 1 Kings 8:39 tells us, *"Thou, even thou only, knowest the hearts of all the children of men."*

Only God knows what's in your heart; Satan does not. He doesn't have access to your heart, although he can find out what's in your heart if he listens to your mouth—because out of the abundance of the heart, the mouth speaks. So watch your words!

Another thing that Satan is *not* is omnipresent. He cannot be in more than one place at the same time. He is in a locality even now, as you are reading the words of this book. He is limited geographically to one locality. Only God is omnipresent.

However, long ago, when Satan was cast out of heaven after leading a rebellion of one-third of God's angels, those heavenly beings, hundreds of thousands of them, were cast out with him. We know them today as fallen angels, or demons, or evil spirits. Now, the angels that fell are divided into two categories. One group of angels is *bound*; that is, they are not free to roam this planet; they are held in chains until the day of judgment because of their Old Testament behavior of being sexual with human women on the earth. God would not tolerate this behavior, and He removed these particular fallen angels from the earth, putting them into chains and reserving them for their future judgment.

> *"God spared not the angels that sinned, but cast*
> *them down to hell, and delivered them into chains*
> *of darkness, to be reserved unto judgment;"*
>
> (2 Peter 2:4)

However, there are still hundreds of thousands of angels in the second category: fallen angels who are *not bound* yet. They will be one day, but for the time being, they are part of Satan's vast army—and these fallen angels/evil spirits seek to possess human beings.

Jesus encountered these possessed people in His ministry on the earth:

> *"When evening had come, they brought to Him*
> *many who were demon-possessed. And He cast out*
> *the spirits with a word, and healed all who were*
> *sick."* (Matthew 8:16 NKJV)

Part of Jesus's ministry was to cast out the spirits with His word and heal those who had been possessed.

Watch out for this tactic. The enemy seeks willing vessels whom he or his evil spirits can possess, and then he is able to more effectively work through them.

Device #9 of the Enemy: Operate in Deception

All of Satan's works involve deception. He is a deceiver:

> *"So the great dragon was cast out, that serpent*
> *of old, called the Devil and Satan, who deceives*
> *the whole world; he was cast to the earth, and his*
> *angels were cast out with him."* (Revelation 12:9 NKJV)

This passage tells us that Satan has deceived the whole world. He's a deceiver. The fact is that when Jesus died on Calvary, Satan lost his legal right to do anything on this planet. Because of that, he really is quite limited today. He must get the cooperation of human beings to do anything on this earth—because he doesn't have the legal right to make things happen here anymore. To do this, he can only influence people by lies and deceit. If we give in to his deception, then we give him legal access to wreak havoc in our lives.

On the other hand, when Jesus took back the legal rule of the planet on the cross, in turn He said to us, "I'm going to give you the authority that I've got. And you will walk on scorpions. You will cast out devils. All authority is given unto Me, and as the Father has sent Me, I am giving this authority to you. Now you can have power over all the works of the devil."

Now, that's really good news! This becomes an issue of authority. Do you know the difference between *authority* and *power*? Consider a policeman standing at a street corner where the lights aren't working. When he holds his hand up, all the cars stop. That is *authority*. Does the man actually have the physical power to stop that car? Probably not; the driver could step on the gas and mow that policeman down. The driver and the vehicle itself may have the *power*, but *authority* stops them. Now, if the driver did try to use the power of the vehicle, then the policeman might tap into his own resources and stop the car with his weapon. That's power.

But authority is demonstrated when the policeman holds up his hand and everybody stops.

Jesus has given you *authority* over all the works of the enemy. Did you know that you can stop what Satan is doing in your life? You have that authority! But remember: you're dealing with a deceiver. You're dealing with somebody who wants to make you believe you don't have authority. He wants to make you believe that you have to do what he tells you to do. So he tries to deceive you. Deception is one of his primary devices. But you have not only the authority but the power!

Device #10 of the Enemy: Plant Wicked People in Churches

Satan is not after Buddhists. Satan is not after those who follow the teachings of Confucius. Satan is not after atheists or secular humanists. He's already got those people. Satan is after the Christians.

There are only two sides in this battle: God and Satan, light and darkness, the kingdom of God and the kingdom of Satan, those who are for Christ and those who are against Him. The enemy is not concerned about any of those who are already on his side. His strategy is to plant enemies of believers *inside* the Christian Church to wreak havoc and confusion:

> *"Another parable He put forth to them, saying,*
> *'The kingdom of heaven is like a man who sowed*
> *good seed in his field;*
>
> *but while men slept, his enemy came and sowed*
> *tares among the wheat and went his way.'"*
>
> (Matthew 13:24–25 NKJV)

Jesus told this parable about the kingdom of heaven. It is like a man who sowed seed in the field, but while he slept, his enemy came and sowed tares among the wheat and then went on his way. Jesus gives the explanation:

> *"The field is the world, the good seeds are the sons*
> *of the kingdom, but the tares are the sons of the*
> *wicked one.*
>
> *The enemy who sowed them is the devil, the harvest*
> *is the end of the age, and the reapers are the*
> *angels."*   (Matthew 13:38–39 NKJV)

Jesus said that the good seeds are the children of the kingdom, but the tares are the children of the wicked one, and the enemy who sowed them is the devil. One way the enemy seeks to destroy the kingdom of God is by infiltrating it, sowing tares among the wheat, putting wicked people in with the children of the kingdom.

I'm going to present two scenarios to you. I know of only two, but there may be others. It is possible for the tares to take over a church entirely—*en masse.* When a so-called Christian denomination votes against the principles of the Bible and against Jesus Christ, in favor of what Jesus Christ is against, that church has been taken over by the "tares." Entire denominations have fallen along the way due to the satanic plants that were in the church who were able to take over and multiply until no true believers remained. The other scenario occurs when both the church leadership and the people exercise vigilance, practice church discipline, publish standards, and uphold qualifications for membership, including living one's life under the lordship of Jesus. That church will stand—even though every church has been infiltrated in some way by the enemy. Some of the enemy's plants just aren't successful because we are not willing to let the tares overrun the wheat. I want to be in *that* church, don't you?

But this is another of Satan's strategies, to plant wicked people in churches.

Device #11 of the Enemy: Oppress (Vex) God's People

Satan oppresses God's people:

> *"And, behold, a woman of Canaan came out of*
> *the same coasts, and cried unto him, saying, Have*
> *mercy on me, O Lord, thou Son of David; my*

daughter is grievously vexed with a devil."

(Matthew 15:22)

This woman's daughter was "grievously vexed" by a devil. To be vexed means to be distressed, harassed, troubled or annoyed. Our enemy vexes people. But take heart!

> *"How God anointed Jesus of Nazareth with the Holy Spirit and with power, who went about doing good and **healing all who were oppressed of the devil**, for God was with Him."*   (Acts 10:38 NKJV)

The devil is an oppressor and a *possessor*. If people will let him possess them, he will, but if he is not successful at that, he will surely be an *oppressor*. He is going to try to hold you down, get you under his power and in his clutches, and sap all the energy out of you. That's what he does when he "vexes" God's people.

Device #12 of the Enemy: Speak through Other People

Did you know that not every word you hear is actually being spoken by the people around you? One of the enemy's greatest tactics is to speak through people directly to us. He even tried to do this with Jesus Himself:

> *"But He turned and said to Peter, 'Get behind Me, Satan! You are an offense to Me, for you are not mindful of the things of God, but the things of men.'"*   (Matthew 16:23 NKJV)

The devil used Peter's voice—his actual vocal chords!—to speak evil words to the Lord. But Jesus turned and commanded the enemy to get behind Him. Jesus saw that the words Peter was spitting out were actually coming from Satan.

The enemy seeks to speak to us through the people. That's why you need to be careful whom you listen to. Even well-meaning people—like Peter—may be instruments of the enemy, the vocalizations of Satan. How do you know when someone is speaking the words of Satan? Worse yet, how do you know you are being used of Satan (if and when you are)? The answer is wrapped up in the very meaning of the name: *Satanas* means "accuser." When you are accusing your husband, your wife, your children, or your employer or employee, you are being used by the enemy. That's the stuff of the kingdom of darkness. That is coming from Satan. If it happened to Peter, one of the closest disciples to Jesus, it can happen to us. So watch out, because what you could be listening to—or what you could be speaking—could be coming straight from the enemy.

In contrast to this, we follow Jesus who simply said, *"Do not think that I will accuse you..."* (John 5:45). We don't go around blaming people, no finger pointing.

Device #13 of the Enemy: Cause Sickness and Disease

Another of the enemy's tactics is to cause sickness and disease. Now, there are several causes of sickness found in the Scriptures—and there are several ways in the Scriptures of being healed of disease. But one of the primary causes of sickness and disease is the devil. He inflicts God's people with disease:

> *"And as he was still coming, the demon threw him down and convulsed him. Then Jesus rebuked the unclean spirit, healed the child, and gave him back to his father."* (Luke 9:42 NKJV)

When Jesus rebuked the devil in the child and it departed, the child was cured at that very moment. Certain diseases are caused by Satan—and the cure of the disease is not to deal with the disease, but to deal with the devil who's the cause of the disease. That's why you and I have been given the power and the ability to cast out evil spirits—to counter this tactic of the enemy!

Device #14 of the Enemy: Cause Uncleanness

The enemy causes uncleanness. I have seen both physical and spiritual uncleanness in my life. Some of the mission fields I have visited have broken my heart. In Haiti, eight to ten people might sleep in a tiny cardboard hut at night, with a tin roof full of holes. A trench down the middle of the street was what people openly used for their toilet, with barefoot children playing in it. But many of the huts belonging to Christian families I visited were different: they still had dirt floors, tin roofs, and cardboard walls, but everything was neat and orderly. John Wesley once said that cleanliness is next to godliness. I personally think that cleanliness is a *part of* godliness.

As bad as physical uncleanness can be, moral and spiritual uncleanness are worse. What we are experiencing in America, with all our large houses and high "standards of living," is a huge demonic effort to bring uncleanness to our whole nation. We have foul mouths. We have foul television shows, foul music videos, foul jokes, foul conversations. Foul advertising fills our magazines. Pornography is everywhere—it has increased in staggering proportions in the past forty years. The undressing of America has set us up.

We must guard against this tactic of the enemy by cleansing ourselves from all filthiness—of the flesh and of the spirit. Your spirit can be made filthy by demons. Moral filth and impure thoughts will plague us and unleash evil spirits in our lives. Know this: God is holy, but the devil is unholy; God is righteous, but Satan is unrighteous; God is clean, but Satan is filthy. He seeks to fill us with filthy thoughts, filthy ideas, filthy talk—filthy everything, and this is simply the external evidence of the internal working of unclean spirits.

There are specific evil spirits who specialize in moral uncleanness. In fact, they are referred to in Scripture as "Unclean Spirits." What should we do with an unclean spirit?

> *"And when the unclean spirit had convulsed him*
> *and cried with a loud voice, he came out of him."*
>
> (Mark 1:26 NKJV)

Of course, you know the answer to my question: full deliverance. Yes, it takes an exorcism sometimes. Once uncleanness gets in, and if it has attached to the work of an evil spirit, then that spirit has to be cast out. That's what Jesus did.

Beware of this tactic of the enemy! Keep your mind renewed!

Device #15 of the Enemy: Take the Word of God Away

Another device of Satan is to actually take the Word of God away:

> *"When anyone hears the word of the kingdom, and*
> *does not understand it, then the wicked one comes*
> *and snatches away what was sown in his heart.*
> *This is he who received seed by the wayside."*
>
> (Matthew 13:19 NKJV)

This illustration is given to us by Jesus. Do you remember the four kinds of soil He spoke of? There was wayside soil, stony soil, thorny soil, and the good ground. Wayside soil is the packed down walkway around a garden area. The story and thorny soils are obvious. Often those who read this analogy, this parable, wonder what kind of soil they are. Am I wayside, stony, or thorny? And where's the good ground? I've even heard preachers say they can only expect 25% of the people to respond.

Let me digress for a moment. I'm not sure I've ever seen good ground. I personally think all four soils are good ground. Here's why. North of where I once lived you could drive by crop fields that had what appeared to be stone fences around the field. I once asked if the stone fences were to keep someone out or something in? The answer was a great surprise to me. The farmers used stone pickers behind their tractors to move the stones to the edge of the fields. Then they grew their crops. In the parable, Jesus says the rocks are persecutions and afflictions. If you remove the stones and rocks, you've got good ground.

And the thorny ground are those who are overcome by weeds, notably, "the cares of this world, the deceitfulness of riches and the lusts of other things." Guess what! Pull the weeds and you get good ground.

"The wayside" is good soil trampled on so that the seed doesn't penetrate the soil. It just sits on the surface, and Satan like a bird simply comes and steals it away. But if you plow up the trampled on, hardened wayside soil... you get good ground.

Let's consider the wayside soil. This represents those who hear the Word, but then then the devil comes and takes away the Word from their hearts—lest they should believe it and be saved. If Satan can get away with it, he is still practicing this strategy today: he seeks to pull away from us the Word that we receive—right after we receive it! That's why teaching notes can be so important, along with reading and memorizing God's Word. Satan knows that if he can get out of you the Word you have just received, then he has successfully destroyed the very thing that would have brought life, change, power, and victory into your life.

How does Satan take the Word out of you? He might make you question the Word: *Well, the preacher's just a little too fanatical, too radical*, you think, and you rationalize it away. Or Satan will reword the Word you got—he may exaggerate it like he did with Eve in the Garden. He will do whatever he can to get the Word out of you, to discredit what you've heard. Or he will contradict it: He will come to you with an idea contrary to the Word that you've heard, or he'll put a wrong interpretation on the Word that you've received. He does this to take the Word out of our hearts.

Device #16 of the Enemy: Send Disembodied Spirits to Possess Other Bodies

Evil spirits are disembodied spirits. They don't have bodies, so they seek to physically possess a body. Remember how, when Jesus cast the devils out of a man, they entered the swine—and the herd of pigs ran down the side of a cliff and committed suicide:

> *"Now a good way off from them there was a herd of many swine feeding.*
> *So the demons begged Him, saying, 'If You cast us out, permit us to go away into the herd of swine.'*
> *And He said to them, 'Go.' So when they had come out [of the men], they went into the herd of swine. And suddenly the whole herd of swine ran violently*

down the steep place into the sea, and perished in the water." (Matthew 8:30–32 NKJV)

Disembodied spirits will always seek to possess a body. Satan suppresses, represses in order to possess.

Device #17 of the Enemy: Provoke

And then, Satan provokes:

"And Satan stood up against Israel and provoked David to number Israel." (1 Chronicles 21:1)

When Satan stood up against Israel, his strategy was to provoke David to number Israel, or count the number of people he had under his rule, which he was not supposed to do. In another part of the Old Testament, Satan stood up and provoked Joab. Has Satan ever provoked you? He is a provoker, so watch out, because that's one of his devices. He'll provoke you to do evil, he'll provoke you to cuss, he'll provoke you to whatever it is that God tells you not to do. He's a provoker.

Device #18 of the Enemy: Hold People in Bondage

The enemy also loves to hold people in bondage:

*"So ought not this woman, being a daughter of Abraham, **whom Satan has bound**—think of it— for eighteen years, be loosed from this bond on the Sabbath?"* (Luke 13:16 NKJV)

Jesus said it was time for the woman whom Satan had bound for eighteen years to be set free. Satan is an enslaver, and once he's got you, he wants to keep you in his clutches. He wants to hold people in bondage. He doesn't just bind you once; *he keeps you in bondage.* That's why you want to avoid ever being bound by Satan in any area or your life, because once you are bound, he wants to keep you there. Jesus, in contrast, comes to set you free… *"If the Son therefore shall make you free, ye shall be free indeed"* (John 8:36).

Device #19 of the Enemy: Empower Evildoers

Satan empowers evildoers, those who work evil. He is ultimately the one behind all of it:

> *"Then Satan entered Judas, surnamed Iscariot,*
> *who was numbered among the twelve."*
>
> (Luke 22:3 NKJV)

It wasn't until Satan entered into Judas Iscariot that this disciple of Jesus set in motion the plan to betray the Lord. In fact, the devil is the one who put into the heart of Judas Iscariot the plan to betray Him in the first place:

> *"And supper being ended, **the devil having already***
> ***put it into the heart** of Judas Iscariot, Simon's son,*
> *to betray Him."* (John 13:2 NKJV)

The enemy is the one who empowers evildoers. I've been to Haiti three times, and each visit was shocking. Voodoo is the national religion in Haiti. Haiti's in terrible condition because so many people there worship Satan. During my first trip there, I was walking down the street, and I came to a building with open walls and a thatched roof. Inside, a drum band was playing voodoo music, and voodoo dances were going on. People had congregated there to watch, and as I wandered in, I had difficulty believing what I was seeing. The women were down on all fours, nose to nose with several goats. The women were rubbing their noses in pigeon dung on the floor—and then they would stand up and dance. One woman began to dance absolutely uncontrolled, with movements that were physically impossible for the human body to perform. She bent over backward with her head on the jetting out rugged rocks that held up to the center pole of the thatched roof. I watched her with her feet jumping up and down and her head bouncing off the rocks, spinning 360 degrees. I realized that I was watching someone move who was completely controlled by the devil.

Now, when we here in the Church talk about the anointing of the Lord, we do so with respect and care because the Holy Spirit comes to empower the believer to do what we *should* do. But I have seen, on the other side, the enemy "anoint" people to do evil. One of his devices is to give spiritual aid to people who are intent on doing evil. Some people actually receive supernatural help from the devil to cheat, lie, steal, and conduct evil business. The enemy empowers evildoers—and that is one of his favorite tactics.

Device #20 of the Enemy: Attempt to Control So He Can "Break Down"

The enemy will attempt to control you so he can break you down:

> *"And the Lord said, 'Simon, Simon! Indeed, **Satan has asked for you, that he may sift you as wheat:** But I have prayed for you, that your faith should not fail; and when you have returned to Me, strengthen your brethren.'"* (Luke 22:31–32 NKJV)

Fortunately, Jesus Himself intercedes for us to thwart this plan of the enemy.

Device #21 of the Enemy: Seek to Kill and Destroy

The enemy of our souls desires to kill. It is one of his primary motives on the earth:

> *"You are of your father the devil, and the desires of your father you want to do. **He was a murderer from the beginning**, and does not stand in the truth, because there is no truth in him. When he speaks a lie, he speaks from his own resources, for he is a liar and the father of it."* (John 8:44 NKJV)

The devil was a murderer from the beginning. Do you think that Cain slew Abel without the devil operating in his life? I don't think so. The enemy is a murderer. He wants to kill you. Beware of this tactic.

Device #22 of the Enemy: Keep from the Truth

There is *no truth* at all in the enemy. Let's look at the same verse again:

> *"You are of your father the devil, and the desires*
> *of your father you want to do. He was a murderer*
> *from the beginning, and does not stand in the truth,*
> *because **there is no truth in him**. When he speaks*
> *a lie, he speaks from his own resources, for he is a*
> *liar and the father of it."*   (John 8:44 NKJV)

From the beginning, the devil was a liar; there is no truth in him. The devil will never give you the truth. He may give you a *part of* the truth, but that is not the truth. The enemy has no truth in him whatsoever.

Device #23 of the Enemy: Use Lies, Lies, and More Lies

Did I mention that the enemy is a liar? John 8:44 reminds us that when Satan speaks a lie, he is speaking of his own. He uses lies, lies, and more lies because he is a liar and the father of lying. Satan is the one who gets people to lie. And if we're not careful, we can end up with a lying spirit, unable to tell the truth. Remember Ananias? He was the one in the New Testament who lied to the Holy Spirit, and the leaders of the church asked him, *"Why has Satan filled your heart to lie?"* (Acts 5:3). Satan uses lies.

Device #24 of the Enemy: Promote All Sorcery

Satan is the one behind all sorcery in the world:

> *"But Elymas **the sorcerer** (for so his name is*
> *translated) withstood them, seeking to turn the*
> *proconsul away from the faith.*
> *Then Saul, who also is called Paul, filled with the*
> *Holy Spirit, looked intently at him*
> *and said, 'O **full of all deceit and all fraud, you***
> ***son of the devil, you enemy of all righteousness,***

> *wilt you not cease perverting the straight ways of*
> *the Lord?'"*   (Acts 13:8–10 NKJV)

Elymas was a sorcerer. Paul said that he was full of mischief and that he was an actual child of the devil. Our enemy is the enemy of all righteousness, and he will never cease trying to pervert the right ways of the Lord.

But the sorcery issue is greater still. The word *sorceries* in Revelation comes from the Greek word, *pharmakeia,* the word from which we get pharmacy, or specifically drugs that are mind altering and have witchery effects. The Scriptures say that this drug taking and marketing is the deceiving power affecting all nations. Here's the Scripture:

> *"...thy merchants were the great men of the earth;*
> *for by thy sorceries were all nations deceived."*
>   (Revelation 18:23)

Device #25 of the Enemy: Disguise Himself and His Followers

Satan is the master of deceit, and his final tactic is to disguise himself and his minions of evil. Contrary to popular belief, he doesn't come dressed in a red suit, with horns on his head and a pitchfork in his hand. He disguises himself:

> *"And no wonder! For **Satan himself transforms***
> ***himself into an angel of light."***
>   (2 Corinthians 11:14 NKJV)

Satan will transform himself into an angel of light—but his followers also are transformed:

> *"Therefore it is no great thing if **his ministers***
> ***also transform themselves into ministers of***
> ***righteousness**, whose end will be according to their*
> *works."*   (2 Corinthians 11:15 NKJV)

Satan will transform himself into an angel of light—and his ministers transform themselves as well, to look like ministers of righteousness. We will be deceived by his tactics if we are not careful. Satan can come dressed in religious robes and using religious jargon. Watch out!

———

Those are just some of the devices of Satan that we are warned about. We must beware of the things that God tells us to beware. We must take heed and proactively guard against the things God has warned us against. We must arm ourselves with both defensive and offensive weapons, and we must maintain an awareness of these tactics of the enemy.

Because we are Satan's high-value targets, all these strategies are important to him. But we are not left to our own devices. When we recognize the True Light, who is always with us, guarding us and protecting us, we can move forward without fear.

Our next step is to learn how to distinguish this True Light from the false light that the enemy uses to try to deceive us. Read on!

Chapter 7

Recognize the
True Light

Amissionary, home on leave, was shopping for a globe of the world to take back to her mission station.

The clerk in the store where she shopped showed her a reasonably priced globe and then another one with a light bulb inside.

"This one is nicer," the clerk remarked, pointing to the illuminated globe, "but, of course, a lighted world costs more."

The Light of the World came to this earth and brought us His light—but it did cost more. In fact, it cost Him everything. He gave His very life to bring us this light, and He is now the True Light that we must follow.

Unfortunately, in this war between kingdoms—the kingdom of light versus the kingdom of darkness—the false light will try to impersonate the True Light and deceive us into following the enemy.

That enemy, Satan, typically will not come to us looking like a devil. The Word of God tells us that he transforms himself into an angel of light. Isaiah 5:20 describes for us his *modus operandi*:

> *"Woe to those who call evil good, and good evil;*
> *who put darkness for light, and light for darkness;*
> *who put bitter for sweet, and sweet for bitter!"*

(Isaiah 5:20 NKJV)

This is precisely what the enemy does, and that is why he is so treacherous. Evil can be tricky to spot because he transforms himself into an angel of light. His false prophets come to us disguised as ministers of righteousness. They look like they are part of God's family, but they are not a part of us. They look like they belong in church, but they do not. This is the treachery of Satan.

The kingdom of darkness is Satan's kingdom—but isn't it wonderful that we've been taken out of the darkness and brought into the marvelous light of the Gospel? We no longer live in darkness—we live in the light—but a dark kingdom still surrounds us. And there is a gray area in between that is a mixture of dark and light. The kingdom of Satan extends into the light through the gray darkness that surrounds us. The Bible teaches that there is True Light, and the kingdom of Satan extends right up to the light. He comes as an angel of light. His ministers come as ministers of righteousness. And in fact, his apostles come as apostles of Christ. This is the danger each of us must face.

True Light

The *True Light* is so important to us as high-value targets:

> *"This is the message which we have heard from*
> *Him and declare to you, that God is light and in*
> ***Him is no darkness at all.***" (1 John 1:5 NKJV)

What is the True Light? We are told that God is light, and that in Him there's no mixture of light and dark. In fact, there is no darkness at all in God; He is the True Light:

> *"Again, a new commandment I write to you,*
> *which thing is true in Him and in you, because*
> *the darkness is passing away, and the true light is*
> *already shining."* (1 John 2:8 NKJV)

The darkness is gone, and now the True Light shines!

142

> *"That was the true Light which gives light to every man coming into the world."* (John 1:9 NKJV)

Do you know this True Light? His name is Jesus. He is the True Light for everyone in the entire world.

False Light

While Jesus is the True Light, we must beware the false light, the false apostles who transform themselves into the apostles of Christ. They speak the name of Jesus, they call themselves Christians, and they are even called ministers of the Gospel. They transform themselves into ministers of Christ, and they will look like Christians to us if we are not careful. They are followers of their leader, Satan himself, who is transformed into an angel of light.

Despite his pretense of following the Lord, Satan works in the false light. This false light is how he is able to get inside, infiltrate, and penetrate the Church of the Lord Jesus. His goal is to bring it to damnation. He masquerades as an apostle of Christ, a minister of the right, and he pretends he's part of us—but he is not. We need to understand this and be aware of his schemes because the works of darkness extend from the depths of the darkness right up through and including this false light, including the very light grays or soft other colors.

The works of darkness are transformed into the light. They *look like* light. Out of the darkness comes Satan, the false apostles of Christ, the false ministers of righteousness. They come into the Church and pretend to operate in the light. But the fact is, they are from beneath, not from above. It is the enemy within.

James tells us there are two kinds of wisdom: the wisdom that comes from beneath and the wisdom that comes from above. Satan's goal is to change the characteristics of the light. In my own lifetime I have seen the enemy take what God calls in His Word an "abomination," which is the act in which a man lies with a man, and a woman with a woman—homosexual activity—and bring it into the church, presenting it as if it's acceptable behavior.

This has become a grave tragedy in America right now. The Church has been taking the lead in the acceptance of this behavior that God calls an "abomination." But what "church" is it? It's not God's Church! It's not the Church that has been called out of darkness into His marvelous light. No, it is the false church, in the false light, and it has led the way toward the moral bankruptcy we now have in our nation. We are supposed to be *"the light of the world."*

I am writing under the fear of God when I say that the modern church is in big trouble—because it is being led in part by an angel of light who is really Satan. He is spewing out of the depths of hell all kinds of blasphemy and abominations, and the watered-down church says, "Well, it can't be all that bad." Some Christians choose to stay in these lukewarm churches, and they honestly believe that they can be a voice for the Lord in that circumstance. The fact is, they won't; instead, they will become just as watered-down as everyone else. Beware of the false light that is infiltrating the Church! Pay close attention, and follow only the True Light, especially in this day and age.

The Church has become filled with fornication. Pornography has infiltrated the minds of our young people; it is not just a matter of the printed page or the videos we can now access on the internet with a swipe of our finger. No, it is a condition of the mind, a condition of the heart, a condition of our depraved thought life. According to Proven Men Ministries, 62 percent of evangelical men view porn, compared to 64 percent of the general population.[9] How can this happen? It's because some pastors are living in the gray zone, outside the True Light, and in that place, Satan will bring up all kinds of moral uncleanness.

In America today, even among our churches, a mass phenomenon of demonic possession is taking place. The kinds of evil spirits that run with Satan, a whole group of them, are called *unclean spirits*—and the "uncleanness" does not refer to physical

---

9   "Porn in the Pew: How Churches Should Help Members Dealing with Addiction," Samuel Smith, *The Christian Post*, March 26. 2020, https://www. christianpost.com/news/porn-in-the-pew-how-churches-should-help-members-dealing-with-addiction.html.

dirt; it refers to the moral bankruptcy we are seeing take place in our nation.

> *"And there shall be, **like people, like priest**: and I will punish them for their ways, and reward them their doings.*
>
> *For they shall eat, and not have enough: they shall commit whoredom, and shall not increase: because **they have left off to take heed to the LORD**.*
>
> *Whoredom and wine and new wine take away the heart.*
>
> *My people ask counsel at their stocks, and their staff declareth unto them: for **the spirit of whoredoms hath caused them to err**, and **they have gone a whoring from under their God**."*
>
> (Hosea 4:9-12)

In the midst of this morally bankrupt culture, Christians have become worldly. We look like non-Christians now. We dress like them. We listen to the same music they listen to. We think we sanctify it by adding a few "religious words." No longer does sin slink in the back door of the Church or relegate itself to certain districts of town. It now walks in the front door of the Church and sits right down in the front rows—and nobody says a thing. We've *become* like the world. We've learned to talk like them. We've developed their mannerisms. Church has become big business now. Church has gone Hollywood. We are living in the industrialized church era. Even some modern Bible translations can no longer be trusted, as the copyrights are now owned by large secular companies that do not care about compromising Scripture. They mess with the text, with the meaning of the Word, and eventually desecrate it.

Even Christian songs now have double meanings. Twenty years ago, Christian music changed, when music producers started moving toward "crossover music." Little did they know how well it would work. The problem was, it wasn't the world that crossed over to the church; it was the church that crossed over to the world. The problem has since become so prevalent that our friend, the late David Wilkerson, stood up in a contemporary youth rally and, empowered by the Holy Spirit, decried the ungodliness of the music. He yelled into the microphone, "Ichabod! Ichabod! The glory has departed!"

In our modern church today, there is a lot of light that's false, and it can be hard to tell the difference between it and the True Light. The Bible tells us that to be friends with the world is to be the enemy of God. Could anything be plainer than that? Yet, somehow today, we have been infiltrated and penetrated by false prophets, false teachers, and false ministers of righteousness who have eroded our standards. In new and modern churches, the crowd has become more important than the standard because, you see, standards eliminate people. And we want our new Gospel to be one of what we call "inclusion." We don't want to exclude anybody. We don't want to hurt anybody's feelings.

Jesus doesn't want to exclude anybody, either, but He doesn't offer forgiveness without repentance. These are dark days because Satan has brought worldliness into the church. We have become lovers of self more than lovers of God, lovers of pleasure more than lovers of holiness. And many churches are now designed to make people feel good. We have been infiltrated by false teachers who have said that the criterion for what you do, what you read, and what you study is whether or not it feels good.

Forms of False Light

There are different forms of false light that the enemy tries to pass off as part of the True Light. The Scriptures make it pretty clear what these forms of false light are:

> *"Do you not know that the unrighteous will not inherit the kingdom of God? Do not be deceived. Neither fornicators, nor idolaters, nor adulterers, nor homosexuals, nor sodomites,*
>
> *nor thieves, nor covetous, nor drunkards, nor revilers, nor extortioners will inherit the kingdom of God."* (1 Corinthians 6:9–10 NKJV)

The Bible tells us continually to *not be deceived.* Truth is narrow. We need to make sure we aren't following deception. Fornicators, idolators, adulterers, those who practice homosexuality, thieves, those who covet what other people have—none of these will inherit God's kingdom. Neither will drunkards, extortioners, nor abusers, whether they inflict verbal, physical, or sexual abuse. These are sobering words!

Galatians 5:19 adds others to the list: adulterers, those who are unclean, who act promiscuously. And verse 20 includes those who practice idolatry, witchcraft, hatred, wrath, strife, and heresies. Now, when many of us think of the term "witchcraft," we may think of voodoo or some deep, dark occult behavior. Of course, that is certainly witchcraft, but what is more prevalent in our day and age: witchcraft is bringing about even good things by evil power. Witchcraft is manipulation. And it goes right along with hatred—not getting along with other people. Emitting evil ideas and thoughts. Being filled with wrath and consumed by acts done in vengeance. Strife and sedition, sowing discontent about someone who is in authority, whether a husband sowing discontent about his wife or the wife sowing discontent about the husband to the children. Sedition occurs when church members sow discontent about the church leaders in authority over them.

Galatians 5:21 goes on with the list of "false light" behavior:

> *"Envy, murders, drunkenness, revelries, and the like; of which I tell you beforehand, just as I also told you in time past, that those who practice such things will not inherit the kingdom of God."* (NKJV)

People who do these things shall not inherit the kingdom of God. These are all forms of false light.

How to Know the False Teachers

How can we recognize those who are bringing false light rather than living in the True Light? Here are four clues to follow:

1. By their fruit

The first test is to ask this question: Is their fruit holy? Is what they produce in their lives actually of God?

> *"You will know them by their fruits. Do men gather grapes from thornbushes or figs from thistles?*
>
> *Even so, every good tree bears good fruit, but a bad tree bears bad fruit.*
>
> *A good tree cannot bear bad fruit, nor can a bad tree bear good fruit.*
>
> *Every tree that does not bear good fruit is cut down and thrown into the fire.*
>
> *Therefore by their fruits you will know them."*
> (Matthew 7:16–20 NKJV)

Every good tree brings forth good fruit, but a corrupt tree brings forth evil fruit. A good tree cannot bring forth evil fruit, and a corrupt tree cannot bring forth good fruit. Look at the fruit of those who are influencing you to see if they are of the True Light or of the false.

2. By their doctrine

False teachers can also be spotted by their doctrine:

> *"But you have carefully followed my doctrine, manner of life, purpose, faith, longsuffering, love, perseverance."*   (2 Timothy 3:10 NKJV)

Be sure to check the doctrine. The church will not wander into the false light without following the wrong doctrine:

> *"Take heed to yourself and to the doctrine. Continue in them, for in doing this you will save both yourself and those who hear you."*
> (1 Timothy 4:16 NKJV)

Once again, there are ideas that don't sound terrible, and they come from the "gray areas" because Satan moves ideas from darkness into the gray areas. Then he'll move them from the darker gray areas to the lighter areas, creeping closer and closer to the light until what had been in the deep darkness now becomes normal and accepted. This is called *desensitization*, and if we fall for it, we end up with false light because of the doctrine that we have followed.

3. By their manner of life

Third, we can identify these false teachers by observing their manner of life. Let's look at the verse in 2 Timothy again:

> *"But you have carefully followed my doctrine, manner of life, purpose, faith, longsuffering, love, perseverance."*   (2 Timothy 3:10 NKJV)

The industrialization of the church is caused by leadership being primarily interested in financial profits and numbers as indicators of success. *"Men of corrupt minds, and destitute of the truth, supposing that gain is godliness: from such withdraw thyself."* Or as the Message puts it, *"truth is but a distant memory. **They think religion is a way to make a fast buck"** (1 Timothy 6:5).

In contrast with this, when a leader displays the traits of faith, longsuffering, love, and patience, it is more likely they are living in the light rather than the darkness.

4. By their spirit

And finally, you will know them by their spirit:

> *"And the spirits of the prophets are subject to the prophets.*
>
> *For God is not the author of confusion but of peace, as in all churches of the saints."*
>
> (1 Corinthians 14:32–33 NKJV)

No one can hide the condition of their spirit. God is not the author of confusion, and the Spirit of God knows who is truly following Him and who is a follower of deception:

> *"For what man knows the things of a man*
> *except the spirit of the man which is in him?*
> *Even so no one knows the things of God except*
> *the Spirit of God."*   (1 Corinthians 2:11 NKJV)

How to Recognize the "True Light"

As high-value targets, it is extremely important for us to recognize whether we are in the True Light:

> *"This is the message which we have heard from*
> *Him and declare to you, that God is light and **in***
> ***Him is no darkness at all.** "*   (1 John 1:5 NKJV)

The Scripture defines *True Light* as light having no darkness in it at all. That is how we can know whether something is of the True Light. God is light—and in Him there is *no darkness at all*:

> *"I have come as a light into the world, that*
> *whoever believes in Me should not abide in*
> *darkness."*   (John 12:46 NKJV)

Jesus is the light who has come into the world, and whoever believes in Him will not continue in the ways of darkness:

> *"The night is far spent, the day is at hand.*
> *Therefore **let us cast off the works of darkness,***
> ***and let us put on the armor of light**."*
>   (Romans 13:12 NKJV)

> *"For it is the God who commanded the light to*
> *shine out of darkness, who has shone in our hearts*
> *to give the light of the knowledge of the glory of*
> *God in the face of Jesus Christ."*
>   (2 Corinthians 4:6 NKJV)

The surefire way we know that we are in the light is because *Christ is in us*. Because of Him and His Spirit living in ous, we walk in darkness no more!

> *"For **you were once darkness, but now you are light** in the Lord. Walk as children of light."*
>
> (Ephesians 5:8 NKJV)

Do you remember when you lived in the darkness—before you discovered the Truc Light? Our life is now a battle—the kingdom of darkness versus the kingdom of light. And oh, a battle it is.

> *"For we do not wrestle against flesh and blood, but against principalities, against powers, against the rulers of the darkness of this age, against spiritual hosts of wickedness in the heavenly places."*
>
> (Ephesians 6:12 NKJV)

As children of the light, who do we now wrestle against? It's not flesh and blood—the other people we encounter every day. No, we wrestle against principalities and powers—and against the rulers of *the darkness of this world*, against spiritual wickedness in high places. The light always stands in opposition to the darkness. That is who and what we are fighting against!

> *"You are all sons of light and sons of the day. We are not of the night nor of darkness."*
>
> (1 Thessalonians 5:5 NKJV)

How to Know If We Are in the True Light

So, how can we know when we are walking in the light?

> *"Then Jesus spoke to them again, saying, 'I am the light of the world. He who follows Me shall not walk in darkness, but have the light of life.'"*
>
> (John 8:12 NKJV)

Anyone who follows Him will not walk in darkness. He or she will instead have the light of life. This only comes from following Jesus Christ.

There are some clues that we are walking in the light. Here are twelve of them:

1. We do not walk in darkness of any sort.

Here's the proof that we are in the light: we do not walk in darkness of any sort. A lot of people want to give up most of their sin, yet they still hold onto two or three of their "smaller sins." But just one sin is enough to destroy you. We know we're in the light because we don't walk in darkness—we don't tolerate sin of any sort in our lives.

2. We have the light of life.

Second, we know we're in the light because we have the light of life. We have the holy, pure, wonderful Jesus walking with us—not the dressed-up Jesus of the modern, watered-down church. They have chopped Jesus up into all kinds of pieces, and they offer the pieces to the masses as if we had a smorgasbord-buffet kind of religion, where you can take what you want and leave what you don't want. "Oh," they say, "I'll take Jesus as my Savior, but I'm not taking Him as my Lord." That is the "cafeteria" approach to the Gospel. This is a doctrine of the devil, my friend. It is an evil, false apostle who brings the message that offers people Jesus without presenting Him as Lord. The word *Lord* means "master," and it is used 7,738 times in the Bible. The word *Savior* is used thirty-six times. The question is, is Jesus your Lord? If He's your Lord, He'll also be your Savior. If He's your Lord, He'll be your Healer. If He's your Lord, He'll be your Baptizer. If He's your Lord, He's your coming King. If He's your Lord, He is your Peace.

We can't take only the pieces of Jesus that fit us. The true Gospel says God has a wonderful plan for your life. The erroneous Gospel says God has wonderful life for your plan. We have reversed the Gospel and watered it down to

152

"Santa Claus evangelism." "Come to Jesus and get whatever you want," we say. This is an abomination. We have turned the supreme God of the universe into the servant of our selfishness. What could be a greater abomination than that?

The goal of prayer is not to get my will done on earth through heaven; prayer has to do with getting His will done on earth through me. Prayer is not twisting God's arm to get Him to do what I want Him to do. And that is why so many people don't pray anymore. They've tried to influence God through coercion, and it doesn't work:

> *"If we say that we have fellowship with Him,*
> *and walk in darkness, we lie and do not*
> *practice the truth."* (1 John 1:6 NKJV)

If we say we have fellowship with Him, but we walk in darkness—if we practice uncleanness in any area of our lives—we're lying!

> *"But if we walk in the light as He is in the*
> *light, we have fellowship with one another,*
> *and the blood of Jesus Christ His Son cleanses*
> *us from all sin."* (1 John 1:7 NKJV)

What does it mean to walk in the light? Watch closely what the Scriptures tell us: "Walk in the light as He is in the light." We must follow the ways of Jesus. Christlikeness is God's intention for each and all of us.

> *"But you are a chosen generation, a royal*
> *priesthood, a holy nation, His own special*
> *people, that you may proclaim the praises of*
> *Him who called you out of darkness into His*
> *marvelous light."* (1 Peter 2:9 NKJV)

He has called us, the chosen generation, the royal priesthood, the holy nation, the peculiar people, to show forth His praises. He has called us out of darkness into His *marvelous light*! We must have a zero-tolerance policy for

153

darkness, whether it has to do with being worldly, with doctrine, or with practices that are seemingly okay but are not. There must be a demarcation line between them and us. We must walk in the light as He is in the light.

3. We practice truth.

If we walk in the light, we will practice truth in our lives. Let's look at 1 John again:

> *"If we say that we have fellowship with Him,*
> *and walk in darkness, we lie and do not*
> *practice the truth."*   (1 John 1:6 NKJV)

If we walk in darkness but say we are walking in the light, we are not practicing the truth. But the opposite is true, too: we practice the truth as we continue to walk in the light. After all didn't our Blessed Lord say He was the way, the Truth and the Life? He is the Way—you'll never get lost. He is the Truth—you will never be confused. He is the Life— you'll never be depressed.

4. We have fellowship with Him and one another.

When people don't have true fellowship, they don't talk about the things that really matter in life. Instead, when they get together, they talk about the NFL, the movies, or current events. When people are walking in the light as He is in the light, we have fellowship with one another. We have a vertical relationship with God that spills over into our horizontal relationships with other people. But without walking in the light, there's no vertical fellowship with God. God becomes a theory. God becomes a technicality. God becomes a theological system. God becomes religion. But when you walk in the light as He is in the light, there's sweet fellowship, and you are never alone ever again. He walks with you, and He talks with you. He tells you that you are His own. You never go through any trouble without His power. You never face perplexity without His peace. You never face problems without His wisdom because greater is He who is within you than he that is within the world. We have fellowship with Him, and we have true fellowship with His people as well. When we get together, we may talk about the football score from the game last night, but our true fellowship is all about Jesus and His Word. He is the common denominator. He is the real bond we share. The Jesus in you identifies with the Jesus in me, and I love the Jesus Christ in you. Any two persons connected to Jesus are by Him, connected to each other. What a bond!

5. We are cleansed of all sin.

When we live in the light, the blood of Jesus Christ cleanses us. He doesn't leave us stuck in our sins. He cleanses our sin out of existence. They don't call Jesus "Savior" by chance! He is the Savior because He's the One who knows what to do with sin:

> *"If we confess our sins, He is faithful and just to forgive us our sins and to **cleanse us from all unrighteousness**. "* (1 John 1:9 NKJV)

The God that we serve is the God who can create something out of nothing—because that's what He did. Remember? He spoke, and the worlds existed. He said, "Let there be light," and then there was light. But listen to this: never doubt that the God who can speak *something* out of *nothing* can also speak *nothing* out of *something*. That's what He does with our sins: He takes them away. If we were still stuck in your sins, how could we call Him the Savior? But He saves *to the uttermost* all of us who come to Him by Christ Jesus.

Were you a sinner? I know I was. Have you been washed? Have you been cleansed? That is what our wonderful Jesus came to do. He came to earth so that the whole world through Him would be saved. He wants to walk out of the pages of the Bible and right into your heart, right into your mind, right into your thoughts today—and never leave you again. He will rearrange you from top to bottom, from the inside out. Your thoughts will be new. Your heart will be new. Your feelings will be new. Your habits will change—because if any person is in Christ, he or she becomes a new creation. Old things pass away, and everything becomes new. He is the Savior. How do we know we're in the True Light? Because we have been cleansed from our sin.

6.   **We love our brothers.**

> *"Again, a new commandment I write to you,*
> *which thing is true in Him and in you, because*
> *the darkness is passing away, and the true*
> *light is already shining.*
> *He who says he is in the light, and hates his*
> *brother, is in darkness until now."*
>
> (1 John 2:8–9 NKJV)

If we say we are in the light, but we hate people around us, we are actually a part of the darkness. But the darkness should have passed, and the True Light should now shine:

> ***"He who loves his brother abides in the light,***
> *and there is no cause for stumbling in him."*
>
> (1 John 2:10 NKJV)

We know we're in the light because we love the people around us. When we have no malice, no bitterness, no hatred in our hearts, we're walking in the light like He is in the light.

7.   **We abide in the light.**

Let's look at that verse again:

> *"He who loves his brother **abides in the***
> ***light,** and there is no cause for stumbling in*
> *him."*   (1 John 2:10 NKJV)

To know we are in the light, we must abide—or remain, stay—in the light. We don't just get in the light and then duck back out of it. We take up a position, guard, and maintain a readiness. This is a way of life for us. We abide in the light. To abide means to remain or stay put.

8. We cause no stumbling to others.

Another important point in 1 John 2:10: when we walk in the light, we don't tempt or provoke others to failure. A person who's walking in the light doesn't want to cause anybody else to stumble. We aren't living to see how close to the world we can get and still stay in the kingdom. Our lives don't reflect any kind of compromise. Why? Because we care about people. Instead of trying to see how much we can get away with, we're trying to see how holy we can become before Almighty God. We're trying to be righteous, which simply means, "right!" We're trying to do what God wants done. We are careful not to cause others to trip or even be in danger of falling by any bad example on our part.

> *"He that loveth his brother abideth in the light, and **there is none occasion of stumbling in him**."* (1 John 2:10)

9. We know exactly where we are going.

> *"But he who hates his brother is in darkness and walks in darkness, and does not know where he is going, because the darkness has blinded his eyes."* (1 John 2:11 NKJV)

If we hate our brother, we are not only living in darkness, but we do not know where we are going. The darkness is blinding our eyes. A person who is bitter towards someone can no longer think, look, or make decisions without being biased by that bitterness. But because we are in the light, we know exactly where we are going. We know the difference between good and evil, right and wrong, up and down, forward and backward. We know how to test the spirit of a man, the spirit of a song, the spirit of a message. We know these things precisely—because we're not even walking in the gray areas nor are we walking in false light. We're walking in the True Light.

10. We have no fellowship with darkness.

Listen to the command of our Lord: do not be unequally yoked together with unbelievers:

> *"Do not be unequally yoked together*
> *with unbelievers. For what fellowship has*
> *righteousness with lawlessness? And what*
> *communion has light with darkness?"*
>
> (2 Corinthians 6:14 NKJV)

We are to completely separate ourselves from the darkness. And that is why many people accuse us of being narrow-minded. They prefer a broad way, not a narrow road. Yet Jesus told us that we are to travel the narrow road and pass through the narrow gate.

> *"...wide is the gate, and broad is the way,*
> *that leadeth to destruction, and many there*
> *be which go in thereat: Because strait is the*
> *gate, and narrow is the way, which leadeth*
> *unto life, and few there be that find it."*
>
> (Matthew 7:13-14)

11. We separate ourselves from the darkness.

Again, we must separate ourselves from the darkness. We are not to go around flaunting some holier-than-thou attitude because that wouldn't be holy. But we must obey the command of our Lord that says to come out from among them and separate ourselves from them. We are to be in no way unclean. When we separate ourselves from the world, He promises that He will receive us.

We don't fellowship with darkness, and we separate ourselves from it. This is the meaning of His command, *"Have no fellowship with the unfruitful works of darkness."*

12. We reprove the unfruitful works of darkness.

In fact, we are to go a step further—we are to *reprove* (express disapproval of) the unfruitful works of darkness:

"And have no fellowship with the unfruitful works of darkness, but rather expose them."

(Ephesians 5:11 NKJV)

We are to have zero fellowship with the works of darkness. *Zero.* But we are not only to withdraw from fellowship that relates to such activities; we are to *reprove* them. The world may point their fingers at us and call us all kinds of names. They will call us hypocrites and all kinds of things, because we refuse to obey anybody but the Commander in Chief.

———

As for me, I want to obey Jesus more than I want to do anything else on this planet. And if He says to come out from among them, to be separate, to touch not the unclean, then I say, "Yes, Sir." I will not mix with the darkness, or the gray areas of life. I choose to live and walk only in the light. A quote from my family Coat of Arms is, "I'd rather stand with God and be judged by the world than to stand with the world and be judged by God."

Living in the light is the safest place to be. As a high-value target, you cannot afford to dabble in areas of compromise, the "gray areas" of darkness. That opens you up to the subtle attacks of the enemy, who masquerades as an angel of light. You must stay in the light to be able to discern the works of darkness.

How prepared are you at this point to defend yourself against the attacks of the enemy? You have learned to do the following:

- Beware of his offensive strategies.

- Take heed of the dangers, moving in an offensive posture against him yourself.

- Put on the full armor of God, from head to toe.

- Discern the most common tactics of the enemy.

- Remain in the True Light, where the attacks that come against you become well-lit and obvious.

Now let's move on to another way to prepare to defend yourself as a high-value target of the enemy—to understand the mission that God has set before you.

Chapter 8

Understand Your Mission

William Carey was a man on a mission.

True, he was just an average shoemaker in a small, forgotten English village. But in the evenings, when he had finished his work, he diligently studied Greek, Hebrew, and other modern languages. He pored over the pages of Captain Cook's *Voyages*, feeling the tug to move beyond the confines of his current situation and expand his horizons.

The young man was a dreamer, the villagers said. But in fact, young William wasn't just a dreamer. He was called by God.

Early in his life, William Carey knew that his mission was to reach the millions of unbelievers outside Europe, and his studies were to that end: to learn how he could reach them with the Gospel.

With God's help, the plan slowly unfolded for him. He left for India to serve as the first Protestant missionary of the modern era, and his life and witness ultimately inspired a generation of missionaries—Adoniram Judson, Hudson Taylor, and David Livingston, to name a few—to follow in his footsteps. Because one young shoemaker living in a back-woods, impoverished English village decided to follow his mission, large parts of the world that might never have otherwise heard the Gospel have large populations of Christian believers today.

What's Your Mission?

The mission that God has for you is likely the reason you became a high-value target to begin with. Understanding this mission will give you greater insight into how to defend yourself against the attacks of the enemy.

How can you begin to discern the mission that God has set before you, your purpose, the very reason you were placed on the earth at this time?

1. Recognize the real enemy.

First, to understand your mission, you must know who the real enemy is. We have entered a combat zone, and we have been living in it for some time. The enemy has been launching his attacks at us, but we have been learning how to fend off the adversary, learning how to be the aggressor and begin to conquer instead of being defeated. We are beginning to see where the light overcomes the darkness, and the kingdom of God overcomes the kingdom of Satan. It's an exciting time to be alive!

It is important to remember that the enemy of our soul, the true enemy, the one who is at the root of all the destructive forces in our lives—is *not other people*. God never sets us against other people. Each and every human being has been made in His image, and each person is someone for whom Jesus gave His life. Your enemy is never a person. Never, never, never. If we make this mistake, and start attacking other people as our enemy, the real enemy has already severely diverted us from our mission:

> *"For we do not wrestle against flesh and*
> *blood, but against principalities, against*
> *powers, against the rulers of the darkness of*
> *this age, against spiritual hosts of wickedness*
> *in the heavenly places."*　(Ephesians 6:12 NKJV)

Our enemy is Satan himself and all the fallen angels he dragged down out of heaven with him, who are now the principalities and powers of darkness:

> *"Plead my cause, O Lord, with those who*
> *strive with me; fight against those who fight*
> *against me."*   (Psalm 35:1 NKJV)

David knew the secret of not making other people the enemy. When other human beings came against him, he prayed, "Please, my God, plead my cause with those who are trying to strive against me!" In other words, he said, "I'm not going to do it; I want You to do it!" Now, there will be people who will try to fight against you, but if you don't enter the conflict, there won't be strife because it takes two to tango. Leave those kinds of people alone. Instead, we need to bring God into our mission. This is not a human endeavor we're taking on; this is a conflict of kingdoms. This is a battle between darkness and light. This is the kingdom of God versus the kingdom of Satan.

"Love your enemies; Do good to them that hate you; Bless them that curse you;" says our Commander in Chief. These instructions are completely out of step and foreign to humanistic thinking. The logic of love is not well understood. We never do evil back to those who do evil to us. Here's why. Here is the logic of God, the logic of love:

> *"Dearly beloved, avenge not yourselves, but*
> *rather give place unto wrath: for it is written,*
> *Vengeance is mine; I will repay, saith the Lord.*
>
> *Therefore if thine enemy hunger, feed him; if*
> *he thirst, give him drink: for in so doing thou*
> *shalt heap coals of fire on his head.*
>
> *Be not overcome of evil, but overcome evil*
> *with good."*   (Romans 12:19–21)

2. Know the status of people.

If the enemy is never people—and it isn't; it is always Satan and his forces—then what is the status of the people with whom we are involved on this mission?

The people we encounter may be captives:

> *"God perhaps will grant them repentance, so that they may come to their senses and escape the snare of the devil, having been taken captive by him to do his will."*
>
> (2 Timothy 2:26 NKJV)

Many people have already been captured by the enemy and caught in his snare. When a person assumes the lordship of his own life—that is, plays God in his own life—he is acting just like the devil because that's how the devil became the devil. He was once a good angel. But he said, "I will be exalted. I will be like the Most High God. I'll exalt my throne above the stars of the heavens." And he tried to take over God's position.

When we do that as humans, we are following the example of Satan. We place ourselves squarely in the same kingdom as Satan. And when a person is in the same kingdom as Satan, whoever is the leader has the legal right to rule. That's why I want to live in the kingdom of God. I want God to have the legal right to rule in my life! I want Him to have the legal right to tell me what to do. The proof that I'm in His kingdom is that I obey His instructions—and I do it gladly! I say, "Yes, Sir," I click my heels, and I obey immediately—with joy. That's what it means to be in His kingdom: you are under a new King, a different Ruler. You operate by a different set of laws.

But the person who has usurped God's rightful position in his life is actually living in the kingdom of Satan, and no matter how nice he smiles, no matter how nice his clothes are, no matter how much money's in his bank account, and no matter how socially acceptable he looks, he has the same condition of heart. He has been captive at the will of the enemy. He is ensnared by the enemy:

> *"In humility correcting those who are in opposition, if God perhaps will grant them repentance, so that they may the truth."*
>
> (2 Timothy 2:25 NKJV)

Unfortunately, these people are not only ensnared by the enemy; they are also at war against themselves. They make decisions that are self-destructive. Their basis of decision making is no longer genuine intelligence.

But our job is to not strive with them; instead, we are to be gentle with them, willing to teach them, patient, and instructing those who oppose themselves. They are against themselves. We need to let them know the truth: when they say there's no God, they have just wiped out their own eternal future. They have made a decision not only against God, but against themselves. When they reject the Ten Commandments, the laws of God, they have made a decision against themselves. They don't break the laws; the laws break them. When people disagree with God, they have chosen, in that rejection of God, a way of life that is destructive and detrimental, at best.

3. **Understand the mission.**

Paul defines our mission the best. His definition includes seven aspects of the mission that we need to be aware of. He introduces our mission with these words:

> *"But rise and stand on your feet; for I have appeared to you for this purpose, to make you a minister and a witness both of these things which you have seen and of the things which I will yet reveal to you."* (Acts 26:16 NKJV)

As Paul testifies to the mission, he tells the Church to rise and stand on its feet. The true Church in America is being called to rise up and stand tall. We have been lying on a bed of roses for decades, and our inertia has caused our decline. Rise! Come on, soldier, get up! It's time to sound the trumpet. Awake those who have fallen asleep and rise up to your mission in Christ.

What is that mission? First, as we just saw in Acts 26:16, it is to make you a minister. Every man is to be a minister. Every woman is to be a minister. This is not a pastor's job; this is a people job. But one of the devices of Satan is to make the Church believe that the mission of the kingdom of God is only for the leaders. But that is not how a military operation works! An army cannot be made up of only the generals; imagine having only the executives involved in the battle, and no soldiers. But unfortunately, many of our leaders believed this lie. So the pulpit has been used to feed the egos of leaders instead of raising up a holy people who will be mighty in spirit and rise up as the army of God.

The second part of our mission is to make us witnesses to the things of God. Let's look at Acts 26:16 again:

> *"But rise and stand on your feet; for I have*
> *appeared to you for this purpose, to make you*
> *a minister **and a witness** both of these things*
> *which you have seen and of the things which I*
> *will yet reveal to you."* (NKJV)

You and I are witness to two things: first, what we have seen God do in our lives, in our family's lives, in our spouse's life, and in our children's lives. There's a lot of power in your personal testimony! Second, we will testify to Jesus Himself:

> *"But you shall receive power when the Holy*
> *Spirit has come upon you; and you shall be*
> ***witnesses to Me*** *in Jerusalem, and in all Judea*

and Samaria, and to the end of the earth."
(Acts 1:8 NKJV)

That is where the power comes in: when we are witnesses unto Him. This witness will flow out unto the uttermost parts of the earth. Who knows where your ministry's going to go? He calls you to minister, and this is the mission: to be a minister, and second, to be a witness to what you've seen yourself; and to be a witness of Him.

When God makes you a minister and a witness, He also says that He will appear to you. When you have a chat with God, you receive things from Him you couldn't even have imagined. Thoughts will come to you from God that are so holy, so right, so biblical. God is going to show up in your life. He is going to do things through you. He is going to give you something worth talking about. He is going to give you profound ideas that could only come from Him.

Third, He will deliver you from the people He has sent to you:

> *"**I will deliver you** from the Jewish people, as well as from the Gentiles, to whom now I send you."*
> (Acts 26:17 NKJV)

Whomever God sends you to in this mission, He will deliver you from their power over you. They will not influence you; you will influence them.. Those who appear to be your enemies will be taken off guard by you because your mission is defined by God, and it is not the traditional way of doing war. There will be no strife. All will be done in gentleness, and you will have no fear. This absence of fear allows you to have confidence. Confidence—not cockiness. And this allows us to open the blind eyes of the people:

> *"**To open their eyes**, in order to turn them from darkness to light, and from the power of Satan to God, that they may receive forgiveness of sins and an inheritance among*

167

those who are sanctified by faith in Me."
(Acts 26:18 NKJV)

The people who are held in captivity, blindfolded, need to have their eyes opened. When they took the blindfolds off Patty Hearst, she still couldn't see. She had been held captive so long that her eyes would no longer work properly. The same is true of the people you and I are sent to on our mission: they have been in the camp of the captor too long.

The Scriptures tell us that Satan, the god of this world, has blinded them, lest the glorious Gospel should shine into their hearts. They haven't been able to receive the Gospel. They have an enemy—who is also your enemy. You and I must deal with this enemy to open their eyes. As the Scriptures say, we must turn them from darkness to light.

Some prisoners of war have been so influenced by their captors that if a redeeming soldier shows up to set them free, they actually don't want to be set free; they have been so fooled. It's as Voltaire described, "It is difficult to free fools from the chains they revere." (I'll repeat this quote again later because it is so apropos.)

That's where our mission comes in. When you're dealing with a captive who has been so taken over by the enemy of our souls, the blood of the Lamb and the Word of His testimony is the only thing that can set that person free.

Next, we must turn them from the power of Satan over to God. Those whom we are called to reach are in the clutches of the power of Satan. Jesus taught us the power we have over the enemy, however, when He said this:

"Behold, I give you the authority to trample on serpents and scorpions, and over all the power of the enemy, and nothing shall by any means hurt you." (Luke 10:19 NKJV)

Satan's power is nothing when compared to that of the King of Kings and the Lord of Lords! Our Lord has given us power over all the power of the enemy—and nothing shall by any means hurt us. The devil is easier to deal with than other people? We usually think the opposite is the case, but God didn't give you power over people—He gave you power over the devil.

As part of our mission, we are to cause people to receive forgiveness and the inheritance that God has prepared for them. The ultimate goal of our mission: that other people may receive forgiveness of sins. When people come out of captivity by the enemy, the first thing they receive is forgiveness for everything they did while they were in captivity. Forgiveness of sin is one of the main messages of the Scriptures and one of the main messages of God. As Jesus told the story, as soon as the prodigal son showed any sign of coming home, his father was running out to meet him! There is no problem on God's side of receiving His children back to Himself: the party is easy; the reception and the killing of the fatted calf is not where the issues usually lie. The departure from the pigpen is the difficult part. But our mission is to turn people from Satan to God so that they may receive forgiveness of sins.

In addition to forgiveness, these newly released captives also receive an inheritance. And wouldn't you know it? They get the same inheritance as you! There's so much joy in heaven over each sinner who repents. When somebody crosses over from darkness to light, all the angels get together—and they party! How can you pass from darkness to light and not know it? How can you come out of death into life and not know it? When we live in a blurred kingdom, full of gray spaces of compromise, we are really living in the kingdom of darkness. But when we enter the light, all of heaven is shouting, angels are clapping, and the people of God rejoice. Those once captive receive forgiveness and the same inheritance as you and I who have been saved through faith and set apart.

4. Understand your role in the mission.

Fourth, we need to understand our role in this mission.

The first element in the mission is that there is to be no strife. You don't want to check out right at the beginning of the mission with a wrong attitude toward another person because you think they're the enemy. They are not the real enemy, and we are not to engage in strife with other people:

> *"And a servant of the Lord must not quarrel*
> *but be gentle to all, able to teach, patient."*
>
> (2 Timothy 2:24 NKJV)

In fact, it is honorable to actively walk away from strife and conflict:

> *"It is honorable for a man to stop striving,*
> *since any fool can start a quarrel."*
>
> (Proverbs 20:3 NKJV)

Nothing will be accomplished through strife. Nothing, nothing, ever, ever, ever—zero. Again, let me repeat, *there can be no godly achievement from strife*—ever. In this kingdom, we don't do strife. We don't do strife. Ever. With anyone, ever! Strive introduces a contest of wills, a contest of egos. The real issues are left unexamined.

> *"For where envying and strife is, there is*
> *confusion and every evil work."*   (James 3:16)

When we engage in strife, there will be confusion. The facts of the case get lost because now what's going on is conflict. Now it becomes "a" versus "b"; now it's one against the other. Now it's an argument. Now it's a contest of egos and what becomes more important than *what's* right is *who's* right. The man who really knows what's right doesn't have to shout, scream, holler, and throw a fit to get his point across. He just presents the facts. He holds his peace. This is not a contest of wills with other people. That's not part of the mission. Where there is strife, there's confusion, as well as every other evil work going on.

The second element of the mission is to be gentle. A real Christian is a "gentleman." Look at 2 Timothy 2:24 again:

> *"And a servant of the Lord must not quarrel* **but be gentle to all,** *able to teach, patient."*
>
> (NKJV)

Living in Florida as I do, I like manatees. I've swum with a few, even given a head rub to several in my day, before that practice was outlawed for their protection. Years ago, I visited Crystal Springs, and I lay at the bottom of that body of water with my scuba tank on for more than twenty minutes, just rubbing this one manatee's face. This creature weighed at least eighteen hundred pounds, but they call manatees the "gentle giants" for a reason. This manatee's head was right next to me, and he would just open his eye, look at me, and then close his eye. He did that over and over again. We can learn a lesson from the manatee: the real "bigness" in a man is shown in his ability to be gentle. The guy who is always pumping his muscles and showing off his physical strength is actually the weakest. What makes a man the biggest is his gentleness. Isn't that how the Lord has dealt with us? It is no wonder that the psalmist David said of God, *"Thy gentleness hath made me great"* (Psalm 18:35).

Many people will try to pull us into strife, but we must choose to be gentle. The verse just ahead of the one above is this, *"But foolish and unlearned questions avoid, knowing that they do gender strifes. And the servant of the Lord must not strive; but be gentle unto all men..."*

A further admonition comes from Titus 3:9, *"But avoid foolish questions, and genealogies, and contentions, and strivings about the law; for they are unprofitable and vain."*

We must also be able to explain the message, be "able to teach":

"And a servant of the Lord must not quarrel
*but be gentle to all, **able to teach**, patient."*
(2 Timothy 2:24 NKJV)

We must build a relationship in which we help people understand the message or share what God has done for us. It's not just a matter of them saying yes to our three questions, repeat a short, memorized prayer, and then it's over. I submit to you that rarely does anybody come out of darkness and into the light in that situation. We need to be able to explain salvation, step by step, and be patient with people as they seek to understand.

These captives we are bringing into the light are not notches on our belt. And the name of the game is not how to get the most numbers attached to your "ministry." This is about being a true and faithful witness, someone who helps others to be delivered from the power of the enemy, turning them from darkness to light, from the kingdom of Satan to the kingdom of God.

Along with this patience, a final part of our mission is to practice meekness:

*"**In humility** correcting those who are in*
opposition, if God perhaps will grant them
repentance, so that they may know the truth."
(2 Timothy 2:25 NKJV)

I love the character quality of meekness. It has been defined as "our strength under God's control." Meekness involves submitting all we've got, everything we've learned, everything we are, all our ambitions; placing them under God's control; and then reaching out to others with wisdom, discretion, and deference to their needs. It is meekness that prevents escalation to strife. Note the admonition of the Lord, *"Who is a wise man and endued with knowledge among you? let him shew out of a good conversation his works **with meekness of wisdom**"* (James 3:13).

And finally, we guide them to recovery from the traps of the enemy:

> *"And that they may come to their senses and*
> *escape the snare of the devil, having been*
> *taken captive by him to do his will."*
>
> (2 Timothy 2:26 NKJV)

The squad we're on has broken through the enemy lines, we have marched into enemy territory, and we have found a shed in which captives are being held. We have sent the enemy scattering, and now it's time to pull the captives out of the enemy territory, leading them to the helicopter that's waiting to fly them to safety. At that moment, whoever is willing to go can go. But whoever is not willing to go can't go. The captives have a role to play in their own rescue. They help to *"recover themselves"* out of the snare of the one who took them captive. We can guide them to recovery, but we cannot force them to come along. If they're not willing to leave the darkness, then they won't. There is a critical moment when people must exercise their own wills to respond to God so that they may recover themselves.

————

In conclusion, our mission is to function as ambassadors. An ambassador is one who has been commissioned by a higher authority to convey the message on behalf of that authority.

> *"Now then **we are ambassadors for Christ**, as*
> *though God did beseech you by us: we pray you in*
> *Christ's stead, be ye reconciled to God."*
>
> (2 Corinthians 5:20)

The mission of an ambassador is the ministry of reconciliation. That's our mission!

> *"Now all things are of God, who has reconciled us*
> *to Himself through Jesus Christ, and has given us*

the ministry of reconciliation."

(2 Corinthians 5:18 NKJV)

When we're talking to those who are in captivity, we are talking to them in Christ's stead. His authority, His way, His wisdom, His words, His feelings, His attitudes...we are representing all these aspects of Christ to them. We must do nothing with them that isn't Christlike. And in Christ's stead, our goal is for them to be reconciled to God.

We're the freedom fighters who come to set the captives free. That is our mission, and that is our cause.

Chapter 9

Deal with the Devil

The church visitation team had just spent twenty minutes explaining the Gospel to a young woman whose heart was open to the things of God. When she was asked, "Are you ready to receive Jesus Christ as your Lord and Savior?" she responded, "Yes, I am!"

The leader of the group said, "Then simply pray after me, 'Father, I thank You for sending Your Son…'"

The young woman started repeating, "Father, I thank—" but before she could go on, her car, parked nearby, started honking. The noise of the horn was so loud and deafening that the woman could not even hear the words of the group leader who was trying to direct her in prayer.

The group stopped the prayer and walked over to the car to investigate. They opened the hood, beat on the horn, and finally shut the engine off entirely. Only then were they able to resume praying with the woman—but at that point, she had become so distracted by the honking of her car's horn that it was a struggle to get through the prayer.

Many people would conclude that a mechanical failure had set off that car's horn—and that is entirely possible. But it is also not out of the realm of possibility that that "mechanical failure" was a subtle attempt by the enemy to distract this new believer from accepting the Gospel message.

Not every negative event has a demonic source. Some, however, do. The enemy is alive and active in our world. As a high-value target in the kingdom of God, you must be prepared at all times for an attack against you from this enemy.

God Has Equipped Us to Deal with the Devil

You don't have to constantly maintain a defensive posture, waiting for the enemy to send his fiery darts against you. No, your calling and mission—should you choose to accept it—is to move into an offensive posture and take the fight to the devil. We must learn to deal with the devil and his tactics—and defeat him!—as we press forward in the mission to which our High Commander has called us.

We can deal with the devil in a number of different ways. Let's look at three of them.

1. **We must recognize that Satan has already been dealt with judicially.**

    We first must recognize that Jesus has already dealt with Satan, long ago on the cross. This is where it begins in dealing with our adversary, the devil. Do you know the present-day status of Satan? His status has been changed.

    The Book of Job opens with God and Satan having a conversation. Yuk! That always bothered me. If God is so good and Satan is so evil, why are they on talking terms? By the way, the Book of Job is a most interesting book and story line. Its content deals with many philosophical aspects of life. Worth the read!

    So why are God and Satan even talking? The answer is that God is a God of law and order and follows lawful and legal principles. Satan, at that time, had authority, meaning legal administrative power and control within a certain jurisdiction over the earth. It appears it was turned over to him by Adam.

    Remember when Satan tempted Jesus. They're on an "exceedingly high mountain." Satan shows him *"all the kingdoms of the world and the glory of them."* Satan, then tempting Jesus, makes him an offer. *"All these things will I give thee, if thou wilt fall down and worship me"* (Matthew 4:9). If they weren't Satan's to give, where would be the temptation? All Jesus would have had to say was, "Devil, they are not yours to give."

Satan had legal authority but all that changed... and guess where and how... Calvary! The Day of Salvation through the death and resurrection of Jesus Christ, the Lord of Glory. Satan used to have access to heaven (because of his *legal* standing) and he was always accusing the people of the earth to God. That's why he was called the *Accuser.*

Here now is the Scriptural proof of the cause and time of his loss of legal standing.

> *"And I heard a loud voice saying in heaven,*
> **Now is come salvation**, *and strength, and the*
> *kingdom of our God, and the power of his*
> *Christ: for* **the accuser of our brethren is cast**
> **down**, *which accused them before our God*
> *day and night."* (Revelation 12:10)

Jesus said it this way, *"Now is the judgment of this world: now shall the prince of this world be cast out"* (John 12:31). At His being nailed to the cross the Scriptures say, *"having spoiled principalities and powers, he made a shew of them openly, triumphing over them in it"* (Colossians 2:15).

Had the enemy known the power of the crucifixion to legally destroy their power, the Scripture says, *"...none of the princes of this world knew: for had they known it, they would not have crucified the Lord of glory"* (1 Corinthians 2:8).

Now you've got it. Satan's legal status is now *defeated.* He has been kicked out of heaven and no longer has access to the throne of God. He no longer can accuse you before the Father day and night like he used to do. He is not on talking terms with God, and he has no legal connection to the Father that obligates God to speak with him.

This is due to Jesus's sacrifice on the cross:

> *"Having **disarmed principalities and powers**, He made a public spectacle of them, triumphing over them in it."*
>
> (Colossians 2:15 NKJV)

Jesus has spoiled the principalities and powers, and—I love this!—He has made a show of them openly, triumphing over them. Back in the Roman era, when these words were originally written, when the Romans defeated a people, they took all the conquered enemy soldiers, chained them together, and made those defeated soldiers march through the main streets of the cities. The Romans made a show of them in their captured condition, and this same picture is precisely what is used to show us what Jesus did to the devil. He made a show of the devil and his minions openly:

> *"Which none of the rulers of this age knew; for had they known, they would not have crucified the Lord of glory."*
>
> (1 Corinthians 2:8 NKJV)

The Bible goes on to say that had the princes of this world known what they were doing, what was going to happen in the end, how it would ultimately seal their doom, they would never have crucified the Lord of Glory. But in His death and resurrection, Jesus absolutely destroyed Satan. So the enemy has already been dealt with.

His power now is merely that of lying, tempting and deceiving in an attempt to entice mankind to his narcissistic philosophy, his darkness.

2. **We must understand that Jesus's authority and power has been transferred to us.**

> *"As my Father hath sent me, even so send I you."*
> (John 20:21)

Because the authority and power over Satan have been transferred to us, we now have the right, the authority, and the power to deal with the enemy:

> *"Then the seventy returned with joy, saying, 'Lord, even the demons are subject to us in Your name.'"*
> (Luke 10:17 NKJV)

Seventy of Jesus's disciples returned from their preaching assignment, and they were filled with joy because the devil had been subject to them when they used the name of Jesus as the authority. It is Jesus who has all authority and all power, but He has given us the right to use His name, which means we can act on His behalf, with His authority, and with His power. Even the devils are subject to us through His name.

Jesus also gave us further authority:

> *"Behold, **I give you the authority** to trample on serpents and scorpions, and **over all the power of the enemy**, and nothing shall by any means hurt you."*
> (Luke 10:19 NKJV)

We have the power to tread on serpents and scorpions, both of which are symbols of the devil and his demons. Jesus has given us authority over all the power of the enemy, and nothing will by any means hurt us. This is really important news. The weakest Christian has more power than the strongest devil! You do not need to fear the enemy—ever. Your children should not fear Satan. They should not fear demons. They should not fear evil spirits. They should not fear sorcerers or any of the works of the devil. They should never be afraid of any of them because the Christian on his or her knees has more power than Satan himself because of Jesus's authority.

> *"I would have you wise unto that which is good, and simple concerning evil.*
>
> *And the God of peace will crush Satan under your feet shortly. The grace of our Lord Jesus Christ be with you. Amen."*
>
> (Romans 16:19-20 NKJV)

To have power over Satan, we must not study Satan. To have power over evil, we must not study evil. The worst mistake a novice can make about dealing with the devil is to study the devil instead of studying God. To study evil instead of studying good. To study sinfulness instead of righteousness. Curiosity about evil leads to investigating evil, which leads to our spiritual pollution. We need to instead keep our focus on the Lord and His goodness:

Notice that the crushing of Satan under our feet is preceded by the instruction to study good and be simple about evil.

3. We must learn to discern the spirits.

We need to discern the spirits, or we won't know how to deal with a situation—because dealing with depends on what kind of a spirit is involved. Thank God that He has gifted us with what we need in this regard:

> *"But the manifestation of the Spirit is given to each one for the profit of all ... the discerning of spirits."*
>
> (1 Corinthians 12:7, 10 NKJV)

The manifestation of the Holy Spirit is given to every single one of us—and for what purpose? To profit with. One of the ways we profit is through the discerning of spirits. The Holy Spirit gives us the ability to discern the truth about a sentence that's spoken, an idea that's put forth, an emotion that's displayed, or a facial expression—to understand what spirit is behind it. Behind every idea is a presenter of the idea. And behind every presenter, there is a spirit:

> *"But earnestly desire the best gifts."*
>
> (1 Corinthians 12:31 NKJV)

Covet earnestly the best gifts. Covet the gifts you need to help you discern the different kinds of spirits that are involved in a situation.

Four Kinds of Spirits

There are only four kinds of spirits that we will encounter in any given situation.

1.   The Holy Spirit

First, there is the Holy Spirit. And the discerning of spirits includes discerning what the Holy Spirit is doing. What is He behind? Who is He supporting?

2.   Angelic spirits

The second kind of spirits are the angelic spirits. These are the angels, the good spirits that kept their alliance with God when Satan led the rebellion long ago.

3.   Demonic, evil spirits

The third kind of spirits are demonic spirits. These are the evil spirits that we are waging war against. There are two categories of evil spirits. The first are here on this planet; they have a measure of freedom, or mobility on the planet. They work under the leadership of Satan. The second group of evil spirits are the ones that are already bound in chains; they will be there until the final judgment. You can catch the entire story line of their attempt to enter the human race in Genesis 6:1-2 and referred to in 2 Peter 2:4.

> *"And the angels which kept not their first estate, but left their own habitation, he hath*

reserved in everlasting chains under darkness unto the judgment of the great day." (Jude 1:6)

4. Human spirits

Finally, there are human spirits. You are a spirit who lives in a body. You have an intellect and emotions, but you are a spirit. God breathed into Adam the breath of life, and he became a living soul. This soul is what sets you apart from the animals. An animal has a measure of intelligence and a measure of emotion, but it doesn't have a spirit. What makes you different, what makes you non-animal, is this: that God is called the Father of spirits. When a man and a woman come together and a child is created, that which is born of flesh is flesh. But there's no person in the child's body unless God puts the spirit in there. So God puts the spirit in the person. And when you die, your spirit goes back to your God who gave it to you. God is your Creator. He created you— the person, the spirit. And He placed you in your body while inside your mother's womb.

Why is it important to know these four kinds of spirits?

First of all, if you know the Holy Spirit is moving in your life, you can better cooperate with Him. You want to discern what the Holy Spirit is doing so you can be an instrument of His righteousness and do what the Holy Spirit wants done.

Second, you want to know about the angelic spirits because you want to receive whatever God is sending to you through them. The writer of Hebrews gives us a glimpse of their particular mission:

*"Are they not all **ministering spirits** sent forth to minister for those who will inherit salvation?"* (Hebrews 1:14 NKJV)

God commissions angelic spirits to minister on our behalf and to make things happen in the unseen world for us what we ourselves can't do.

Third, you want to know when a demonic spirit is involved so you can exercise your power over that spirit. As we have discussed, we have been given authority from Jesus, our Commander in Chief, to cast down the evil spirits in His name.

And finally, we must be able to discern whether something is from a human spirit; so we can make an appeal to that human spirit on behalf of God and point that person in the direction of the kingdom of God.

4. Stay true, and stay sanctified.

To deal with the devil, we must stay true, and we must stay pure and sanctified:

> *"For to this end I also wrote, that I might put you to the test, whether you are obedient in all things."*   (2 Corinthians 2:9 NKJV)

Paul wanted to find proof in the Corinthians, evidence that showed whether they were obedient in all things. That's the crux of the matter—our obedience:

> *"Now whom you forgive anything, I also forgive. For if indeed I have forgiven anything, I have forgiven that one for your sakes in the presence of Christ."*   (2 Corinthians 2:10 NKJV)

In the very next verse, Paul sought to determine whether the Corinthians were forgiving one another. And then, finally, he wrote this:

> *"Lest Satan should take advantage of us for we are not ignorant of his devices."*
> (2 Corinthians 2:11 NKJV)

The Corinthians were to be obedient in all things and specifically to be forgiving, *so that Satan would not gain an advantage over them*. We must always walk in forgiveness, so that Satan cannot gain an advantage over us. Without being forgivers, we will have bitterness and bitterness opens us up to anger, wrath, retaliation, resentment, revenge… and Satan damages our well-being.

5. **Take a "no compromise" position with Satan.**

From the above admonition to be forgiving in place of anger we get the following addendum: to give *"no place to the devil."*

> *"Be ye angry, and sin not: let not the sun go down upon your wrath:*
>
> *Neither give place to the devil."*
>
> (Ephesians 4:26-27)

We must not give the enemy any place whatsoever in our lives. If you give Satan an inch, he'll take a mile. If you give him any place at all, you give up legal territory to him, and from that legal territory he will launch an assault on other areas of your life. In warfare, we want to win every hill, take all the territory, and never compromise with the enemy at all. We must do what Jesus said in Luke 19:

> *"And he called his ten servants, and ...said unto them, **Occupy till I come**."*   (Luke 19:13)

The word *occupy* is actually a military term that means to hold the hill, hold the jurisdiction, occupy the hill. We are to occupy the territory until He returns. We are to never let Satan have any territory that is under our jurisdiction whatsoever. That means no discussions with Satan. Don't talk to him and don't let him talk to you. Have no tolerance of Satan whatsoever. Do not yield to Satan. Do not receive any of his ideas whatsoever. He comes to steal, to kill, and to destroy. He comes to accuse and to condemn, to put us down.

We must refuse to give any space at all to those ideas or thoughts. No allowances. Satan is not allowed in this place.

Satan must not be allowed in your marriage; not allowed in your church; not allowed in your home; not allowed in the lives of your children. He is not allowed anywhere that is under your authority. There can be no compromise. He cannot be allowed in your body. He cannot be allowed to have any place in your mind, nor can he have any place in your heart. He cannot be allowed to have any of your affections. He is not allowed in your life—at all. Instead, Jesus has all authority in this place. You belong to Him. Every word you speak, every motive of your heart, every action you undertake—all of it belongs to God.

The enemy's strategy is to get you to give in, just an inch. How many immoral thoughts will you allow to enter your mind? Your answer should be "None." How much maliciousness will we commit? None. How much unforgiveness will you allow to fester in your heart? How much bitterness? How much resentment? How much strife? *None! Zero!*

Often in an attempt to be "relevant" we have compromised. Yes, we are in the world, but we are like the ship that is in the midst of the sea. Jesus prayed these words concerning His Church:

> *"I do not pray that You should take them out of*
> *the world, but that You should keep them from*
> *the evil one."* (John 17:15 NKJV)

It's okay for the ship to be in the sea, but it's not okay for the sea to be in the ship! In other words, it's okay for the Church to be in the world, but it is not okay for the world to be in the Church:

> *"Adulterers and adulteresses! Do you not*
> *know that friendship with the world is enmity*
> *with God? Whoever therefore wants to be a*

> *friend of the world makes himself an enemy of*
> *God."* (James 4:4 NKJV)

The world is part of the enemy's territory. Satan is called the god of this world. In a world of compromise we must not!

6. Submit to God and resist the devil.

To deal with the devil, we must not just resist him; we must also submit to God:

> *"Therefore **submit to God. Resist the devil***
> *and he will flee from you."* (James 4:7 NKJV)

When we submit ourselves to God, as we resist the devil, he will flee from us. I cannot tell you how many times I've had people tell me that they have resisted the devil and the devil did not flee. The answer to that problem is not complicated. Resisting the devil is only half the command. Satan does not flee when we resist him. He flees only when we submit to God and *then* resist him. Submitting to God is the greatest deterrent to the devil. We are not for sale! Like it says in the Warrior's Creed (author unknown):

"I am part of the fellowship of the Unashamed!
I have the Holy Spirit's power!
The die has been cast!
I've stepped over the line!
The decision has been made!
I won't look back, let up, slow down, back away or be
   still.
My past is redeemed, my presence makes sense, my
   future is secure.
I am finished and done with low living, sight walking,
   small planning, smooth knees, colorless dreams,
   tamed visions, mundane talking, cheap living!
Yes! I no longer need preeminence, position, promotion,
   or popularity.

I don't have to be praised, recognized, regarded, or
  rewarded.
I now live by faith, lean on His presence.
I walk by patience. I live by prayer. I labor by power!
My face is set!
My gate is fast!
My mission is clear!
My goal is heaven!
My road is narrow!
My way is rough! My companions are few BUT my
  God is reliable.
With God's help, I will not flinch in the face of sacrifice,
  hesitate in the presence of the adversary, negotiate
  at the table of the enemy, ponder at the pool of
  popularity.
I won't give up, shut up, or let up and preached up for
  the cause of Christ.
I am a disciple of Jesus Christ.
I must go 'til He comes, give 'til I drop, work 'til He
  stops me, and preach until ALL know, and when
  He comes, He will have no trouble recognizing me.
  My banner is clear."

It is significant that the verse before the admonishments
to "submit to God. Resist the devil" is a vital key that assures
God's participation in us... humility!

> *"But He gives more grace. Therefore He says,*
> *'God resists the proud, but gives grace to the*
> *humble.'"* (James 4:6 NKJV)

Here's the bottom line: submit yourself **humbly** therefore
to God, resist the devil, and he will flee. We must not miss
the context of humility. God resists the proud. Anyone who
thinks they can resist Satan proudly and flippantly are sadly
mistaken because we block the grace that we need.

7. **Cast out devils.**

To deal with the enemy and his evil spirits, first cast him out. We must learn to cast out spirits. As we move into our mission of setting people free who are enslaved by Satan—whether they are relatives, friends, or acquaintances—we must remember that the deliverance of people is twofold: We must deal with the captor, but we must also deal with the captive. We must deal with the devil, but we must also deal with the person. If we try to deal with the person without dealing with the devil, we will get nowhere because the person is ensnared by the devil.

But if we deal with the devil without dealing with the person, we may free him or her to an extent, but do we know what Jesus says? He said that seven devils even more vile than the first will come back to torment that person. Why? We must learn to deal both with the devils and with the people. Dealing with the devil stops his power, but then we must deal with the person to keep him or her free in the future:

> *"And He said to them, 'Go into all the world and preach the gospel to every creature.*
>
> *He who believes and is baptized will be saved; but he who does not believe will be condemned.*
>
> *And these signs will follow those who believe: In My name they will cast out demons; they will speak with new tongues;*
>
> *they will take up serpents; and if they drink anything deadly, it will by no means hurt them; they will lay hands on the sick, and they will recover.'"* (Mark 16:15–18 NKJV)

Casting out devils is part of our mission. We are to go into all the world, preaching the Gospel to every creature, casting out devils, speaking with new tongues, and laying hands on the sick so that they shall recover. It's part of our mission.

Clash between the Kingdoms

"If I cast out demons by the Spirit of God, surely the kingdom of God has come upon you."

(Matthew 12:28 NKJV)

When the God who is in you and the Satan that is in the world confront each other, there is a clash of kingdoms. But this doesn't have to frighten us:

*"You are of God, little children, and have overcome them, because **He who is in you is greater than he who is in the world."***

(1 John 4:4 NKJV)

Fear not, my friend, because greater is He that is in you than he that is in the world. Fear not, my friend, because God has given us the victory!

In addition, casting out devils is not a matter of prayer, nor is it a function of the mind. You cannot *think* devils out of a person; they don't come out by thinking. They don't work in the realm of thoughts. Nor do they come out by prayer. Prayer is when you speak to God and God speaks to you. Casting out spirits happens when we speak our *words* to them:

*"When evening had come, they brought to Him many who were demon-possessed. And **He cast out the spirits with a word**, and healed all who were sick."*

(Matthew 8:16 NKJV)

Jesus cast out spirits with His Word. In the same way, we cast out spirits with our own words—in His authority and in His name.

This is accomplished through the faith that is released through our words. That is what gets rid of Satan:

> *"And when He had come into the house, His*
> *disciples asked Him privately, 'Why could we not*
> *cast it out?'*
>
> *So He said to them, 'This kind can come out by*
> *nothing but prayer and fasting.'"*
>
> (Mark 9:28–29 NKJV)

Spirits are exorcised and removed by faith-filled words:

> *"It is the Spirit who gives life; the flesh profits*
> *nothing. The words that I speak to you are spirit,*
> *and they are life."* (John 6:63 NKJV)

The words that Jesus has given to us are spirit, and they are life. There is life in our words when we speak forth and exercise the power and authority that Jesus transferred to us.

Our words of faith become effective when they are spoken in the authority of Jesus's name:

> *"... Paul, greatly annoyed, turned and **said to the***
> ***spirit**, 'I command you in the name of Jesus Christ*
> *to come out of her.' And he came out that very*
> *hour."* (Acts 16:18 NKJV)

When Paul spoke to the spirit, it was not a prayer; he was not talking to God. He was confronting the enemy firsthand. He commanded the spirit *in the name of Jesus Christ* to leave—and the spirit obeyed. As we walk in the power and the authority of Jesus Christ, we do not have to scream and shout in a ridiculous religious show to exercise our authority over the enemy. But neither do we need to withdraw into a religious lukewarm orthodoxy that's afraid of devils. God wants you and I to walk without any fear of Satan whatsoever. He has made the evil spirits subject to us through His authority:

> *"Then He healed many who were sick with various*
> *diseases, and cast out many demons; and He did*

not allow the demons to speak, because they knew Him." (Mark 1:34 NKJV)

When Jesus cast out devils, He forbade them to speak. Do not let Satan speak back to you through other people. Jesus didn't allow the demons to speak, and then He sent them fleeing. When we deal with spirits, they are subject to us because of the transferred authority of Jesus Christ. You can tell the devil that is harassing you that he must go—and he will go. It is that simple. All power is given to you in this area. *Start dealing with the devil.*

Let us begin to cast out Satan—out of our thinking, out of our emotions, out of our hearts, out of our homes, out of our marriages. Get rid of everything that has to do with Satan. Give no place whatsoever to the devil. Instead, take authority over him. Jesus died to give that authority to you.

Noted American humorist Will Rogers was once asked to account for the success of the theater business and the failure of the Church. This is what he said: "The theater business takes what is make-believe and acts it out on stage like it's real life. But the church takes what is real in life and acts like it is make-believe." The devil—and the battle we find ourselves in—is reality; it is not make-believe. It is time for us to deal with the devil—in our hearts, in our minds, in our homes, and in our relationships.

When we do, we can turn to the final part of our mission, and the reason we were called in the first place: to set people free.

Chapter 10

Further Strategies for Handling the Enemy's Attacks

Satan is our enemy, and it is certain that he will attack each of us at some point. So, with this in mind, we need to ask ourselves, what does God want us to do when we recognize that we are under attack?

The Scriptures give us sixteen different strategies for handling the attacks of the enemy and overcoming them in such a way that victory is assured. Let's look at each one in detail:

1.   Correct any wrongdoing.

The very first thing we should do when we realize we are under attack is to correct any wrongdoing we are presently involved in or have been involved recently. Being involved in sin—of any kind, regardless how "big" or "small"—gives the adversary space to operate in our lives. So, if we've been doing something wrong, we need to stop it and repent right away. If we'll do that, we will limit the enemy's work in our lives in an immense measure:

> *"And herein do I exercise myself, to have*
> *always a conscience void of offence toward*
> *God, and toward men."*   (Acts 24:16)

Paul's words are helpful to our understanding. When he wrote, "I exercise," it means that he put some effort into it. Today, to "exercise" means to go to the gym and work out. Paul means something similar to that. He was going to work on it, to make sure he got this task right. He also said he would *always*, not just part of the time, have a good conscience. His work was to always have a good conscience without any offense. If I have done wrong, my mental, emotional, and spiritual being knows I have done wrong, and my conscience bothers me. That's a good thing! We should welcome a conscience that is active, that bothers us when we get out of line. The worst condition people can get in is when their conscience no longer bothers them anymore. That is a spiritual condition called a seared conscience. "Seared" means dried up, withered away, cauterized, incapable of feeling. Yikes!

> *"...having their conscience seared with a hot*
> *iron."*   (1 Timothy 4:2)

But it can get worse than a seared conscience, where a person can do wrong without it bothering them. A person can become reprobate which means to become unruly, and degenerate to the point of reversing good and evil. This is really big big trouble! So troublesome that God puts a "woe" in front of the description. "Woe" means to be in a condition of misery, suffering, emotional distress, and misfortune.

Here is reprobation, the reversing of good and evil defined:

> *"Woe unto them that call evil good, and good*
> *evil; that put darkness for light, and light for*
> *darkness; that put bitter for sweet, and sweet*
> *for bitter!"*   (Isaiah 5:20)

> *"And even as they did not like to retain God*
> *in their knowledge, God gave them **over to a***
> ***reprobate mind**, to do those things which are*
> *not convenient."* (Romans 1:28)

Reprobate means "unprincipled." Why does reprobation happen? Because we can get into a place that the Bible describes as being past feeling guilt over sin, when they have given themselves over to a reprobate mind. A reprobate mind is a mind that believes that what is wrong is really right and that what is wrong is really okay. That is the condition of a perverted mind.

Having a clear conscience has two dimensions. First, there is a *vertical* dimension, which involves keeping right with God. Second, there is the *horizontal* dimension, which involves keeping right relationships with other people. It is important for us to continually conduct a self-evaluation, and if there's any wrongdoing in our lives between God and us or between others and us, we should clear it up and repent. It would be wrong to underestimate the importance of this:

> *"... sent you out **to battle for the right armed***
> ***only with your faith and a clear conscience.***
> *Some, alas, have laid these simple weapons*
> *contemptuously aside and, as far as their*
> *faith is concerned have run their ships on the*
> *rocks."* (1 Timothy 1:18–20 PHILLIPS)

Paul wrote these words to a young preacher, Timothy, and shared with him the importance of two simple weapons: looking after his faith and keeping a clear conscience. Without these two weapons in place, so many people run their ship onto the rocks. We must always keep an eye out to see if we have done something wrong, and if we have, we must correct it right away.

2. Get the truth on every related matter.

Second, you and I need the truth on every related matter. Jesus said this:

> *"And ye shall know the truth, and the truth shall make you free."* (John 8:32)

When we know the truth, it will make us free. So often, the enemy will try to attack us in our minds, especially by putting error in our thoughts. But the antidote for error is always the truth—the whole truth and nothing but the truth: We must love the truth. Only truth is the anecdote to error.

> *"And with all deceivableness of unrighteousness in them that perish; because they **received not the love of the truth, that they might be saved.**"* (2 Thessalonians 2:10)

3. Replace your own thoughts with biblical patterns.

Third, we need to replace our own thought patterns with biblical patterns. Remember, the attack of the enemy is often indicated by the intrusion of unscriptural ideas or thoughts. We have to counteract them. So we turn to those portions of Scripture that are the opposite to those of the enemy. This is so important because out of our thinking comes our emotions and out of our emotions comes our actions and out of actions comes the consequences. It all starts in the mind. And that's why the Scripture says:

> *"...be ye transformed by the **renewing of your mind,** that ye may prove what is that good, and acceptable, and perfect, will of God."* (Romans. 12:2)

> *"Let this mind be in you, which was also in Christ Jesus."* (Philippians 2:5)

> *"Casting down imaginations, and every high thing*
> *that exalteth itself against the knowledge of God,*
> *and **bringing into captivity every thought** to the*
> *obedience of Christ."* (2 Corinthians 10:5)

We must bring into captivity every thought that has to do with the knowledge of God and obedience to Christ. This is the point of power. When we grasp and do this, we suddenly experience freedom, and we will conquer the adversary. Satan speaks to the mind to get to the heart. God speaks to the heart to reach the mind. Jesus affirmed this principle in both Matthew 4:4 and Luke 4:4—both verses say the same thing; they are identical:

> *"But he answered and said, It is written, Man shall*
> *not **live** by bread alone, but **by every word that***
> ***proceedeth out of the mouth of God.**"*
> (Matthew 4:4, Luke 4:4)

4.   Make no compromise with the devil.

Fourth, as detailed in the previous chapter, we must not compromise at all in our lives. There needs to be *zero* compromise. This is not something we can play loosely and freely with. The stakes are way too high. Paul wrote this to encourage us as believers:

> *"Neither give place to the devil."*
> (Ephesians 4:27)

Don't give place to the devil. Don't give him an inch. Do not give him a millimeter. Do not give him a nano portion. Don't leave him any space. If you leave the devil any space at all in your thinking, in your mind, in your heart, in your relationships, in your behavior, if you leave the devil a little space, he's going to build on that land, in that space you've allowed him to have. He's going to build a castle, a fortress, a stronghold. And you'll have a hard time tearing it down later.

That's why the Scriptures are clear that if something's going wrong, you should not put it off. Deal with it decisively. Be proactive.

5. **Raise your standards.**

Learn to set high standards.

> *"So shall they fear the name of the Lord from the west, and his glory from the rising of the sun.* **When the enemy shall come in like a flood, the Spirit of the Lord shall lift up a standard against him.** *"*
> (Isaiah 59:19)

Back in the days of Hurricane Katrina, people built levies to keep out the flood water. If we don't have a high enough levy, the waves will wash right over the top, come in, and do damage. The Scripture is telling us that when the enemy is coming at us, we need to build a higher levy. You want to raise a standard higher so when the flood comes, it hits that levy and can't come into your life. That levy for you is your standard.

Families ought to sit down together, and fathers and mothers should set standards for the household. What is allowed inside the doors of your home, and what is not? Do we have standards for our children, for our marriages? Do we have standards for what's allowed on the television in our homes? If we do not have high standards, and we allow television programs in without high standards, the devil's going to come in like a flood. We're asking for big trouble. We don't even have to ask for it; it's coming to us.

So, what stops the enemy from coming into our homes via video, music, the airwaves—and that includes radio, television, and the internet? If we don't have standards when we go on the internet, we're going to be in trouble. As we raise our standards, we prevent the devil's access to our lives. Raise the standards because when you're under attack, the standards are what will stop the enemy from entering your life.

6.   Hold to the profession of your faith.

Sixth, you need to have a grip. You need to hold fast. You need to hold the profession of your faith without any vacillating whatsoever:

> *"Let us hold fast the profession of our faith without wavering; (for he is faithful that promised.)"*
> (Hebrews 10:23)

Remember, the enemy is after us. And what's he going to attack? He's going to attack our faith, to try to get it defused, off track, or misdirected. We need to hold our faith tight with a secure grip. As you know, ours is a faith battle, and faith is the victory that overcomes the world. More specifically, faith is the victory that overcomes the devil. God, the One who has made the promises to us, is faithful. And because we know He's faithful, we can hold fast to our faith. The Scriptures tell us that we have become partakers of His divine nature. How do we do that? How do we become a partaker of His divine nature? We hold on to those things by our faith in His promises:

> *"According as his divine power hath given unto us all things that pertain unto life and godliness, through the knowledge of him that hath called us to glory and virtue:*
>
> *Whereby are given unto us exceeding **great and precious promises**: that **by these ye might be partakers of the divine nature**, having escaped the corruption that is in the world through lust."*
> (2 Peter 1:3-4)

> *"But let him ask in faith, nothing wavering. For he that wavereth is like a wave of the sea driven with the wind and tossed.*

> *For let not that man think that he shall receive*
> *any thing of the Lord."* (James 1:6–7)

He who wavers is like a wave in the sea. This is what will happen to you if you waver in your faith: you will be driven with the wind, and you'll get tossed around. Someone who is like that will not receive anything from the Lord. A double-minded man is unstable in all his ways. But the key to overcoming all this is to *hold fast the profession of your faith.*

7. Keep your confidence.

If we make decisions when we're not confident, they will tend to be wrong decisions. God intends for us to have poise. He wants us to be able to walk with our heads held high— but not our noses! He wants us to have composure, no matter what circumstances we face:

> *"Cast not away therefore your confidence,*
> *which hath great recompence of reward.*
> *For ye have need of patience, that, after ye*
> *have done the will of God, ye might receive the*
> *promise."* (Hebrews 10:35–36)

Confidence will bring great rewards. Confidence is the mental attitude of trusting, or relying, a sense of certainty, and assurance which gives rise to fearlessness and courage.

Confidence is not presumption but rather is certainty based on the integrity of God who is going to give us a stable platform to make wise, intelligent decisions. Don't quit on your confidence. Have patience, which is simply a calm self-imposed waiting or endurance. This is the essence of perseverance. AFTER we have done the will of God we WILL receive the promise. Be steadfast which means to be firmly fixed, not moved or displaced.

8. Keep praising.

Keep praising the Lord! The Bible tells us this:

> *"Let the high praises of God be in their*
> *mouth,and a two-edged sword in their hand."*
>
> (Psalm 149:6)

Let the high praises of God be in our mouths. We have two weapons. One of them is a two-edged sword in our hand, which is the Word of God. Our second weapon is just as powerful: we also must keep the praises of God in our mouths, because they will keep us from speaking anything negative against God or His plans!

9. Make spiritual music.

Every person is to be a musician—every single one of us, regardless of our musical talent. Don't let anybody else make the music for you; learn how to make spiritual music for yourself. Now, spiritual music has a great deal of power, and it can be of great benefit to us when we're under attack. Let's look at the story of David and Saul:

> *"And it came to pass, when the evil spirit*
> *from God was upon Saul, that David **took an***
> ***harp, and played with his hand**: so Saul was*
> *refreshed, and was well, and the evil spirit*
> *departed from him."*   (1 Samuel 16:23)

Saul was being oppressed with an evil spirit, but notice what David did that helped ease his distress: David took a harp and played it for the king, and that music did something to Saul. Saul was refreshed—the spiritual music not only refreshed him, but he actually became well. He was healed! The Bible says that the evil spirit departed from him when the music was played. Now, that's God's idea of music!

Spiritual music has the power to send devils fleeing. Spiritual music has such a God-nature about it that demons don't want to be around it. Spiritual music refreshes us. It will actually help us to get well when we're sick, and the evil spirits that are after us will depart from us when we are in the presence of spiritual music. They can't stand to be around it!

Unfortunately, the opposite is also true: unspiritual music can attract devils into our lives. Unspiritual music can bring the demons to our door. It accommodates them. It creates a comfort zone for them. So, beware of what music you allow in your life:

> *"And be not drunk with wine, wherein is excess; but **be filled with the Spirit;***
>
> ***Speaking to yourselves in psalms and hymns and spiritual songs, singing and making melody in your heart to the Lord;***
>
> *Giving thanks always for all things unto God and the Father in the name of our Lord Jesus Christ."* (Ephesians 5:18–20)

These are interesting verses. We are told not to be drunk with wine, but we are to be filled with the Spirit. What a comparison here between being filled with the Spirit and being drunk with wine! Why do you think they call alcoholic drinks "spirits"? Because they are a substitute for the Holy Spirit! Some people get on an airplane, and they have to have a drink to get their courage up to get through the flight. Not me. I'm already "drinking"! I have *the* Spirit…and because of that, I already have all the courage I need. Wine and spirits are a poor substitute for the Holy Spirit. We are not to be drunk with wine; we are to be filled with the Spirit.

One of the best ways to do this is to speak to ourselves. Talking to yourself is a very important activity. David wrote this in Psalm 103:

> *"Bless the Lord, O my soul: and all that is within me, bless his holy name."* (Psalm 103:1)

David actually instructed his soul to bless the Lord. We are to do this, as well: *"Come on, soul. Bless the Lord, O my soul. Stand up and bless the Lord!"* Talk to yourself. Talk to your soul when it is down and discouraged. The psalms are a good place to find examples of this:

> *"Why art thou cast down, O my soul? and why
> art thou disquieted in me? hope thou in God:
> for I shall yet praise him for the help of his
> countenance."*   (Psalm 42:5)

Speak to yourself in psalms. Repeat the words of the psalms, personalizing them to encourage yourself.

Second, speak to yourself with hymns. Next to your Bible, have an old-fashioned hymnal to refer to. If you don't like the tunes, don't worry about it. Just read the words. Those good, old hymns are chock-full of strong, doctrinal declarations of the faith because the great men and women of God in yesteryear had deep experiences of faith that they wrote and sang about. And when they wrote the lyrics of these hymns, it was so that you and I would get to participate in that richness. Let's be careful that we be not attracted to entertaining music. Especially let's be alert to spiritual words that contemporary musicians might defile by the use of carnal sounds. Not all Christian music is Christian.

Finally, we are to sing spiritual songs, songs that are spiritually based, spiritually motivated, spiritually flavored, and spiritually accompanied. I like to put on instrumental music in the background of my house. I don't want anyone else to do my singing for me; I sing along to this music with words I am using to address the Lord. Find a way to make up your own melodies in your heart to the Lord. Make spiritual music, and you will send the devil packing.

10. Lock arms with a fellow believer.

When you're under attack, it is always a great idea to join up with someone else—you may physically lock arms with them, but you may also spiritually, symbolically, lock arms, as well. You need to come together spiritually, mentally, and emotionally. Get a fellow believer to stand with you:

> *"**Two are better than one**; because they have
> a good reward for their labour.*

> *For if they fall, the one will lift up his fellow:*
> *but woe to him that is alone when he falleth;*
> *for he hath not another to help him up…*
>
> *And if one prevail against him, two shall*
> *withstand him; and a threefold cord is not*
> *quickly broken.* " (Ecclesiastes 4:9–10, 12)

Solomon said that two are better than one. If you link up with somebody else, you will have a good reward for your endeavor. It's a good thing to do. If one of you falls, the other can lift up his or her friend. It's not good for a person to be alone—God has said this since the beginning. People ought to get married. There are a few exceptions, but in a true marriage, the two will become one, in fact better than one.

This is called *synergism*, the interaction between two persons that produces a greater effect than that obtained merely by the addition of the two. Synergism doesn't merely apply to chemicals, pharmacology, toxicology, microbiology, or ecology. In Scripture we learn that if *"one can chase a thousand then two can put ten thousand to flight."* When two or three agree the results are multiplied.

Synergy is not just for marriage (although it is that). It's true for Christian comrades—godly friends in your life with whom you can lock arms and stand together. Notice the "threefold cord" in the Scripture. God seems to prefer in some cases to be the third one in. Here's an example. Jesus made it clear, *"that if two of you shall agree on earth as toughing any thing that they ask, it shall be done of them of my Father which is in heaven"* (Matthew 18:19).

If one can put a thousand to flight, and two can put ten thousand to flight, imagine how many you could put to flight when God is part of that relationship!

11. **Don't underestimate the power of God.**

With God on your side, you will never have to fight alone:

> *"For it is God which worketh in you both to will and to do of his good pleasure."*
>
> (Philippians 2:13)

God is the One who works in you, both to show you direction and to do His good pleasure. Don't underestimate the power of God. It's greater than the power of Satan:

> *"For the weapons of our warfare are not carnal, but mighty through God to the pulling down of strong holds."* (2 Corinthians 10:4)

The weapons we use to fight the enemy are not carnal; they are mighty as God pulls down those strongholds. Don't underestimate the power of God working in your life!

12. Walk by faith, not by sight.

> *"For we walk by faith, not by sight."*
>
> (2 Corinthians 5:7)

If we walk by what we see in the natural realm, we are not responding in the spiritual realm. Our greatest enemies are spiritual—not other people, but the devil and his demons who are trying to wreak havoc in our lives.

13. Keep your armor on, and never give up.

Keep your armor on, and don't quit fighting:

> *"Wherefore take unto you the whole armour of God, that ye may be able to withstand in the evil day, and having done all, to stand.*
>
> *Stand therefore, having your loins girt about with truth, and having on the breastplate of righteousness."* (Ephesians 6:13–14)

Winston Churchill was asked to be the keynote graduation speaker at a college in the United Kingdom. Thousands were in attendance to hear the prime minister speak. As he walked forward to the podium, he received a standing ovation. When the crowd finally sat down, they were treated to a speech that was only five words long, but they were the most important five words he could have spoken at that time in history: "Never, never, never give up." Then he turned around and sat down.

If I could pass one encouraging word to you, from the words of Winston Churchill, I would say this: Never, never, never give up. No turning back! Keep standing. Never give up:

> *"And he called his ten servants, and delivered*
> *them ten pounds, and said unto them, Occupy*
> *till I come."* (Luke 19:13)

Jesus's statement here contains an important word, a military term, the word *occupy*. When soldiers capture a hill, they then *occupy* the hill. It means to hold on to the territory they've acquired. When Jesus told us to occupy until He returns, He is telling us to take territory from the devil and then hold our ground. Never, ever give up!

14. Remember the God factor.

Finally, don't ever forget God:

> *"What shall we then say to these things? If*
> *God be for us, who can be against us?"*
> (Romans 8:31)

The answer is no one—not even the devil himself! Always remember the God factor. We need Him and we have Him. It's as Jesus said, *"Without me, ye can do nothing"* (John 15:5) and it is also true, *"we can do all things through Christ which strengtheneth us"* (Philippians 4:13).

Chapter 11

Set People Free!

In 1965, Charles Krulak was a young second lieutenant who had just gotten married after graduating from the United States Naval Academy. He and his new bride moved to Quantico, Virginia, home of the school where officers learned about honor, courage, and commitment. At the time, young Charles shared a room with another married naval officer, John Listerman. John was a Christian—which meant nothing at the time to Charles, other than that he came to see John as a really nice guy. Because of John, it seemed to Charles that Christians were good people, but nothing more came of it than that.

After graduating from the basics, both John and Charles were sent to Camp Pendleton, in California, where they also joined the same battalion that was preparing to go over to Vietnam. John Listerman soon began to show himself to Charles as a tremendous leader, one who was both aggressive and technically proficient. The troops under his command loved him. He was committed to his men, and his troops were committed to him, in turn.

In December 1965, John and Charles were sent to war. For Charles, the war lasted several years. For John, it lasted just one day.

While they were on patrol moving through the jungle, they came around a corner on the trail and were immediately ambushed. John took a .50-caliber round in his kneecap, which threw him into the air. The second round that hit him entered his body just below his heart and exited his side.

Charles was also wounded—but not mortally. He was able to crawl about thirty meters over to John's side, but before he could even ask, "Are you okay, John? Where were you hit?" his leader grabbed on to Charles's sleeve and said, "How are you doing, Chucker? Are you okay?"

When Charles reassured him that he was, John's next question was, "Are my men safe?"

Charles told him, "Your people are okay." Then John turned his head toward the sky and repeated over and over, "Thank You, Lord. Thank You for caring for my people. Thank You for watching over them."

John Listerman was airlifted from the jungle that day, and Charles Krulak was evacuated soon thereafter. John's care and concern for his troops—for his people—that day ultimately led Charles to become a Christian later in life.

John was a high-value target—not only in the jungles of Vietnam, but also because of his witness for the Lord.

You, too, are a high-value target! A mission from the Lord of heaven and earth has been passed to you, and the enemy knows it. He trembles in fear over the authority that your Commander in Chief has given you. You have been taught his tactics, you have put on your armor, and you have studied your mission. It's time to go forth and fulfill the calling. It's time to follow the mission of Jesus and begin to set people free.

The mission of Jesus was, and still is, setting people free. That's what He came to do. That was His entire purpose, and it is what Jesus still does today. He comes to set people free. Is that good news or what? If you were ever in prison, the best news, I think, would be that you were being set free. Freedom has been made possible through the sacrifice of Jesus on the cross:

> *"Therefore if the Son makes you free, **you shall be free indeed**."* (John 8:36 NKJV)

This freedom Jesus came to bring to us is no mere emotional sentiment; it is no mere theory or a theology. It is factual. It is practical. It is freedom, indeed; He has *absolutely* set us free.

Jesus makes us free from every bondage, every false idea, every emotional stress, every spiritual fracture, every mental limitation, every psychological chain. When people are not free, they have to consider everything they do: *What will people think?* They live in self-condemnation and self-degradation. They have to pretend. When they can't be real, they have not been set free. When we have to premeditate what we're going to do in front of others, when we are living a pretense, we are bound up in chains of our own making.

But Jesus brought us good news when He spoke these words:

> *"The Spirit of the Lord God is upon Me, because*
> *the Lord has anointed Me to preach good*
> *tidings to the poor; He has sent Me to heal the*
> *brokenhearted, to proclaim liberty to the captives,*
> *and the opening of the prison to those who are*
> *bound;*
>
> *to proclaim the acceptable year of the Lord, and*
> *the day of vengeance of our God; to comfort all*
> *who mourn,*
>
> *to console those who mourn in Zion, to give them*
> *beauty for ashes, the oil of joy for mourning, the*
> *garment of praise for the spirit of heaviness; that*
> *they might be called trees of righteousness, the*
> *planting of the Lord, that He may be glorified."*
>
> (Isaiah 61:1–3 NKJV)

Jesus has come to comfort all who mourn. He gives us beauty for ashes, the oil of joy for mourning, the garment of praise for the spirit of heaviness. Jesus will do such a work in us that we will no longer carry a spirit of heaviness anywhere we go. Our feet will be like the feet of a deer, as we hop, run, and skip through life. As the Scriptures tell us, we run upon the high places of the earth. Jesus comes to take away the spirit of heaviness. He wants us to dance, and jump, and skip—He wants us to be filled with life.

Whatever is pulling you down and destroying you, Jesus has come to destroy. He comes to destroy the destroyer, to take it out of our lives. He's going to turn you into a tree of righteousness, and you will become solid like an oak. Fruit is going to flow out of your life, and blessings will come out of your circumstances. All kinds of benefits are going to flow through you because of what the Lord has done.

When Jesus came to the earth, He began His mission to set people free. But His work is continued on the earth through you and through me. His mission is our mission. I don't have a ministry. Jesus has a ministry, and I can't tell you how delighted I am to be a part of His ministry.

What It Takes to Set People Free

What does it take to set people free? Let's look at seven of the basic ingredients, all prescribed in God's Word.

1.   Have the Spirit of the Lord upon you.

First, to continue the mission of the Lord and set people free, you need to have the Spirit of the Lord upon you. Don't ever think you can do this without Him!

> *"The Spirit of the Lord is upon Me…"*
> (Luke 4:18 NKJV)

It is not necessarily a difficult thing to have the Holy Spirit operating through you. Did you know that He is more zealous to come upon you than you are to have Him come upon you? The Holy Spirit wants more of you than you are giving Him. The Holy Spirit is the One who brings into existence all the benefits of what Jesus did on the cross.

I want the Holy Spirit to be the leader in my life. I want His leadership in my ministry. I want His guidance. I want His empowerment. And that's not hard to gain because He *wants* to give it to me—and to you:

> *"If you then, being evil, know how to give*
> *good gifts to your children, how much more*
> *will your heavenly Father give the Holy Spirit*
> *to those who ask Him?"*   (Luke 11:13 NKJV)

If we ask God for bread, do you think He'll give us a stone? Of course not. The Holy Spirit has been poured out on us. He didn't come to give you a little sprinkle; no, He came to pour out His Spirit on you:

> *"'And it shall come to pass in the last days,*
> *says God, that **I will pour out of My Spirit** on*
> *all flesh: your sons and your daughters shall*
> *prophesy, your young men shall see visions,*
> *your old men shall dream dreams.'"*
>
> (Acts 2:17 NKJV)

Develop a thirst for God! "*Blessed are they which do hunger and thirst after righteousness: for they shall be filled*" (Matthew 5:6).

2. Be anointed to preach the Gospel.

Our second qualification is to be anointed to preach the Gospel. The anointing given in the Old Testament differed from the anointing that was given in the New Testament. In the Old Testament, the anointing came on a person to do a specific task—and then it lifted. But in the New Testament, the anointing stayed upon the believer, and it taught and instructed that person all the things of God:

> "But **the anointing** which you have received
> from Him **abides in you**, and you do not
> need that anyone teach you; but as the same
> anointing teaches you concerning all things,
> and is true, and is not a lie, and just as it has
> taught you, you will abide in Him."
>
> (1 John 2:27 NKJV)

"Anointing" literally means "to rub in." Oh my, isn't this wonderful!

3. Heal the brokenhearted.

There are a lot of broken hearts in the world. But do we know what breaks hearts? Sin. A ten-year-old girl who is conned by a fifteen-year-old boy gets a broken heart. The broken condition of people's hearts today doesn't start when people turn eighteen or twenty or thirty—although they get broken hearts, too. But the enemy is after our children, and he is working to break their hearts at a younger and younger age. That is why God called biblical parents to be the protectors of their children's hearts. There's no reason for you to have a broken heart and live your adult years fragmented. The devil comes to steal, to kill, and to destroy, but we can have God's abundant life instead. Jesus comes to heal broken hearts. That's why they call Him the Great Physician. Whatever brokenness you've been carrying, Jesus comes to heal it.

Freedom requires an intact condition of the heart. The heart needs to be happy to be free. You should have a joy-filled heart, not one that's so cracked that it leaks tears, remorse, and regret. Setting people free takes the Spirit of God, an anointing to preach, and the ability to bind up broken hearts.

4.   Preach deliverance to the captives.

Fourth, we are to preach deliverance to the captives. Now, remember that our enemy is never people. The true enemy is Satan:

> *"Be sober, be vigilant; because your*
> *adversary the devil walks about as a roaring*
> *lion, seeking whom he may devour."*
> (1 Peter 5:8 NKJV)

Our enemy is never people—but they sure can come across like our enemies. We have to deal with the devil, but we also have to preach to the captives for them to gain complete freedom. Again, it is impossible to set somebody free who does not want to be set free. As Voltaire said, "It is difficult to free fools from the chains they revere." Because God knows this, He has instructed us to preach deliverance to the captives, to those who are being held by Satan. This "preaching" is important!

*"For the message of the cross is foolishness
to those who are perishing, but to us who are
being saved it is the power of God."*
(1 Corinthians 1:18 NKJV)

God's method for reaching the captives is preaching—which many find foolish—but it is not:

*"For it is written: 'I will destroy the wisdom
of the wise, and bring to nothing the
understanding of the prudent.'"*
(1 Corinthians 1:19 NKJV)

So many times, we assume that we need a lot more wisdom and understanding than we have before we can effectively share the Gospel. The truth is, we are not going to get people out of captivity and into the kingdom of God, out of prison and set free, by some intellectual process. If reason didn't get them there, reason will not get them out. If a person is doing serious drugs, all the psychology in the world will not rescue him or her from that addiction until you address the cause behind the drugs. Whatever got them there has to be dealt with to get them back out again:

*"For since, in the wisdom of God, the world
through wisdom did not know God, it pleased
God through the foolishness of the message
preached to save those who believe."*
(1 Corinthians 1:21 NKJV)

God's method is preaching. It is not music. It is not skits, plays, and dramas. It is not even the printed page. He didn't say to go into all the world and print the Gospel. It isn't colored ink. It's preaching.

God, in His wisdom, reduces the whole solution down to this. Here's what you do to set the captives free: you preach to them:

> *"For Jews request a sign, and Greeks seek*
> *after wisdom;*
> **but we preach** *Christ crucified, to the*
> *Jews a stumbling block and to the Greeks*
> *foolishness."* (1 Corinthians 1:22–23 NKJV)

What are we to preach? We preach that Christ was crucified. It's pretty simple. God is not looking for super intellectuals, because our intellect would get in the way of the simplicity and power of the Gospel. A lot of people aren't saved because they think they're too smart. If the facts were in, though, their smartness is their stupidity. It is not smart to say there's no God. You have to be stupid to think that:

> *"The fool has said in his heart, 'There is*
> *no God.' They are corrupt, they have done*
> *abominable works, there is none who does*
> *good."* (Psalm 14:1 NKJV)

5. Preach recovery of sight.

When we preach the Gospel, we preach deliverance and the recovery of sight:

> *"The Spirit of the Lord is upon me, because*
> *he hath anointed me to preach the gospel*
> *to the poor; he hath sent me to heal the*
> *brokenhearted, to preach deliverance to the*
> *captives, and* **recovering of sight to the blind,**
> *to set at liberty them that are bruised."*
> (Luke 4:18)

Sight gets recovered from preaching. The captives need preachers. That's what will move them from captivity to delivery, from bondage to freedom, from blindness to eyesight. Every human walking on this planet has a way of seeing the world around him or her. We got that way of seeing because of our experiences, relationships, and education—

everything we went through from the time we were children. Everybody develops a way of seeing.

The question isn't whether or not we have a way of seeing. The question is, are we blind? The blind try to lead the blind. Your education is only as effective as the one who educated you. That's why parents are told to train up their children according to the Scriptures, because that is what enables people to see straight. That's our job—to preach for the recovery of sight to the blind.

6.   Preach to set at liberty the bruised.

Let's look at Jesus's words again, as quoted by Isaiah:

> *"The Spirit of the Lord is upon me, because*
> *he hath anointed me to preach the gospel*
> *to the poor; he hath sent me to heal the*
> *brokenhearted, to preach deliverance to the*
> *captives, and recovering of sight to the blind,*
> ***to set at liberty them that are bruised."***
>
> (Luke 4:18)

Liberty comes from preaching. This is the greatest need in America today: preachers of true liberty. Do you know what the Founding Fathers of this nation preached? Liberty. Do you know what they believed we were endowed with from our Creator? Liberty.

Unfortunately, blindness has begun to run rampant in America today. When a false concept of liberty is promoted, then the people will see liberty through the wrong eyes. Americans today see liberty as the right to do evil. But what we have called *liberty* has led us to slavery because God never intended freedom to be the right to do evil. He intended freedom to be the right to obey Him. As Daniel Webster said, "Liberty is not the right to do evil, but the power to do what you ought to do."

If the Christian Church in America does not get back to preaching the Word of God, America will never regain her liberty. God's message to His Church in America is to wake up, to shake free from your lethargy, to get up, get out, and preach. Liberty comes from preaching. This is what it takes to set people free.

7. Preach the acceptable year—right now.

> *"To preach the acceptable year of the Lord."*
> (Luke 4:19)

And what are we supposed to preach? We are to preach the acceptable year of the Lord. The captives not only have to have liberty preached to them, and the recovering of sight preached to them, and deliverance preached to them, and the Gospel preached to them—but they need to know that this liberty, deliverance, and recovery of sight is for *right now*.

The acceptable time is now. *"Behold, now is the accepted time; behold, now is the day of salvation"* (2 Corinthians 6:2). There will never be a better time and place. The best time for salvation is right this minute. Oh for the appeals we once made, the songs we once sang, the tears we once shed when we implored the people.

> *"Almost persuaded" now to believe;*
> *"Almost persuaded" Christ to receive;*
> *Seems now some soul to say,*
> *"Go, Spirit, go Thy way,*
> *Some more convenient day*
> *on Thee I'll call."*
>
> *"Almost persuaded," come, come today;*
> *"Almost persuaded," turn not away;*
> *Jesus invites you here,*
> *Angels are ling'ring near,*
> *Prayers rise from hearts so dear;*
> *O wand'rer, come!*
>
> *Oh, be persuaded! Christ never fails—*
> *Oh, be persuaded! His blood avails—*
> *Can save from every sin,*

Cleanse you without, within—
Will you not let Him in?
Open the door!

"Almost persuaded," harvest is past!
"Almost persuaded," doom comes at last;
"Almost" cannot avail;
"Almost" is but to fail!
Sad, sad that bitter wail—
"Almost—but lost!"

Be now persuaded, oh, sinner, hear!
Be now persuaded, Jesus is near;
His voice is pleading still,
Turn now with heart and will,
Peace will your spirit fill—
Oh, turn today!

Lyrics and music by Philip Paul Bliss (1838-1876)

How to Set People Free

What's the bottom line? Our mission on this earth is to set people free.

How do we do this? Through the four directives given by our Commander in Chief.

1. Proclaim liberty.

Number one, we must proclaim liberty. Those in captivity need to know the Good News that we have come to bring. They need to know that this is their moment—and that their response to this moment will define their lives. To *proclaim* is to call out an intelligently understood message. The captives need to be told what they can intelligently understand, that Jesus comes to set them free—free from selfishness, free from fear, free from hatred, free from bitterness, resentment, a broken heart, everything in their lives that is holding them back.

We start with the proclamation of liberty. Proclaim to people that this Jesus has come to set them free:

> *"Now the Lord is the Spirit; and **where the Spirit of the Lord is, there is liberty**."*
>
> (2 Corinthians 3:17 NKJV)

2. Preach that Christ was crucified and is risen.

We not only proclaim liberty, but we preach the Gospel. We preach Christ. We preach that Christ was crucified and risen on their behalf. He's the liberator. To preach means to set forth the message with earnest exhortation; to advocate calling listeners to respond.

> *"But **we preach Christ crucified**, to the Jews a stumbling block and to the Greeks foolishness,*
>
> *but to those who are called, both Jews and Greeks, Christ **the power of God and the wisdom of God**."* (1 Corinthians 1:23–24 NKJV)

This kind of preaching brings the power of God into the situation. The truth of the matter is that people are in bondage, but we in and of ourselves don't have the ability to set them free. All we can do is take them to the One who can. I can't save them, but I can bring them to the Savior. That's why we preach Christ—because that's where the power is. It is the fact that He is alive today. His death on the cross reconciled us to God but it's His present indwelling life that empowers, transforms and sets free.

> *"For if, when we were enemies, we were reconciled to God by the death of his Son, much more, being reconciled, **we shall be saved by his life**."* (Romans 5:10)

Isn't Jesus what really changed you? It wasn't some psychological system; it certainly wasn't religion. What changes people is Jesus. He still walks the aisles today. He still comes into the hearts of those who respond. He will be everywhere He is preached. Preaching brings the presence of Jesus to people. Christ in you is the hope of glory, the One whom we preach.

3. Persuade.

Third, we must persuade. That is the purpose of preaching. If we preach God's way, we will persuade. Being persuaded is what it's going to take to set the captive ones free. Proclaim—let them know why we're there—and then preach Christ, the Liberator, doing so with persuasion.

> *"Now when the congregation had broken up, many of the Jews and devout proselytes followed Paul and Barnabas, who, speaking to them, **persuaded them** to continue in the grace of God."*   (Acts 13:43 NKJV)

When the many people who were following Paul and Barnabas talked to them, they were persuaded to follow the ways of the Lord. Our job is to persuade others in the same way:

> *"Knowing, therefore, the terror of the Lord, **we persuade men**..."*   (2 Corinthians 5:11 NKJV)

There's no such thing as being too persuasive with the things of God. There is such a thing as being too emotional, however. You can persuade emotions but not persuade the person. There's a difference. You can persuade a person intellectually and still lose his or her soul. Persuasion is not a function merely of emotion or of intellect; persuasion is a function of the spirit.

4. Persist.

There is no other name whereby we must be saved. Only Jesus. There is no other way. We must persist in the faith and persist in sharing the faith with others.

Jesus came to set the captives free. It is our mission to do so as well.

Chapter 12

Called to Be a Soldier!

"Thou therefore endure hardness, as a good soldier of Jesus Christ. No man that warreth entangleth himself with the affairs of this life; that he may please him who hath chosen him to be a soldier. And if a man also strive for masteries, yet is he not crowned, except he strive lawfully."
(2 Timothy 2:3-5)

What Is a Soldier?

1. One who participates in warfare

A soldier is one who contends in a battle; who fights on behalf of a cause and generally represents a higher-up authority. In our case it's the Most High. We are to be the "Good Soldier of Jesus Christ":

> *"Thou therefore endure hardness, as **a good soldier of Jesus Christ**."* (2 Timothy 2:3)

Here are a few of many passages that affirm we are in a fight and are at war:

> *"**I have fought a good fight**, I have finished my course, I have kept the faith."* (2 Timothy 4:7)

"This charge I commit unto thee...

*that thou by them mightest **war a good
warfare.**"* (1 Timothy 1:18-19)

The visible wars are everywhere; persons against persons, nations against nations; race against race; gender against gender; social class against social class; killing; massacres; hatreds; shootings, knifings; bombings, verbal abuses and on and on *infinitum*! But none of these is our war! Our warfare is an invisible war! Our war is against the mental, emotional, social, philosophical and spiritual powers that cause the visible wars.

If the invisible wars are won, hatred, malice and hostilities will cease and peace, calm, and tranquility will govern motives, attitudes, and behaviors. The first rule of warfare, as enunciated by Sun Tzu, is "know thy enemy." It means to know who is behind the conflict and really pulling the strings. In the invisible war there is no armistice—no cessation of hostilities. Our war plan is a continuum until judgment day.

There are only two sides in the invisible war: good and evil, right and wrong, God and devils. And everyone is on one side or the other. There is no middle ground. To be ambivalent, indecisive or irresolute on matters of good and evil is to be morally complicit. Silence is an act of complicity.

The challenge issued by Moses to the people of his day, "Who is on the Lord's side?" is the question of our day. A Christian soldier is a warrior, engaged in the warfare on the Lord's side!

2. **One who separates him or herself from many civilian enterprises**

*"No man that warreth entangleth himself
with the affairs of this life; that he may please
him who hath chosen him to be a soldier. "*

(2 Timothy 2:4)

A wartime economy differs vastly from business as usual. The allocation of the assets of time, energy, and substance are drastically modified in order to achieve victory while also meeting the basic vital domestic and consumer demands. Rationing is common. It is necessary to limit consumption in order to focus on winning the war. Fixed quantities are assigned to various aspects of life. These can include financial purchases, amounts of time consumed, attention given and distractions avoided.

The Christian soldier of today is generally left to make his or her own decisions. Most church denominations have little sway over congregants. Those that do might risk cultish attributes. But let it be known that cults are identified by the obsessive giving of reverential homage to mere human leaders, as opposed to that honor which only belongs to God.

Lacking formal structured authorities to lead us into biblical soldiership is fine, especially when we consider that each of us is to be directly connected to God ourselves and not connected to God through anyone else. There is only *"one mediator between God and men, the man Christ Jesus"* (1 Timothy 2:5).

Thus, each of us must discipline ourselves, exercise self-control in appropriating financial and time elements that enable us to participate in the war without unnecessary distractions. Be undistractable. Watch out for amusements. "Muse" means to think, to spend times of thoughtfulness, reflection, and contemplation. "Amuse" as in "amusement" means to be mentally distracted, to have one's attention diverted so that mental, emotional, and spiritual waste occurs.

William Wordsworth penned it thus:

The world is too much with us; late and soon
Getting and spending we lay waste our powers...
We have given our hearts away, a sordid boon!

Let us be careful lest the description by Sir Walter Raleigh becomes the story of our lives:

Even such is time, that takes in trust
Our youth, our joys, our all we have,
And pays us but with age and dust;
Who, in the dark and silent grave,
When we have wandered all our ways,
Shuts up the story of our days.

We soldiers must spend our time, talent, and treasure in view of the war lest narcissism with its pitiful compensation becomes our lot in life. Question: How many hours of each week are you directly involved in the war? Think about it.

3. **One who lives by commandment**

Can you imagine a soldier who doesn't follow lawful orders? The consequences range from dishonorable discharge to forfeiture of all pay and allowances, confinement for five years, and if it's in a time of war, it could be death or such other punishment as a court-martial may direct. NJP or Non-Judicial Punishments may be applied without court proceedings.

Consider some of the aspects of a Christian who lives by commandment. First of all, we must ask, "Is there any other kind of Christian other than an obedient one?" I have not been able to find such an option. We are speaking here of willful, deliberate, and habitual disobedience. Oh, one might happen to inadvertently disobey. And if we do, *"We have an advocate with the Father, Jesus Christ the righteous"* (1 John 2:1). Thank you, Jesus!

However, two verses later it says,

> *"And hereby we do know that we know him, **if we keep his commandments**.*
>
> *He that saith, I know him, and keepeth not his commandments, is a liar, and the truth is not in him."* (1 John 2:3-4)

Obedience is the evidence of being genuinely Christian. Here's the proof!

> *"...He became the author of eternal **salvation unto all them that obey him.**"*   (Hebrews 5:9)

> *" And we are his witnesses of these things; and so is also **the Holy Ghost, whom God hath given to them that obey him**.*
>
> *When they heard that, they were cut to the heart, and took counsel to slay them."*
>
>   (Acts 5:32-33)

When they heard that the Holy Spirit is given to them that *obey* they threw a fit and decided to kill them that held such a view. Do you think the times have changed? Suggest this in your local church and see what kind of reaction you get. Generally speaking, the theology of our day lets Christians think they are going to heaven without much real change in conduct; salvation *in* sins versus salvation *from* sin.

Don't make any mistake here. Let's not mix up cause and effect. We don't become a Christian by doing what's right; instead, because we are Christians, we do what's right. How much of the time? All of the time and in every situation. Dietrick Bonheoffer said it most clearly, "Only those who really believe obey, and only those who obey, really believe."

God doesn't really need me to explain this. He does it clearly in Scripture, but let's see the Scriptures one more time (after all, repetition is the classic method of learning)! Get ready soldier! The evidence is love and obedience!

> *"And **hereby we do know that we know him, if we keep his commandments.***
>
> *He that saith, I know him, and keepeth not his commandments, is a liar, and the truth is not in him.*

> *But whoso keepeth his word, in him verily is*
> *the love of God perfected hereby know we that*
> *we are in him."* (1 John 2:3-5)

What makes the war so dangerous is not the devil, nor those merely controlled by the devil, but the enemy within, the fake, the hypocritical particularly among leadership. *"grievous wolves enter in among you, not sparing the flock"* (Acts 20:29). Jesus Himself warned us, *"Beware of false prophets, which come to you in sheep's clothing, but inwardly they are ravening wolves"* (Matthew 7:15).

We should know it is a joy to live by commandment!

First, here is what it means to live by commandment when Christ is indeed our Commander in Chief!

> Before we decide, speak, or act in any given situation, we first check to see if God has a command that applies. If so, we obey that commandment immediately, joyfully and without compromise.

Memorize this definition! I mean it! Memorize it!

About 17 or 18 years ago a new family, father, mother, son and daughter, was visiting our church. That Sunday I was teaching on "The Joy of Living By Commandment." I cited the above definition a number of times. Later that week, the family was driving, and Dad and Mom were in the front seat debating some issue. Suddenly the seven-year-old boy from the back seat poked his head into the front and said, "Dad, this is not complicated. 'Before we decide, speak, or act in any given situation, we first check to see if God has a commandment that applies. If so, we obey that commandment immediately, joyfully and without compromise.'"

The shocked parents decided immediately to join the church. If their seven-year-old could pick that up in one visit, they were coming back. Those parents are still in the church occupying a noble seniority. Their daughter married. She, her husband, and their two children are in the church. I look forward to seeing them every Sunday. The son married and moved away but stays in touch.

So tell us, Teacher, "What's so joyful about 'Living By Commandment'?"

1. The Commands Are Delightful

> *"Make me to go in the path of thy commandments; for therein do I delight."*
>
> (Psalm 119:35)

2. The Commands Are Loveable

> *"I will delight myself in thy commandments, which I have loved."* (Psalm 119:47)

> *"I love thy commandments above gold; yea, above fine gold."* (Psalm 119:127)

3. The Commands Are Faithful

> *"All thy commandments are faithful."*
>
> (Psalm 119:86)

4. The Commands Are Desireable

> *"I opened my mouth, and panted: for I longed for thy commandments."* (Psalm 119:131)

5. The Commands Are Right and Faithful

> *"Thy testimonies that thou hast commanded are righteous and very faithful."* (Psalm 119:138)

"*My tongue shall speak of thy word: for all thy
commandments are righteousness.*"

(Psalm 119:172)

6. The Commands Are Truthful

"*Thou art near, O LORD; and all thy
commandments are truth.*"   (Psalm 119:151)

7. The Commands Are Not Irritating

"*We keep his commandments: and his
commandments are not grievous.*"   (1 John 5:3)

8. The Commands Give Wisdom

"*Thou through thy commandments hast made
me wiser than mine enemies: for they are ever
with me.*"   (Psalm 119:98)

9. The Commands Give Understanding

"*a good understanding have all they that do
his commandments.*"   (Psalm 111:10)

10. The Commands Are the Whole Duty of Man

"*Let us hear the conclusion of the
whole matter: Fear God, and keep his
commandments: for this is the whole duty of
man.*"   (Ecclesiastes 12:13)

Can you see how a joy-filled life can be by simply
"Living By Commandment"? You will always have accurate
direction for every life situation. In contrast to this, let it be
known, that the man who does not do what he believes does
not believe what he believes.

4. One with weapon familiarity

> *"For though we walk in the flesh, we do not war after the flesh:*
>
> *(For the weapons of our warfare are not carnal, but mighty through God to the pulling down of strong holds;)*
>
> *Casting down imaginations, and every high thing that exalteth itself against the knowledge of God,*
>
> *and bringing into captivity every thought to the obedience of Christ;*
>
> *And having in a readiness to revenge all disobedience, when your obedience is fulfilled."* (2 Corinthians 10:3-6)

The warfare is spiritual, moral, ideological, and social as opposed to physical. Therefore our weapons are not guns, knives, clubs, mace, landmines, bombs, grenades, flamethrowers, or improvised explosive devices. We need no cannons, rockets or missiles. Biological and chemical dispersions have no place; no DEWS (Direct-Energy Weapons); no EMs (ElectroMagnetic Launchers); no HPMs or RF weapons (High-Power Microwaves or Radio Frequency weapons); no lasers or particle-beam weapons! None!

> *"The very **weapons we use are not those of human warfare** but powerful in God's warfare for the destruction of the enemy's strongholds. **Our battle is to bring down every deceptive fantasy and every imposing defence that men erect against the true knowledge of God.** We even fight to capture every thought until it acknowledges the authority of Christ."* (2 Corinthians 10:3-6 PHILLIPS)

We must not be mistaken about the nature of our war or we will be gravely misguided about our weapons. We are not haters of men but lovers of men. We are not life-takers but life-givers. We are not destroyers of humanity but constructive of all peoples in all places and at all times.

Beloved, don't miss the Scriptures. The most important content of this book are the direct quotations from Scripture. Let it be as Jeremiah the prophet emphatically announced: *"His word was in mine heart as a burning fire shut up in my bones"* (Jeremiah 20:9). Don't miss the fire. This is not merely about pen and ink, alphabet and words, noun and verb, phrase and clause, sentence and paragraph, diction and eloquence. It's about the Spirit behind and embedded in the words. Catch the Spirit! Catch the fire!

The warfare is not solely about academics, intellectualisms, world views, or pedantics. Behind every idea is a motive; behind every motive is a person; behind every person is a spiritual condition that predicates the audible, the visible, and every form of propagation.

Here's the Word again!

> *"The world is unprincipled. It's dog-eat-dog out there! The world doesn't fight fair. But we don't live or fight our battles that way—never have and never will. The tools of our trade aren't for marketing or manipulation, but they are for demolishing that entire massively corrupt culture. We use our powerful God-tools for smashing warped philosophies, tearing down barriers erected against the truth of God, fitting every loose thought and emotion and impulse into the structure of life shaped by Christ. Our tools are ready at hand for clearing the ground of every obstruction and building lives of obedience into maturity."*
>
> (2 Corinthians 10:3–6 MSG)

Here are several of our weapons and tools listed herein these texts:

1. We follow well-regulated codes of conduct.

2. We cast down imaginations.

3. We cast down everything that sets itself above God and His Word.

4. We hold every proper thought processes in our minds.

5. We are obedient, qualifying us to take revenge on disobedience.

We will be covering the codes of conduct. For the moment let's consider the issue of imaginations. Imagination is the power and/or capacity to form internal images or ideas of objects and situations not present at the moment but intending their fulfillment. Imaginations unchecked will generally usurp the power of will and intrude forcibly and without just cause. The power of imagination should not be underestimated.

In Genesis 11:6, the people got crazy ideas which became imaginations. About them, God said:

"Now nothing will be restrained from them, which they have imagined to do."

Wickednesses of every description are first conceived in the imagination of the heart. Lusts are first conceived, born in the imagination and become overpowering and overmastering desires.

"But every man is tempted, when he is drawn away of his own lust, and enticed.

Then when lust hath conceived, it bringeth forth sin: and sin, when it is finished, bringeth forth death. Do not err, my beloved brethren."

(James 1:14–16)

Evil starts in the unsanctified imaginations of the heart. Left unconquered (not cast down), it bears rule, control, sway and dominates with a commanding influence over rational thinking. So what's the cause of evil imaginations?

There are three causes that work in combination. They are listed as, 1) the rejection of God; 2) the refusal to allow God's influence; and 3) not being thankful for what He has provided and done for them. The results are vain imaginations, darkened hearts, and the false belief that though they are fools they believe themselves to be smart.

The biggest fool in the world is the fool that fools himself. Our soldierly mission is not only to exercise the five strategies listed above in our own lives but to apply these to others that they may be set free. The condition of the world right now is not much different than the condition in Genesis:

> *"And GOD saw that the **wickedness of man was great in the earth**, and that **every imagination of the thoughts of his heart was only evil continually**.*
>
> *And it repented the LORD that he had made man on the earth, and it grieved him at his heart."*   (Genesis 5:5-6)

5. One who pleases his Enlisting and Commanding Officer

> *"No man that warreth entangleth himself with the affairs of this life; **that he may please him who hath chosen him to be a soldier**."*
>
>   (2 Timothy 2:4)

Imagine for a moment, this reality: what you and I do can actually affect God. GOD! GOD!! Bring pleasure to God? Seriously? Nothing can be as solemn as this truth. Nothing! God has a great investment in you. He not only Fathered you but endowed you with giftings, with an ENA.

You are not an automaton, a robot, a mechanical preprogrammed contrivance without active intelligence and creativity, or a machine that resembles and is able to simulate the actions of a human being without actually being one. You are not an android. We are not ruled as animals by instinct. Animals are very limited, confined to embedded impulses and promptings.

There are only three kinds of creation: inanimate, animate, and moral beings.

The animate kingdom is defined as having life and the power of movement or self-locomotion. How is it ruled? You probably guessed it right... by instinct. They are impelled internally, infused with an animating principle that rules their behaviors... so beavers build dams but not automobiles. They are ruled by instinct; thus their behaviors are knowable and predictable.

The third type of creation is that of moral beings, possessing a spirit, a personhood, imaged after God with the ability to create or destroy, bless or curse, do right or do wrong, do good or do evil. How does God rule moral beings? The answer is by moral suasion which is the act of exhorting or encouraging behavior choices by setting consequences of choice. Do this right thing, you will be blessed. Do this wrong thing and you will be cursed. Mankind is generally given an allotted time to make righteous decisions. In fact, mankind has been provided with redemption and recovery from past wrong choices and then empowered by God to go on doing what is right all the time, every time. This we call redemption, which He wrought in Christ by death and resurrection and the sending of His Holy Spirit to empower.

The moral suasion method of control ultimately leads to an eternal destination. There will be a final adjudication of all men. It will be a permanent declaration enforcing the effectiveness of moral suasion. If properly responded... heaven and eternal rewards! If Christ's redemption has been rejected... hell and eternal damnation. But each of us *gets to choose!* And what does heaven do? Rejoice!

> *"I say unto you, there is joy in the presence*
> *of the angels of God over one sinner that*
> *repenteth."* (Luke 15:10)

I am sorry to have to report to you that many theologians support the views of determinism, a philosophical doctrine that human action is not free but necessarily predetermined by either external forces or embedded programming. Then, they blame God for the predetermining. Can you imagine the blasphemy of such an idea... God predetermining specific people to hell... predetermined and programmed to be evil and then held accountable and damnable for doing that which in advance He programmed them to do? What a shame that God should be so misrepresented. It's an absurd slur against the justice of God, the holiness of God, and the love of God.

Did God create the earth? Intelligent people will respond with a hearty "yes," because if there is a creation there must be a Creator. Next question... Did God create the *idea* to create the earth. Most will affirm a "yes," though they may not understand the implications of asserting that God created the *idea* to create the earth. If He created the *idea* to create the earth then there was a time when the idea did not exist.

Pity those trapped with a false concept of God... a God who can think no new thoughts, experience no new feelings, who cannot create but merely carries out in duration of time ideas of which He is not the author. This is fatalism applied to the infinite.

Oh Beloved! Realize you can please God or contrarily disappoint the Commanding Officer of your soul. *"Without faith it is impossible to please Him..."* (Hebrews 11:6).

> *"Furthermore then we beseech you, brethren,*
> *and exhort you by the Lord Jesus, that as ye*
> *have received of us how ye ought to walk and*

> *to please God, so ye would abound more and*
> *more.*"
> (1 Thessalonians 4:1)

6. One who masters appropriate principles needed in Christian soldiership

> *"And if a man also **strive for masteries**, yet is*
> *he not crowned, except he **strive lawfully**."*
> (2 Timothy 2:5)

> *"...if anyone enters competitive games, he*
> *is not crowned unless he competes lawfully*
> *(fairly, **according to the rules laid down**)."*
> (2 Timothy 2:5 PHILLIPS)

A rule is a code of discipline or a body of regulations. Here's the short version... God's work must be done God's way! Christian soldiership cannot be carried out apart from strict observance to Our Master's laws of action. We must *"strive lawfully!"* There can be no breaking or bending of the rules. Lawfully means "in accordance with the laws or rules set down." A rule is "a code of discipline, a body of regulations."

> *"...**according to the measure of the rule***
> *which God hath distributed to us. (We) simply*
> *judge ourselves **by that line of duty which***
> ***God has marked out for us**."*
> (2 Corinthians 10:13 PHILLIPS)

So what is that measure, that rule or body of regulations by which the Christian soldier **must** operate? The answer is simply Christlikeness! We are to represent (re-present) Christ. To represent Christ means we must be qualified and entitled to act and speak on His behalf. Our motives, attitudes, words and actions must be compliant to Christ Himself and His likeness. His deportment must be our deportment; His demeanor, our demeanor!

God has determined that we be Christlike all the time and most particularly whenever we represent Him. The Apostle declared, *"I travail... until Christ be formed in you"* (Galatians 4:19). This is the essence and distinction conveyed upon us:

> *"Now then we are ambassadors for Christ, as though God did beseech you by us:"*
> (2 Corinthians 5:20)

Imagine...we are acting, talking as Christ's personal representatives. Thus we must not vaguely resemble Him but be careful, precise reproductions conforming with strict detail and correctness to Christ's character.

To be painfully truthful with you, I am amazed that Jesus has survived the massive misrepresentations of Him. How many have heard it, "If that's what a Christian is like... I don't want to be one." It would be far too painful to spend pen and paragraph time depicting the false representations of Jesus. How has He survived such fabrications, falsifications, adulterations, and distortions? The answer is because "He Is Alive!"

Jesus is the personification of love, purity, virtue and all holy characteristics. We soldiers must be endowed likewise in order to carry out the war. We must master the principles of God. The essential skills of Christian soldiership are about character! Character has to do with indelible qualities of consistent holy and moral convictions imbedded in the heart, soul and mind of the Christian. Convictions are not for sale. They cannot be enticed, allured or attracted away by offers of pleasure, or advantage. Here are a few of the vitals:*

• Truthfulness vs. Deception
• Loyalty vs. Unfaithfulness
• Obedience vs. Willfulness
• Sincerity vs. Hypocrisy

- Love vs. Selfishness
- Endurance vs. Giving up
- Determination vs. Faint-heartedness
- Discretion vs. Simple-mindedness
- Boldness vs. Timidity
- Sensitivity vs. Callousness
- Cautiousness vs. Rashness
- Tolerance vs. Prejudice
- Meekness vs. Anger
- Availability vs. Self-centeredness
- Decisiveness vs. Double-mindedness
- Punctuality vs. Tardiness
- Wisdom vs. Natural Inclinations
- Compassion vs. Indifference
- Humility vs. Pride
- Persuasiveness vs. Contentiousness
- Contentment vs. Covetousness
- Alertness vs. Unawareness
- Enthusiasm vs. Apathy
- Discernment vs. Judgmentalism
- Patience vs. Restlessness
- Forgiveness vs. Rejection
- Faith vs. Presumption
- Diligence vs. Slothfulness
- Responsibility vs. Unreliability
- Deference vs. Rudeness
- Thankfulness vs. Ungratefulness
- Self-Control vs. Self-indulgence
- Gentleness vs. Harshness
- Reverence vs. Disrespect

- Dependability vs. Inconsistency
- Thoroughness vs. Incompleteness
- Orderliness vs. Disorganization
- Joyfulness vs. Self-pity
- Resourcefulness vs. Wastefulness
- Thriftiness vs. Extravagance
- Generosity vs. Stinginess
- Virtue vs. Impurity
- Attentiveness vs. Unconcern

*These character qualities are further defined and detailed at IBLP.com.

7. One who has spiritual military smarts

"Wisdom is better than strength."

(Ecclesiastes 9:16)

"Wisdom is better than weapons of war: but one sinner destroyeth much good."

(Ecclesiastes 9:18)

It's very true that we are in the fight of our lives. In fact, it's the fight of eternity! The stakes could not be higher because the results of good or evil, true or false, heaven or hell are certain. Destinies are being determined now, nine plus billion of them! The battle rages; the war is on!

Why are we targeted? To keep us out of the war! Missing in Action (MIA). The enemy certainly wants us destroyed, but he is happy to incapacitate us, keep us on the sidelines, preoccupied and absent without leave (AWOL).

Part of the enemy's strategy is to give us a false sense of inferiority; make us feel unfit, incapable, deprived of capacity and disqualified. After all, who am I? That's how Moses responded when asked by God to lead the Jewish nation out of Egyptian bondage:

> *"And Moses said unto the Lord, O my Lord, I am not eloquent...but I am slow of speech, and of a slow tongue."*　　　　(Exodus 4:10)

Are you ready for God's response? It's the same answer he will give you and I.

> *"And the LORD said unto him, Who hath made man's mouth? or who maketh the dumb, or deaf, or the seeing, or the blind? have not I the LORD?*
>
> *Now therefore go, and I will be with thy mouth, **and teach thee what thou shalt say;"***
>
> 　　　　(Exodus 4:11-12)

The false inferiority complexes and sense of inadequacies comes from the unawareness of the "God Factor." Please don't be perturbed when I tell you this, but we, in a shocking sense, have become practical theists. We *believe in God: "In God We Trust."* It's on our license plates, part of our Oath of Allegiance, the official motto of the United States of America. Ever since President Dwight D. Eisenhower, "In God We Trust" has been printed on all paper and coin currency. *E pluribus unum!* But do we? Is God really functional in our day to day living, thinking, decision-making, treatment of one another? Do we live without the God Factor?"

An angel visited the boy farmer, Gideon, to deliver God's faith in him declaring, *"The Lord is with thee, **thou mighty man of valour"*** (Judges 6:12). Gideon voiced his doubts so God by-passed the angel and spoke directly to him:

> *"And the Lord looked upon him, and said, **Go in this thy might**, and thou shalt save Israel."*
>
> 　　　　(Judges 6:14)

Can you guess Gideon's response?

> *"And he said unto him, Oh my Lord, wherewith shall I save Israel? Behold **my***

family is poor…and I am the least in my
father's house." (Judges 6:15)

Dear Reader, it's time for you and I to fess up. What would we have said to God? Better question is, what are we going to God about now regarding the battle before us? I hope we join Gideon's response on getting over our fake inferiorities. Let's learn from Gideon, then we'll go direct to Jesus for the same right answer.

"And the Lord said unto him, **Surely I will be**
with thee…" (Judges 6:16)

God enters the picture affirming, *"I will be with thee…"* Here's how the war had shaped up:

Enemy Soldiers: 120,000

Gideon's Soldiers: 32,000

The **"God Factor"**? Gideon you've got too many soldiers. Your 32,000 are too many even though your enemy has 120,000 soldiers. Send home the fearful. *"And there returned of the people twenty and two thousand; and there remained ten thousand."* Here's the field of battle update:

Enemy Soldiers: 120,000

Gideon's Soldiers: ~~32,000~~

Gideon's Soldiers: 10,000

It gets perceptively worse. God says, *"And the LORD said unto Gideon, The people are yet too many; bring them down unto the water, and I will try them for thee there: Out of the ten thousand only three hundred drank with watchful eyes."* And God says, send the rest home. Battlefield update:

Enemy Soldiers 120,000

Gideon's Soldiers: ~~32,000~~

Gideon's Soldiers: ~~10,000~~

Gideon's Soldiers: 300

And he and God and a mere 300 soldiers took on the 120,000 numbered enemy and won! You can read the God strategy and the outcome in Judges 7:12-22.

The God Factor means the numbers don't count! Don't look at the numbers! Don't be overcome looking at the world situation. Be not dismayed! Don't give up! *"There is no restraint to the Lord to save by many or by few"* (1 Samuel 14:6). With just two men plus God, Johnathan and his armor bearer defeated a whole garrison, 500 stationed soldiers.

> **"There is no restraint to the Lord to save by many or by few."**　　　(1 Samuel 14:6)

Now let's see what Jesus says about soldier smarts, the God Factor, and you and me:

> *"Behold, I send you forth as sheep in the midst of wolves: be ye therefore wise as serpents, and harmless as doves."*　　　(Matthew 10:16)

Go ahead, say yikes! If you and I are going to be in the midst of wolves you'd think the Lord would want us to be bears, mountain lions, pumas, catamounts, or cougars who are the only animals that are the known enemies of wolves. Nope! No such natural advantage! Just a sheep?

Sheep are not known for their conquering ability. The Master must have some real military smarts to give us sheep. In order to save some time and space but not lose accuracy, I'm taking a brief departure from my preferred addiction to the King James Version. I never do so if another translation ever adds to, takes from, or confuses the authenticity of the KJV. So here goes:

> *"Stay alert. This is hazardous work I'm assigning you. You're going to be like sheep running through a wolf pack, so don't call attention to yourselves. Be as cunning as a snake, inoffensive as a dove.Don't be naive.*

*Some people will impugn your motives, others
will smear your reputation—just because
you believe in me. Don't be upset when they
haul you before the civil authorities. Without
knowing it, they've done you—and me—a
favor, given you a platform for preaching the
kingdom news! And don't worry about what
you'll say or how you'll say it. The right
words will be there; the Spirit of your Father
will supply the words.   When people realize
it is the living God you are presenting and
not some idol that makes them feel good,
they are going to turn on you, even people in
your own family. There is a great irony here:
proclaiming so much love, experiencing so
much hate! But don't quit. Don't cave in. It is
all well worth it in the end. It is not success
you are after in such times but survival. Be
survivors! Before you've run out of options,
the Son of Man will have arrived."*

(Matthew 10:16-23 MSG)

We hardly need commentary for the Scriptures speak so clearly for themselves. It's all about the God Factor, all the time every time. The God Factor gets us out of every inkling or even a hint or slight intimation of a sense of inferiority or inadequacy. Whatever we lack, He makes up: *"our sufficiency is of God"* (2 Corinthians 3:5).

Don't let Satan or anyone in your life tell by intimation or outright declaration that you are in any way personally deficient:

*"And God is able to make all grace abound
toward you; that **ye, always having all
sufficiency in all things**, may abound to every
good work:"*   (2 Corinthians 9:8)

Our efficiency may seem like deficiency until we realize we have His sufficiency. Get the facts about you straight. Walk with your head up but not your nose. This is so important to your recovery from past abuses (including self-abuses), your present mental, emotional, spiritual, and social health and your future that we need to linger a moment longer to be sure we've got it!

We go now to where one should always go to find the answers, the truth about life!

> *"For ye see your calling, brethren, how that*
> *not many wise men after the flesh, not many*
> *mighty, not many noble, are called:*
>
> *But God hath chosen the foolish things of*
> *the world to confound the wise; and God*
> *hath chosen the weak things of the world to*
> *confound the things which are mighty;*
>
> *And base things of the world, and things*
> *which are despised, hath God chosen, yea, and*
> *things which are not, to bring to nought things*
> *that are:*
>
> *That no flesh should glory in his presence.*
>
> *But of him are ye in Christ Jesus, who of God*
> *is made unto us wisdom, and righteousness,*
> *and sanctification, and redemption:*
>
> *That, according as it is written, He that*
> *glorieth, let him glory in the Lord."*
>
> (1 Corinthians 1:26-31)

Let's make sure we read where such glorying by us is in writing. Here it is:

> *"Thus saith the LORD, Let not the wise man*
> *glory in his wisdom, neither let the mighty*
> *man glory in his might, let not the rich man*
> *glory in his riches:*

*But let him that glorieth glory in this, that
he understandeth and knoweth me, that I am
the LORD which exercise lovingkindness,
judgment, and righteousness, in the earth: for
in these things I delight, saith the LORD."*

(Jeremiah 9:23-24)

Knowing and counting on God makes you spiritually militarily smart! This is why the primary instruction to us is, *"Finally, my brethren, be strong in the Lord, and in the power of his might"* (Ephesians 6:10). Function in tune and under the power of the God Factor. And what is the God Factor? God Himself!

8. **One who applies the principles of soldiership to his or her Embedded Natural Ability (ENA)**

Every person has an Embedded Natural Ability given to them by their Heavenly Father before they were even born. These are referred to as Spiritual Gifts, seven in number, found in Romans 12:3-8. The full details of this subject and how you can discover your personal ENA can be found in the last half of the book, *Why You Were Born*, which I have written. (Go to www.NothingButTheTruth.org.) Crucial information for anyone wishing to know their purpose in life and the path to life fulfillment.

When you know your gifting, or your Embedded Natural Ability, you will:

- Know your purpose in life
- Know God's will for your life
- Have boundless energy
- Be relaxed just being your real self
- Have fulfillment in life
- Understand your personal worth and value
- Will be stable the rest of your life
- Have direction for personal development

- Be able to choose appropriate vocations
- Be successful and rewarded by God

The seven-fold categorical summary of ENAs are as follows. Remember that joy in life come from discovering your specific gift or ENA, developing it and using it for the highest good. The list mostly includes the King James wording in parentheses:

- Messengers (Proclaiming)
- Helpers (Serving)
- Explainers (Teaching)
- Encouragers (Exhorting)
- Providers (Giving)
- Administrators (Ruling)
- Caregivers (Showing Mercy)

Oh Beloved, you'll never know how much I wish for you to know all the details on how to discover your ENA. You will never know how important you really are without this discovery. The best I could do was to write it in detail (*Why You Were Born*) and also make it available on Audible (https://www.audible.com/pd/Why-You-Were-Born-Audiobook/B08WWJQVDN).

The question here, however, is why and how should soldiership be applied to one's ENA. So let's attempt a definition of soldiership, especially when you consider that we are an Army of Compassion.

Soldiership: Soldiership does not consist, as Wordsworth well said, in "vanity and brainless rage" (*The Task, Book IV*). *The Oxford English Dictionary* merely defines *soldiership* as "a state or condition of being a soldier; the qualities of being a soldier." Unfortunately it is difficult to find a list of the qualities or a description of the condition. The Articles of War are a set of regulations drawn up to govern the conduct of a country's military forces. They are general standards requiring Humanitarian Notification, protection of medical institutions, understanding self-defense and laws of armed conflict, legitimate uses of weaponry, terms of treaty and such like.

To discover a reasonable definition of soldiery, and particularly Christian soldiery, I recommend the reading of the original *Orders and Regulations of the Salvation Army*. It's an impressive 260 page read. Among the prestigious books of my library you could find a short collection of "Army" books with chapter titles like *The Fight Against Formality, Army Making, Army Leading, Desperate Fighting,* and *The Spirit of the Army*. In short, the Army "requires every soldier to give up the use of intoxicants; to keep from any binding habits, company, or language that would be harmful; and to devote all of their leisure time, spare energy and money to the War."

Our mission is not casual. We are in a desperate fight. Every person's life can only go upward from the Cross of Christ. Well-being is at stake. Sanctified sanity is at stake. Eternity is at stake.

Soldiership discipline and the principles thereof must be applied to each ENA. Thus we will have:

• Soldier Messengers (Proclaiming)
• Soldier Helpers (Serving)
• Soldier Explainers (Teaching)
• Soldier Encouragers (Exhorting)
• Soldier Providers (Giving)
• Soldier Administrators (Ruling)
• Soldier Care Givers (Showing Mercy)

There will be an army of love with disciplined persons, each in possession of an ENA with the personally ascribed privilege and duty of using such to win the invisible war.

9. One who endures hardships

> *"Thou therefore **endure hardness, as a good soldier of Jesus Christ.**"*   (2 Timothy 2:3)

In these days of *macho* manhood, genuine strength and toughness has been skewed into a pompous, narcissistic, fake, proud, dominating, aggressive and exaggerated sense of masculinity; a lot of posturing, flexing and big talk. *Macho* is a Spanish word meaning "male animal."

In contrast with this fake manliness, *hardness* means tough, tenacious, not fragile nor easily broken, capable of endurance, not easily tired or impaired. It means hardy, stout, sturdy; having great intellectual, moral, and spiritual endurance. It includes being steadfast, firm, and persistent.

The singular finest outline of this Christian hardness is given to us right out of the Scriptures. Here they are, the characteristics of *hardness* as defined by Scripture!

Giving no offence in any thing that the ministry be not blamed:

We do not offend anyone at any time. Jesus made it plain when He said, *"It is impossible but that offences will come: but woe unto him, through whom they come! It were better for him that a millstone were hanged about his neck, and he cast into the sea, than that he should offend one of these little ones"* (Luke 17:1-2).

Beloved it takes hardness, toughness and discipline not to offend others, any others. And the truth is that no matter what they say or do to us we are not offended. As the Scriptures say of us who love living by the certain laws of God, *"Great peace have they which love thy law: and nothing shall offend them"* (Psalm 119:165). Nothing, absolutely nothing, that others say or do can break through our toughness and cause us to react.

But in all things approving ourselves as the ministers of God,

To live as "ministers of God" means that we exactingly represent God and do so *"in all things."*

In much patience,

Patience is not a waste of time. It's a slowdown zone and a time of contemplation and assessment readying ourselves for the wise, proper timing of a precise bona fide action.

In afflictions,

Soldiers suffer afflictions, which are the inflictions of pain, misery or distress. *"Beloved, think it not strange concerning the fiery trial which is to try you, as though some strange thing happened unto you: But rejoice, inasmuch as ye are partakers of Christ's sufferings; that, when his glory shall be revealed, ye may be glad also with exceeding joy. If ye be reproached for the name of Christ, happy are ye; for the spirit of glory and of God resteth upon you"* (1 Peter 4:12-14). Hardness enables us to stand strong during afflictions.

We soldiers of Christ are not wimpy, frail, delicate, or feeble. We are hard. We understand the mission includes afflictions: *"Many are the afflictions of the righteous: but the LORD delivereth him out of them all"* (Psalm 34:19).

In necessities,

We can do without. In times when the basics are not available, we soldiers keep going. This is another feature of soldier hardness.

In distresses,

Pressure and strain phase us not. Adversity, trouble, sickness, pain, sorrow or anguish that otherwise would affect body, soul or spirit are endured because of soldier hardness.

In stripes,

Punishments by the enemy are a part of the war. Yes, even beatings, physical, verbal, mental, emotional and even spiritual must sometimes be endured. Remember, *"Endure hardness as a good soldier of Jesus Christ."*

In imprisonments,

I have personally visited the Roman prison that held Peter captive. I entered the prison (at least the remains of which) that held the Apostle Paul. I felt the awesomeness of their character that didn't merely sustain them in prison but fired them up to sing on and preach on. What happened? *"And the prisoners heard them. And suddenly there was a great earthquake..."* You need to read the whole drama. Talk about a prison ministry. The "keeper of the prison" tried to commit suicide. Paul stopped him... end of story... the keeper cried, *"What must I do to be saved?"* (Read the story in Acts 16:22-40.)

But imprisonment of Christians is not limited historically to the first century. It is a present-day reality in many countries around the world. And the imprisonment of genuine Christians **is coming to America!** The good guys are becoming the targets. Why? The spiritual wickedness in high places is not merely propagating but demanding agreement, acceptance and compliance to a montage of perversions. When we stand or speak up for righteousness we will be condemned as spreading hate speech. I suggest that if we are imprisoned, we start a prison ministry.

In tumults,

Tumults are public disturbances, commotions by multitudes, uproars, and disorderly rioting. Speeches are designed to stir up agitations and violent emotions. Loudness and confusion abound. Have you checked the news lately? Tumults abound.

In labours,

Christian soldiers often to have to work hard, work long, and work late. Hardness required!

In watchings,

A father was admonishing his daughter to close her eyes while praying. She responded saying, "But Dad, the Bible says we should 'watch and pray.'"

Watching means intentionally staying awake and alert, vigilant and on guard against danger or unexpected intrusions. It simply means to be on the lookout, keeping situations in sight, watching to be aware of any movement or change in order to respond appropriately. It includes being alert to opportunities as well.

In fastings;

Fasting means to abstain from food and sometimes drink. There are two kinds of fasts: voluntary and involuntary. Voluntary fasts are divided into two types, each of which is defined by motive. The soldier must understand Isaiah 58:5-14 which declares in detail the consequences of fasting for selfish reasons versus the benefits of the fast that God chooses.

By purity,

Purity means without mixture, unadulterated, untainted. Pure gold, for example, has no other metals melded in. 14K gold is alloyed with 58.3% gold and 41.7% other metals such as copper, zinc, silver and nickel. 18K gold is 75% gold and 25% other metals. 24K gold is 100% gold with no other metals mixed in.

The Christian soldier must be like 24K gold, no mixture of good and evil, right and wrong. He or she is true from center to circumference and brooks no compromises whatsoever. Any compromise by us embodies peril, hazard, and danger. This is the reason the Scriptures, the soldier's marching orders, declare unequivocally, *"Neither give place to the devil"* (Ephesians 4:27). No place! Zero! It takes hardness to disallow anyone under any circumstances to input or infuse any elements of compromise that destroy purity.

By knowledge,

Knowledge is the apprehension of facts or truth, a clear and certain perception of such in both heart and mind. 100% accuracy is necessary. It's the reason God asked Job, *"Who is this that darkeneth counsel by words without knowledge?"* (Job 38:2). The Christian soldier must forever be alert to assure that the knowledge he or she acts on has not been *darkened* by the enemy.

The major contamination of knowledge comes from iniquity, which is the biblical word for narcissism. *"Have all the workers of iniquity no knowledge?"* (Psalm 14:4 and 53:4). Narcissism, ego dominance, and selfishness contaminates thinking. Its self-centered agenda overrides, twists, and spins one's point of view to favor its agenda. For example, college professors teach "no God" concepts as if they were true. Why would anyone in their right mine conclude that there can be a creation without a Creator? The answer: by eliminating God everyone can do what they want without restraint because there's no one to whom they will be accountable. Intellectual suicide!

By longsuffering,

Suffering, especially longsuffering, requires hardness. More than that, it requires love, for we learn in the Bible that *"love suffers long"* (1 Corinthians 13:4). Love returns us to our motive, our mission, our manner, and to the *modus operandi* of the Christian soldier.

By kindness,

Isn't this a distinguishing element in the army of compassion, the *agape* love force, the Army of the Lord? We Christian soldiers are gentle and tender towards the victims of evil, the captives we seek to set free. The remainder of the verse cited above is this: *"Love suffers long and is kind."* We are tough and tender.

By the Holy Ghost,

Make no mistake about this imperative… the authority, accompaniment, leadership and empowerment of the Spirit of Christ, the Holy Spirit, the Spirit of Truth. Jesus made it plain, *"He dwelleth with you and shall be in you"* (John 14:17). The Christian soldier knows, as P.T. Forsyth so accurately said, that "unless there is within us that which is above us, we shall soon yield to that which is around us." So what has this to do with the hardness of the soldier? Answer: following the Holy Spirit requires the rejection of any and every other spirit, emotion or influence that contradicts or contravenes the leadership of the Spirit. That takes hardness.

By love unfeigned,

It is possible to *show* love without really loving. It's about the essence not merely the mechanics—love without trickery! Not pretended! Not simulated but rather honest, sincere, genuine, true and real. And how shall we define this *agape* love? How about this? "The relentless caring pursuit of the highest possible good for God, His Creation and every person in every situation until it becomes a present tense reality!"

Why does true love require toughness? Because we must resist manipulation, the enemy of realism, veracity and fidelity.

By the word of truth,

This is also referred to as *"the Sword of the Spirit."* It is the chief weapon of the Christian soldier. The hardness of the soldier lies in this: he or she must resist the use of any alternative measures that would replace or usurp the power of God's Word. Here's why: *"For the Word that God speaks is alive and active; it cuts more keenly than any two-edged sword: it strikes through to the place where soul and spirit meet, to the innermost intimacies of a man's being: it exposes the very thoughts and motives of a man's heart"* (Hebrews 4:11 PHILLIPS).

By the power of God,

No other energy is capable of defeating the evil unseen enemies or delivering the captives who are held hostage at the will of our adversary. The soldier must *"Be sober, be vigilant; because your adversary the devil, as a roaring lion, walketh about, seeking whom he may devour: Whom resist steadfast in the faith..."* (1 Peter 5:8-9).

Following the seriousness that must attend the soldier there must come sufficient power to overthrow the enemy and to persuade the captives to come to freedom. Thus the need for the power of God which is given to us.

by the armour of righteousness on the right hand and on the left,

In ancient times soldiers were trained to use the sword in their right hand and the shield in their left hand... the right hand for offense and the left hand for defense. One should comprehensively review the seven pieces of armor given to the Christian soldier, in chapter six of Ephesians.

By honor and dishonor,

It is easier to live with kudos, praise and accolades. The Christian soldier might get some of that from his or her comrades. But the enemy will attempt to dishonor the genuine Christian. Thus we must endure the hardness of the dishonor, rejection, and even mockery. If the enemy speaks well of us, it is either a trap or we're not being viewed as their opponents at all. Soldier: do not expect honor from the enemy. You are their target! It is sufficient to be honored by God, for the Master Himself said, *"How can ye believe, which receive honor one of another, and seek not the honor that cometh from God only?"* (John 5:44).

By evil report and good report:

To be quite frank, soldiers should not care about the opinions of others. If you or I live to make others have good opinions of us, we will be prisoners the rest of our lives, slaves to what people think or say or report. Never had the church so much power over the world as when it had nothing to do with the world. Now contemporary, fake Christianity seeks the approval and adulation of the world. The truth is there is only one opinion of me that matters. This is the meaning of, *"Who art thou that judgest another man's servant? To his own master he standeth or falleth"* (Romans 14:4).

We soldiers may have to endure evil reports of us and we must beware: *"Woe unto you, when all men shall speak well of you! for so did their fathers to the false prophets"* (Luke 6:26).

As deceivers, and yet true;

We might get falsely branded, tagged, marked, and stigmatized. Now our soldiership and hardness is at its finest in returning good for evil, and as the Scripture says, *"Not rendering evil for evil, or railing for railing: but contrariwise blessing"* (1 Peter 3:9). We simply keep living God's way, and few if anybody at all will believe what is said against us. However, *"if ye suffer for righteousness' sake, happy are ye: and be not afraid of their terror, neither be troubled"* (1 Peter 3:14).

Because of the present narcissistic culture of dog-eat-dog behaviors much needs to be firmly grasped when faced with this variety of slander. *"For it is better... that we suffer for well doing, than for evil doing"* (1 Peter 3:17). The Captain of our salvation provided an adequate model for us to follow: *"Who, when he was reviled, reviled not again; when he suffered, he threatened not; but committed himself to him that judgeth righteously"* (1 Peter 2:23).

As unknown, and yet well known;

There are two snares; the fear of man and the praise of man. Each and both of them will cause contortions in our behaviors. *"The fear of man bringeth a snare:*

but whoso putteth his trust in the LORD shall be safe" (Proverbs 29:25). We live indifferent to the popularity cult where everyone seeks to be higher and better than others. *"Do I seek to please men? for if I yet pleased men, I should not be the servant of Christ"* (Galatians 1:10).

As dying, and, behold, we live;

A paradox is a statement that seems to say opposite things but may be true. Here's one: Death brings forth life. A seed must fall into the ground and die before it can bring forth life. The seed rots because of alternating rain, sunshine, dew, shine. When the outside rots or dies, only then can the life that is in it grow forth. The crucifixion of our old narcissistic self allows life, real life, to spring forth. Hardness for the soldier, like all of us, is to let go of the old to receive the new. Jesus said, *"Whosoever will save his life shall lose it: and whosever shall lose his life for my sake and the gospel's shall save it"* (Mark 8:35).

As chastened, and not killed;

To *00* means to correct, discipline, for the purpose of moral improvement. May not seem like a pleasant endeavor to be on the receiving end. It certainly doesn't placate the ego. But who in their right mind would object to being corrected and adjusted if they were heading towards damaging consequences? We see here the need for hardness so that our ways can be amended. Especially to prevent our being killed.

As sorrowful, yet always rejoicing;

There is much sorrow. Who can measure the painful tears being shed around the world like the flowing of the mighty Niagara? Suffering, disappointment, grief, sadness, regret, affliction, trouble, sickness, disease, abuse, and the list goes on and on. We are to be a compassionate army just like Jesus who was *"touched with the feelings of our infirmities"* (Hebrews 4:15). But in spite of this sadness we maintain our mental and emotional posture of rejoicing. The darkness cannot put out the light. We, God's Love Force: we take what we are and have and deliver it to the hurting world.

As poor, yet making many rich;

It has been said, mo' money – mo' problems; mo' money – mo' wants; mo' money – mo' work; mo' money – mo' isolation; mo' money – mo' dissatisfaction. This may not be true of everyone, but I've known a lot of poor rich men: lots of money but broken marriages, broken health, and broken relationships. As wisdom says, *"But they that will be rich fall into temptation and a snare, and into many foolish and hurtful lusts, which drown men in destruction and perdition. For the love of money is the root of all evil: which while some coveted after, they have erred from the faith, and pierced themselves through with many sorrows"* (1 Timothy 6:9-10). It takes hardness for the soldier to say no to temptations.

To be truly rich is to know God and godly people; to know truth and follow it. *"Better is the poor that walketh in his uprightness, than he that is perverse in his ways, though he be rich"* (Proverbs 28:6). The personal economics of the soldier is virtually irrelevant. Our business is to make people truly rich.

As having nothing, and yet possessing all things.

I've never seen a hearse pulling a U-Haul. Job said, *"Naked came I out of my mother's womb, and naked shall I return thither"* (Job 1:21). The Christian soldier is tough enough to say no to the materialism of the day,

"For what shall it profit a man, if he shall gain the whole world, and lose his own soul?" (Mark 8:36). To covet, to clutch, to grasp and come up empty; what a tragedy! In contrast, we have the words of eternal life. As Jesus said, *"I am the resurrection, and the life: he that believeth in me, though he were dead, yet shall he live: And whosoever liveth and believeth in me shall never die"* (John 11:25-26). We've got the goods! (2 Corinthians 6:3-10)

This is the toughness that empowers us to be tender towards others. Our hardness enables us to absorb undeserved punishments in order to live love back even to the instigators. We soldiers overcome evil with good because we endure hardness as good soldiers of Jesus Christ!

10. **One who targets the enemies in order to free their captives**

And how do we do that? Answers:

A. **Know your enemy**

> *"For we wrestle not against flesh and blood, but against principalities, against powers, against the rulers of the darkness of this world, against spiritual wickedness in high places."* (Ephesians 6:12)

B. **The invisible enemies of man**

C. **The enemy has a hierarchical structure**
   i. Principalities (spiritual organizations)
   ii. Powers
   iii. Rulers of darkness
   iv. Spiritual wickedness in high places

Principalities are evil spirits who have been assigned a jurisdiction, a district, a region, a territory, or a position of responsibility in Satan's kingdom. But here's the good news, Jesus is, *"Far above all principality, and power, and might, and dominion, and every name that is named, not only in this world, but also in that which is to come"* (Ephesians 1:21).

Powers refers to evil spirits with specific capacities who carry out the commands and demands of the Principalities. For example, *"the spirit of an unclean devil"* (Like 4:33) and a *"spirit of infirmity"* (Luke 13:11) and a *"spirit of divination"* (Acts 16:16). And again, the good news in the above Scripture is that Jesus Christ is far above the Powers as well as the Principalities.

Rulers of the darkness of this world rule over every aspect of the dark sides. Dark side is an idiom referring to the evil and malevolent, malicious, spiteful, hostile, evil-minded that are motivated to harm others. For example, in present day culture we have the Dark Side, Dark Dealings, Dark Money, the Dark Web, Dark Psychology, and Dark Religion. Even contemporary Christianity has been invaded by darkness—darkness that pretends and poses as light.

> *"For such are false apostles, deceitful workers, **transforming themselves into the apostles of Christ.***
>
> *And no marvel; for **Satan himself is transformed into an angel of light.***
>
> *Therefore it is no great thing if his ministers also be **transformed as the ministers of righteousness**; whose end shall be according to their works. "* (2 Corinthians 11:13-15)

Fake Christianity is everywhere. Pulpits are filled by disguised evil leadership. The institutionalized church has done their market analysis and found out what the people want and offers it to them as Christ. Standards of God and of Scripture are either ignored or explained away. They have made Christianity into an agent of narcissism.

Spiritual wickedness in high places: These spirits are the leaders and have set their sights on human authorities, kings, presidents, cabinet members, governors, senators, congressmen, mayors, corporate giants and all levels of domination. It's a simple strategy. As the leaders go, so will go the people. Perhaps this is one of the reasons we are implored by God as a high priority, *"...first of all, supplications, prayers, intercessions and giving of thanks be made for all men; for kings, and for all that are in authority"* (1 Timothy 2:1-4).

There is a principle in corporate management "Attitudes cascade downwards." Subordinates become like the leaders they follow. From the top down is a management principle. And here is the crux of the matter. All mankind is under assault from evil spiritual powers as well as from corrupt political, educational, corporate, and religious governance.

From the human point of view, international, world and cultural turmoil have one primary cause... the spiritually wicked rulers who are what they are because they reject the Lord God. Here's the proof and it is so important that I want you to see it in two translations:

Why do the heathen rage, and the people imagine a vain thing?

> *"The kings of the earth **set themselves, and the rulers take counsel together, against the LORD, and against his anointed,** saying, Let us break their bands asunder, and cast away their cords from us.'"*   (Psalm 2:1-3)

> *"What fools the nations are to rage against
> the Lord! How strange that men should try
> to outwit God! For **a summit conference of
> the nations has been called** to plot against
> the Lord and his Messiah, Christ the King.
> 'Come, let us break his chains,' they say, 'and
> free ourselves from all this slavery to God.'"*
>
> (Psalm 2:1-3 TLB)

Welcome to America and the United Nations.

Mankind has been kidnapped.

People are not our enemies. They are victims, hunted down, manipulated, coerced into compliance, pushed and pressured by propaganda, compelled to comply and yes, have even joined up and enlisted as perpetrators themselves. And now they are found guilty.

It is for them that we fight. There is no salvation for the devil. Why? Because he, along with other angels, fell from an eternal height and eternal perspective and they made an eternal decision. Their decision was final. There is no recovery for them. No place of repentance!

We fight these spiritual powers in order to free the kidnapped and now imprisoned. They are all sons and daughters of their heavenly Father, the Almighty. They are royalty of the highest order. They, like us, were born into royalty. We were fathered in. It's the plain assertion of Scripture:

> *"Unto him that loved us, and washed us from
> our sins in his own blood, And **hath made us
> kings** and priests unto God and his Father; to
> him be glory and dominion for ever and ever.
> Amen."* (Revelation 1:5-6)

Jesus is the King of Kings. We all know that! But who are the kings over which He is the King? You and I! However, most of humanity has been kidnapped. They've been gone so long they have no idea that they were born royalty, a King under God. They have been abducted, and thoroughly brainwashed (actually mind-polluted) that they have accommodated themselves to their bondage. So let us be clear about our mission.

11. One who is clear on the rescue mission

Our mission is to target and overcome the enemies which bind them, and that's the easy part, because we have been authorized and empowered by the Lord Himself who said:

> *"Behold, **I give unto you power** to tread on serpents and scorpions, and **over all the power of the enemy**: and nothing shall by any means hurt you.*
>
> *Notwithstanding in this rejoice not, that **the spirits are subject unto you**; but rather rejoice, because your names are written in heaven."* (Luke 10:19–20)

Dealing with the devil and evil spirits on a personal level is simple and easy because we have the power and authority to act "In The Name of Jesus" and by the power of His Blood.

Phase two is to intreat, persuade, convince, urge, influence and impel them to leave the enemy, his ways and return unto their Father, the King. Here is the clarity of our mission:

A. **God is everyone's Father:** *"One God and Father of all..."* (Ephesians 4:6). It's the reason Jesus taught us, *"After this manner therefore pray ye: Our Father which art in heaven, Hallowed be thy name* (Matthew 6:9). Certainly we have an earthly father after the flesh. But you are a spirit, and God is the one who created you and placed you in the womb of your mother. *"Shall we not much rather be in subjection unto the Father of spirits, and live?"* (Hebrews 12:9).

B. Every person is born royalty: If God Himself is your Father, and He is, you could not be born into a higher ranking family. You are royalty. Isn't it sad that so many think so lowly of themselves? Most think so lowly they attempt to compensate by artificially exalting themselves when there is no need to, and they end up as narcissists instead. You were born into the same category as God... remember? *"Made in His likeness and created in His image?"*

You must not miss this. You were not only born royalty, but so have all of the rest of humanity. People cannot make people. Only God can make a person, including you, me, and everyone we meet.

> *"Know ye that the LORD he is God: **it is he that hath made us, and not we ourselves**; we are his people, and the sheep of his pasture."*
> (Psalm 100:3)

Race, nationality and gender are irrelevant: *"Of whom the whole family in heaven and on earth is named"* (Ephesians 3:15).

C. People have been kidnapped: Those evil forces we referred to above have taken each one as a hostage. Persons have been abducted, carried off, captured, seized, and shanghaied! The Scriptural term is *"taken captive."*

> *"...that they may recover themselves out of the snare of the devil, **who are taken captive by him at his will.**"*
> (2 Timothy 2:26)

How does Satan do this? The answer is by "blinding the minds."

> *"But if our gospel be hid, it is hid to them that are lost:*
>
> *In whom **the god of this world hath blinded the minds** of them which believe not, lest the light of the glorious gospel of Christ, who is the image of God, should shine unto them."*
>
> (2 Corinthians 4:3-4)

Never underestimate the necessary care of the mind. Satan speaks to the mind to reach the heart. God speaks to the heart to reach the mind. Satan is a liar and there is no truth, zero, in him. He deals in lies, misrepresentations and falsehoods. The hostages have been fed deceptions, prevarications, sham, and counterfeit information. We are dealing with the absence of truth.

Ex falso quodlibet, "From a false preposition, anything can follow." In classical logic it is true that from a contradiction anything can follow. Logic has been dismissed, and any semblance of reason that follows is not reasonable. Valid judgments require a factual basis. An accurate *a priori* must exist for any and every deliberation outcome to be adequate, binding or efficacious.

> *"Ye are of your father the devil, and the lusts of your father ye will do. **He** was a murderer from the beginning, and **abode not in the truth, because there is no truth in him**. When he speaketh a lie, he speaketh of his own: for he is a liar, and the father of it."* (John 8:44)

D. People (all of them) have sided with their captors:
This is not uncommon. The *Stockholm Syndrome* occurs when hostages or abused victims bond with their captors or abusers. It is so named because of a botched bank robbery in Stockholm, Sweden in August of 1973. Four employees were held in the bank's vault for six days, and a bond developed between the captives and the captors. Although it has never been included in the DSM (Diagnostic and Statistical Manual of Mental Disorders), it has been explained by Fairbaim's theory of attachment to abusers.

The most familiar example is the Patty Hearst story. Patty was the granddaughter of the publisher, William Randolph Hearst and was abducted and held hostage by the Symbionese Liberation Army in 1974. Under her new name, Tania, she worked with the SLA to rob banks. She was arrested in 1975 but her pleading of the Stockholm Syndrome was not accepted as a proper defense even though it was presented by one of the best lawyers, F. Lee Bailey. Her seven year sentence was later commuted and she was eventually pardoned by the then President, Bill Clinton.

But who would voluntarily side with the devil? And why? First, they probably don't know it's the devil. Remember he is disguised as a good guy. What they like about Satan is his philosophy. Remember that Satan and those angels that followed his example were once good, valuable, and functional in God's universe. But he changed! To what? To a narcissist (the modern word for iniquity).

"Thou art the anointed cherub that covereth;
and I have set thee so: thou wast upon the

> *holy mountain of God; thou hast walked up
> and down in the midst of the stones of fire.*
>
> *Thou wast **perfect** in thy ways from the day
> that thou wast created, **till iniquity was found
> in thee**."* (Ezekiel 28:14-15)

Satan, then an angel named Lucifer, had access to the stars of the universe (the stones of fire). But he changed! Isaiah 14:12 begins the history: *"how art thou fallen from heaven, O Lucifer."* Five reasons were given and each one begins with, *"I will,"* and each one indicates the take over of God. And just like Satan, everyone wants to play God!

The captives learned to like narcissism, selfishness, iniquity, and the playing of God. They don't want Jesus Christ. They don't want the Bible. They don't want God. People like, yes love, the way of their captors... no God but self.

Narcissism, or iniquity, is the core of human depravity and is now enjoyed by all. We all went that way. Check the Scripture. Going one's own way is the essence of narcissism—iniquity.

> *"All we like sheep have gone astray; we
> have turned every one to his own way; and
> the LORD hath laid on him the iniquity of us
> all."* (Isaiah 53:6)

This is why Jesus came: *"God, having raised up his Son Jesus, **sent him to bless you, in turning away every one of you from his iniquities**"* (Acts 3:26).

E. **Our mission is to rescue them and return them to their Father, the King:** They must do three things:

- Learn

- Turn

- Return

How shall we do this? The Scriptures are clear. Let me list the points and then we'll see them in the Scripture:

- Avoid stupid questions

- No striving (contention or arguing)

- Be gentle (tender, kind, pleasant)

- Be able to explain

- Be patient

- Be meek

- Be instructive

- Call for a proper response for recovery

"Foolish and unlearned questions avoid, knowing that they do gender strifes.

And the servant of the Lord must not strive; but be gentle unto all men, apt to teach, patient,

In meekness instructing those that oppose themselves; if God peradventure will give them repentance to the acknowledging of the truth;

And that they may recover themselves out of the snare of the devil, who are taken captive by him at his will. " (2 Timothy 2:23-26)

Does God give them repentance? This is a theological controversy. Some say God gives repentance to some and not to others based on His selectivity. Some say we can't repent, so God ends up damning us for doing what we can't stop doing. Hardly!

The answer is found in Jeremiah, where we learn that anyone who genuinely wishes to repent will be given the power to repent by God. Here's the Scripture.

> *"...turn thou me, and I shall be turned for thou art the LORD my God.*
>
> *Surely after that I was turned, I repented; and after that I was instructed..."*
>
> (Jeremiah 31:18-19)

F. **Our message must be clear and our manner loving:** Having sided with the enemy they need forgiveness, cleansing, healing, recovery. So we start at the cross, for if love cannot win them, they cannot be won. Our love message is clear and simple, but it must be conveyed lovingly. As I've already mentioned, we are God's Love Force, an army of compassion, soldiers of the Lord Jesus Christ. Their genuine salvation is our goal. There can be no fake gospel, no easy-believism, no Santa Clause evangelism... come to Jesus and you get...! No offer of fulfilled narcissism. Our message is come, die, so you can live again... really live! Jesus must become their Lord (which means master, ruler).

Becoming our Lord means we die to God-playing, narcissism, and selfishness. If Jesus is my Lord, I cease to have an opinion on any matter on which God has already spoken in His Word. Remember they must:

- Turn from the enemy

- Turn from his ways

- Return to their Father, the King

"Seek ye the LORD while he may be found,
call ye upon him while he is near: Let the
*wicked **forsake his way**, and the unrighteous*
*man **his thoughts**: and **let him return** unto*
the LORD, and he will have mercy upon
him; and to our God, for he will abundantly
pardon."   (Isaiah 55:6-7)

God's work must be done God's way. Our war strategies have been clearly set forth. Because the captives have joined with the philosophy and life-style of their captors and now identify as our enemies, they get unusual, atypical, surprising and unexpected treatment by us. We treat our enemies way out of the ordinary in the prescribed by our Commander in Chief.

- If the enemy is hungry we give him or her food!

- If the enemy is thirsty we give him or her water to drink!

- If the enemy is obnoxious, we forgive them!

- If the enemy curses us, we bless them!

- If the enemy spitefully uses us, we pray for them!

- If the enemy does us evil, we do them good!

- If the enemy is feeble-minded, we comfort them!

- If the enemy is confused, we give them godly counsel!

- If the enemy persists in sin, we preach the gospel to them with warnings!

- If the enemy is demonized, we cast the demons out!

- If the enemy is bound, we set them free!

You can find all of the above and more in Romans 12:19-21; Matthew 5:43-47; 1 Thessalonians 5:14; Psalm 1:1. We overcome evil with good. With enemies like us, they don't don't need friends!

Caution: Those like the Prodigal Son in the pig pen are easier to reach and more likely to listen. But know this that God saves from the guttermost to the uttermost (Hebrews 7:25).

The Christian Soldier's Charge

1. **Preach the Word of God.**

2. **Never lose your sense of urgency, in season or out of season.**

3. **Reprove, correct, and encourage, using the utmost patience in your teaching.**

   For the time is coming when men will not tolerate wholesome teaching. They will want something to tickle their own fancies, and they will collect teachers who will pander to their own desires. They will no longer listen to the truth but will wander off after man-made fictions.

4. **For yourself, stand fast in all that you are doing.**

5. **Meet whatever suffering this may involve.**

6. **Go on steadily preaching the gospel.**

7. Completely carry out the commission that God gave you.

I urge you, Timothy, as we live in the sight of God and of Christ Jesus (whose coming in power will judge the living and the dead), to preach the Word of God. Never lose your sense of urgency, in season or out of season. Prove, correct, and encourage, using the utmost patience in your teaching.

For the time is coming when men will not tolerate wholesome teaching. They will want something to tickle their own fancies, and they will collect teachers who will pander to their own desires. They will no longer listen to the truth, but will wander off after man-made fictions. For yourself, stand fast in all that you are doing, meeting whatever suffering this may involve. Go on steadily preaching the Gospel and carry out to the full the commission that God gave you.   (2 Timothy 4:1-5 PHILLIPS)

"Be not afraid, but speak, and hold not thy peace: For I am with thee, *and no man shall set on thee to hurt thee: for I have much people."*   (Acts 18:9-10)

8. Finally my dear reader, "Be of good courage!"

Walk by faith and not by sight. Remember, *"the race is not to the swift, nor the battle to the strong..."* (Ecclesiates 9:11). In this narcissistic dominated age remember, *"Most men will proclaim everyone his own goodness: but a faithful man who can find?"* (Proverbs 20:6-7). It is only required of a steward *"that a man be found faithful"* (1 Corinthians 4:2).

Christian soldiership is not merely analogical, metaphorical, figurative, or symbolical. Our warfare is not a simile. It's a reality! Crimes against humanity abound, and they are instigated, spurred on, incited, provoked, and fomented by a real enemy, the Prince of Darkness whose lifestyle of narcissism has become extremely popular these days.

You are "Called and Chosen to Be a Soldier!" Be a soldier First Class! Stick to your marching orders. You will be affecting eternity. The rewards are out of this world. Let me close with the inimitable words of C.T. Studd, "Only one life 'twill soon be past; Only what's done for Christ will last!" I bid you *adieu*! Soon we will hear the Lord of the Universe say:

> *"Well done, thou good and faithful servant:*
> *thou hast been faithful over a few things, I will*
> *make thee ruler over many things: enter thou*
> *into the joy of thy lord."*   (Matthew 25:21)

Only One Life
by C.T. Studd

Two little lines I heard one day,
    Traveling along life's busy way;
Bringing conviction to my heart,
    And from my mind would not depart;
Only one life, 'twill soon be past,
    Only what's done for Christ will last.

Only one life, yes only one,
    Soon will its fleeting hours be done;
Then, in "that day" my Lord to meet,
    And stand before His Judgment seat;
Only one life, 'twill soon be past,
    Only what's done for Christ will last.

Only one life, the still small voice,
    Gently pleads for a better choice
Bidding me selfish aims to leave,
    And to God's holy will to cleave;
Only one life, 'twill soon be past,
    Only what's done for Christ will last.

Only one life, a few brief years,
    Each with its burdens, hopes, and fears;
Each with its days I must fulfill,
    Living for self or in His will;
Only one life, 'twill soon be past,
    Only what's done for Christ will last.

When this bright world would tempt me sore,
    When Satan would a victory score;
When self would seek to have its way,
    Then help me Lord with joy to say;
Only one life, 'twill soon be past,
    Only what's done for Christ will last.

Give me Father, a purpose deep,
    In joy or sorrow Thy word to keep;
Faithful and true what e'er the strife,
    Pleasing Thee in my daily life;
Only one life, 'twill soon be past,
    Only what's done for Christ will last.

Oh let my love with fervor burn,
    And from the world now let me turn;
Living for Thee, and Thee alone,
    Bringing Thee pleasure on Thy throne;
Only one life, 'twill soon be past,
    Only what's done for Christ will last.

Only one life, yes only one,
    Now let me say, "Thy will be done";
And when at last I'll hear the call,
    I know I'll say "'twas worth it all";
Only one life, 'twill soon be past,
    Only what's done for Christ will last.

If You're a Fan of This Book, Please Tell Others!

- Post a 5-star review on Amazon.

- Write about the book on your Facebook, Twitter, Instagram, LinkedIn, or any social media platforms you regularly use.

- If you blog, consider referencing the book or publishing an excerpt from it with a link back to our website. You have permission to do this as long as you provide proper credit and backlinks.

- Recommend the book to friends, family, and caregivers. Word-of-mouth is still the most effective form of advertising.

- Purchase additional copies to give away to others or for use by your church or other groups.

Learn more about the authors or contact them at
www.NothingButTheTruth.org

ENJOY THESE OTHER BOOKS BY DAVID JOHNSTON

Why You Were Born -
   A Blueprint for Discovering
   Your Life Potential

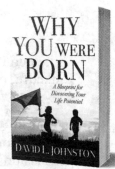

Why are you here on planet earth? Once you know why you were born you will have a new appreciation for your true self, have a known purpose in life and know why you matter. Then, and only then, can you choose a life path, a course of action and eventually a fulfilled life… no disappointments, no pressure to conform to the ideas and expectations of others. You will be free to be you, the real you.

In the second part of this book you will learn how to discover your ENA, your Embedded Natural Abilities. How tragic that some will cross the stage of time, be standing at the exit sign, and look back only to see a wasted life of insignificance. None of us can run a good race on the wrong track. "My Way," only counts if it's the right way.

Read and apply the truths of this book and you will never be a prisoner to your past or the false notions imposed upon you by others. Joy, satisfaction, and fulfillment in life will be yours.

How to Have Peace in Difficult Times - Staying Calm No Matter What's Going on Around You

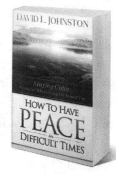

We live in turbulent times. Society sometimes seems like it is teetering on the brink of chaos.

Too often we look towards our circumstances to bring us a sense of peace and calm. Unfortunately, you simply can't control your surroundings and the events that happen to you. All too often they are beyond your control.

This powerful book will give you keys to experiencing peace and staying calm no matter what may be happening to you or around you.

Pastor Johnston uses Scripture to show how God can bring you true and lasting peace.

For example, discover:

- How your words can not only speak peace to others but to your own heart and mind
- The secret to cultivating a lasting peace that cannot be shaken when bad things happen
- The mystical connection between your heart and your mind
- The authority you have to become a "peacemaker"
- How to start making better and wiser decisions
- Beating back anger, resentment, bitterness and strife

When everyone around you is leaning into fear, panic, tension and worry – YOU have the power to walk in peace, even in difficult times.

How You See Yourself -
The Source of Your Struggle
and How to Conquer It

Ever go to a carnival and look into one of those distorted mirrors, you know, the ones that make you look three feet tall and five feet wide? The image of yourself that you see back is distorted. It can produce a good laugh. But many of us struggle with a similar condition – we don't see ourselves accurately. We are hindered from being the best version of ourselves, the version God intended. We are prevented by this insidious thing called iniquity.

Iniquity is mentioned 334 times in the Bible, yet so many remain oblivious to its significant and negative impact on everyday living. Iniquity is the ancient term for narcissism. It's one of the four reason Jesus went to the cross… "He was bruised for our iniquities" (Isa. 53:5). As you journey through the pages of this book you will not only identify the problems iniquity imposes upon us, but you will also discover the solutions.

This book will help you discover:

- How iniquity contributes to mental illness

- How iniquity causes divorce and destroys households

- How conquering iniquity will cause your prayer life to flourish

- How you can finally live without fear and regret

- How to embrace the benefits that come from being free from iniquity and the way it robs you of your God-given potential!

- How iniquity is different from sin

For Every Soldier There Is –
A Time to Kill and a Time to Heal

> *"To every thing there is a season,*
> *And a time to every purpose under the*
> *heaven: A time to be born, and a time*
> *to die…A time to kill and a time to*
> *heal."*   (Ecclesiastes 3:1-3)

This vivid "Gift Book" is written for Veterans. In it they will discover the way to genuine healing.

Your Ultimate Life Management System

One could reasonably argue that the inaugural sermon Jesus delivered to a crowd gathered on a hillside in northern Israel, often referred to as the Sermon on the Mount, may be the most powerful and profound sermon ever preached!

The wisdom, insight, truth and provision that Jesus shared that is chronicled in Matthew's Gospel (chapters 5-7), is artfully unpacked for you in this rich and meaningful message.

This book was written to provide you with a roadmap for living your life in the highest possible way. Truly, the words of Jesus can become life to your soul and a beacon of guidance and comfort for living in this present day and age when we are surrounded by fears and negative forces that can so easily distract, discourage and misdirect us. May this message truly be your ultimate guide to the life God intends for you!

You can order these books at NothingButTheTruth.org, or wherever you purchase your favorite books.

Nothing But The Truth Ministries

Dedicated to the single task of explaining the truth in its simplest and purest form to all peoples of the world.

People matter. YOU matter! Truth is the substance of all wise decision-making. So it's important to know the truth – about you, about why you were born, about every aspect of your life. Truth is wonderful, even when sometimes it may not seem comfortable.

This site is dedicated to sharing God's truth with you – truth that you can apply to your daily life, your relationships, your finances, your choices, your future.

Visit our website at
www.NothingButTheTruth.org and
www.KingofKingsChurch.us